3 WORLDS IN CONFLICT

GOD · SATAN · MAN

3 WORLDS in CONFLICT

THE HIGH DRAMA OF BIBLE PROPHECY

STANLEY A. ELLISEN

Multnomah Publishers *Sisters, Oregon*

3 WORLDS IN CONFLICT
published by Multnomah Publishers, Inc.

International Standard Book Number: 1-57673-354-8

Design by Kirk DouPonce
Cover photo of clouds by Lorentz Gullachsen/Tony Stone Images
Cover photo of open book with globe by Jun Yamashita/Photonica

Printed in the United States of America

For information:
MULTNOMAH PUBLISHERS, INC.
POST OFFICE BOX 1720
SISTERS, OREGON 97759

Library of Congress Cataloging-in-Publication Data:
Ellisen, Stanley A.
Three worlds in conflict / by Stanley A. Ellisen.
p. cm. ISBN 1-57673-354-8 (alk. paper)
1. Bible—Prophecies—End of the world. 2. End of the world—Biblical teaching. I. Title.
BS649.E63E55 1998
236'.9—dc21

98 99 00 01 02 03 04 05 — 10 9 8 7 6 5 4 3 2 1

CONTENTS

EDITOR'S PREFACE

I first met Dr. Stanley Ellisen over twenty years ago when I went to Western Seminary as a student in 1974. I had heard about his teaching before I arrived and looked forward to my time in his classes. I was not disappointed. He was a good teacher and more. He loved God and he loved God's Word. He was a man of prayer and a teacher committed to building a love for God and His Word among his students.

I went back to Western as a faculty member in 1983; Dr. Ellisen was still there and his class in the Gospels was still the high point for many of our students. In the fall of 1997 I was approached and eagerly accepted the opportunity to edit this book. Dr. Ellisen and I talked about his revision to his previous thoughts about these core truths of the faith. I have often thought about our last conversation before his health failed and he went to be with Jesus in November 1997.

As I continued editing this book I often thought how glorious his experiences must be in the presence of God. I would look down at his handwritten comments in the margins of the text before me on heaven, God's plans for His people, or Christ's triumphant return to the earth and wondered about what he was experiencing at that moment.

Dr. Ellisen was a great teacher and in this book he clearly talks about God and God's plans for His people. God reaches out to lost people and has used people of faith throughout the ages to spread His gospel of reconciliation. Jesus is coming again. He was the suffering lamb and will soon be the Lion of Judah; there will be justice. God is patient with you and with me and with all people but soon Christ will return to keep His promises. We can be optimistic in perilous times because those of us who believe have fellowship with the King of the universe. Sin and rebellion will end. Our fallen natures and the temptations of the devil, the world, and our flesh will no longer plague us. We will experience the presence of God purely and for eternity. This is the hope that Dr. Ellisen taught his students and then thought about and wrote about in his last days before he met his Savior face to face.

R. A. Krupp
Naples, Florida
May, 1998

CHAPTER ONE

PROPHECY: GOD'S PREVIEW OF TOMORROW

Back to the future is no longer an oxymoron; it's a fact of life. It's where we live. We all have a bit of the prophet in us as tomorrow keeps crowding in on our agendas.

History is passé and we often neglect its lessons. Our focus is more on the ecstatic hype and hope of tomorrow. This game of trying to beat the odds of the future is one we all play, and for any entrepreneur bent on getting a "leg up" on the competition, it is almost essential. In business, medicine, sports, and entertainment, success very often depends on one's ability to outguess the future. Like it or not, tomorrow with its fears and foibles occupies much of our thinking today.

THE FUTURE: A DIVINE DIMENSION

Futurism is not just a passing fad, peculiar to our age, nor is it a psychological escape mechanism. Rather, it's indelibly ingrained in the human "species" as a product of the Lord's handiwork. God "set eternity in their hearts," as Solomon once expressed it (Ecclesiastes 3:11). In His wisdom the Creator secreted in our complex genes an "eternal time clock." Being made in His image, we were endowed with His awesome dimension of eternity. Risky though it may seem, the Almighty made us for eternity, not as experimental "throw-aways" to play with in His cosmic laboratory.

This future sentinel within plays an important part in our role as the crown of God's creation. It is one of our unique features, distinguishing us from the animals. We're time oriented and the incessant ticks of this clock tick on, refusing to be muffled, slowed, or hurried. As J. G. Holland once observed, "The happiness of the present is largely made up of the delightful prospects of the future." The same might also be said of its anxieties, those debilitating hawkers that compound tomorrow's problems. As the crown of God's creation, we are made to live and plan for an endless tomorrow.

The purpose of this "sixth sense" is highly significant in God's plan and purpose for each of us. He put it there for a reason—to give stability and goal orientation to life. He made us for eternity and designed all life to point in that direction. In many ways life today is a hurried preparation for tomorrow. It is like a "vapor that appears for a little while and then vanishes away" (James 4:14). Ask any older person if this is not so. Stretching out ahead is a vast horizon of eternal ages for which the present life is but a launching pad—a kind of "boot camp" for the future. Without this divine prompt within, life is but a cosmic blip, an accident of chance without real meaning.

FUTURISM: A HUMAN NECESSITY

For some people concern for tomorrow is mystic nonsense. It only generates needless pessimism and is a blight on happiness today. Seneca once said, "The mind that is anxious about the future is miserable." That sentiment is shared by many, painfully reflecting the cynicism of humanity "under the sun." Many people blindly flounder into tomorrow. To fumble toward such an uncertain, foreboding terrain can strike terror and cause depression. Like Seneca, these people find life endurable only by turning off tomorrow.

Such mental manipulations only snub reality and express futility. God has invested each person with this future dimension for a wholesome reason—to alert us to our most basic need. As Jeremiah the prophet once said: "It is not in man that walks to direct his steps" (Jeremiah 10:23, KJV); we need divine guidance. This recognition is meant to incline us toward our Creator. Alone we dimly see in many directions, but we're blind to the future—the very direction we must travel. Our forward visibility is practically zero. This human restriction may seem unfair, but not from the divine view. Its purpose is to turn us to the Lord for help. As the apostle Paul declared, God has designed all things that people should seek the Lord (Acts 17:26–27). Concealing the future is an essential part of that plan.

However, there is a deeper blindness. Without divine revelation, people are blind to the very fabric of life itself. Their view is warped, largely restricted to the material world. Just as music in the airways is lost to one without a radio receiver so true spiritual reality is lost to people without God's revelation. They know little of their true spiritual condition. They need God for the salvaging of their souls. And it is for this essential purpose that God has designed and programmed all things. Though "the heavens declare the glory of God" only His Word can enlighten the heart (Psalm 19:1, 8). The psalmist saw this as an essential purpose of the written Word. As darkness inclines a child to his father's arms, so our limited knowledge of the future is designed to crowd us to the person and Word of God.

HUMANITY'S DIVINE CHART AND COMPASS

This human dilemma is admittedly frustrating, but not without solution. Flying blind into a dark and murky future was not God's intention for anyone. The Lord has provided a grand panel of instruments to illumine and describe the broad structures of His program. Though many resort to horoscopes, ouija boards, and crystal balls, the Bible alone speaks with authority concerning the future. Prophecy is its native soil. Nearly a fourth of its content is predictive, written in the future tense. One can hardly read its pages without being alerted to the future.

This prophetic element is a unique feature of the Judeo-Christian religion. What other religion dares to detail a doctrine of the future? In the Bible we find striking confirmations of its prophecies as compelling evidence that God has spoken. These literal fulfillments are, in fact, their divine credentials. The Lord boldly declared to the prophets that historically fulfilled prophecies would constitute the acid test of true religion (Deuteronomy 18:22; Isaiah 41:21–23). If prophecy has a litmus test, this is it. The flip side, of course, is that this test also exposes and rebukes the false. The Bible is laced with such confirmations, making it unique among the writings of men.

This feature of prophetic hope is not just an accessory but an essential part of the gospel. The apostle Paul saw it as central to the triad of faith, hope, and love. Beginning with faith, it grows in hope and generates love. Without it the gospel is incomplete and hobbled. Ironically, there are some Christians who almost disdain the study of prophecy and question its value. They class it with the cults who often distort some feature and make it their stock in trade. Repulsed by the many celebrated distortions, they see the study of prophecy as irrelevant and only divisive.

The Bible's answer is that true faith is not daunted by these caricatures. It expects to be counterfeited. These cultic fascinations with prophecy should simply alert us to the devil's strategy of distorting the works of God. Such preoccupation by the cults only emphasizes the fact that prophetic hope is part of the warp and woof of true Christianity. It is silly to oppose them by "throwing the baby out with the bath water." Though Paul often confronted heresies, he refused to pair down his prophetic message. He simply saw these bogus quacks as tools of God to further approve and establish the faith (1 Corinthians 11:19). While alert to error, we should guard against overreactions that divest the gospel itself of its unique features, especially its prophetic hope.

HOW RELIABLE AND PRACTICAL IS PROPHECY?

The study of Bible prophecy inevitably raises the question of accuracy. Are its predictions really reliable? Anyone with a fertile imagination can pretend to hear from an angel and conjure up animated predictions. With the Bible's multitude of prophetic forecasts, some valid test of authenticity is essential. Can we really trust them?

Its Reliability

Providentially, this challenge was anticipated and met by the Lord early in the Old Testament. He declared that the badge of a true prophet in

Israel was the accuracy of his fulfilled prophecies (Deuteronomy 18:22)—did he have a convincing track record? His predictions had to be 100 percent on target. In Israel's later history, many such fulfillments did take place in great detail, at times brutally so.

In the New Testament this test was also used by Jesus to demonstrate the convincing proofs of His messiahship (Matthew 11:4–5). Those proofs were obvious, clear, and irrefutable. It is difficult, in fact, to think of any that were fulfilled in any other way. The blind did see; the dead were raised—literally. If such accuracy characterized fulfilled prophecies, we have every reason to expect the same of those yet unfulfilled.

This record of biblical accuracy is a proof of miracles in itself, especially when compared with other would-be prophets. It is a unique phenomenon in the history of human literature. What other religion even claims such a record? Were these fulfillments dependent on chance, the odds against them would be so prodigious as to be inconceivable. Dr. Charles Ryrie has illustrated the improbability of sheer chance achieving such accuracy by the common game of flipping coins. The earth's population has grown since he wrote, but the power of his words remain.

> If slightly more than a thousand people were all flipping coins, the probability is that only one of them would turn up heads 10 times without any tails in the sequence. To achieve 20 heads in an unbroken succession would take more than a million people, and a run of 30 heads would take more than a billion. That is, if more than one-fourth of the earth's total population were flipping coins, we could expect only one to come up with 30 heads in 30 tosses. A run of 40 would happen by chance less than once in a trillion times. Or, if all the people on 250 earths like ours were flipping coins, only one of them could come up with 40 uninterrupted heads in 40 tosses. (Charles C. Ryrie, *The Bible and Tomorrow's News,* 62)

He goes on to point out that by the law of chance it would require over 200 billion earths, populated with four billion people each, to come up with one person who could achieve 100 accurate predictions without any errors in the sequence. But the Bible records not 100, but over 300 fulfilled prophecies in Christ's first coming alone. John Gerstner has calculated the possibility of this happening by sheer chance as one over eighty-four followed by 123 zeros. Mind boggling! For chance to equal that phenomenal record, the coin-flippers would need to keep flipping for eternity.

With such an imposing record of accuracy in fulfilled prophecies, the chances are slim indeed that the remaining prophecies of the Bible will err in their intended fulfillments. The reason, of course, is that God, not chance, is the author of Bible prophecy.

Its Practicality

Granting its accuracy, there are many who would question its usefulness. They see it as mere religious entertainment for the piously curious who like anointed puzzles. Rather than study the "sweet by and by," they feel we should concentrate on the "nasty here and now." Why worry about the details of some future "666" world dictator? Does the study of prophecy really enhance Christian living? Does it make us more loving and useful in our world today?

The answer lies in the character and purpose of the prophets. They were invariably a doughty and down-to-earth lot. They addressed the nitty-gritty world of common people. None were mere glassy-eyed mystics caught up in some kind of Nirvana or dream world. Rather, they spoke to the everyday problems of godly living where the sandals met the cobblestones of life. Their words flowed from a context of exhortation to righteous living, pointing to the future with this in mind. This was true of both the Old and New Testament writers; rarely do you find it otherwise.

Paul, who touched on many prophetic themes, never lost sight of his practical mission. After solidly confirming the doctrine of the resurrection in 1 Corinthians 15, for instance, he immediately showed its relevancy: "Therefore, my beloved brethren, be steadfast, immovable, always abounding in the work of the Lord" (v. 58). To further impress his point, he applied it to their need for generosity in giving to the poor. The same was true in his Thessalonian epistles where he stressed the Lord's return. In these prophetic classics, Paul continually exhorted them to holy living, urging them to abound more and more in love and holiness.

Likewise, Peter the fisherman could hardly be accused of being a dreamy visionary or mystic. As he electrified his readers in 2 Peter 3:11 with a cataclysmic description of final judgment, he made his application with characteristic bluntness: "Since all these things are to be destroyed in this way, what sort of people ought you to be in holy conduct and godliness."

The same could be said of the apostle John, the one through whom Christ gave His final words to the churches. In speaking of the Lord's return and our transformation into His image, he said: "And every one who has this hope fixed on Him purifies himself, just as He [Christ] is pure" (1 John 3:3). Using this prophetic word concerning the future, he sought also to promote, if possible, a preemptive strike of holiness here and now.

The Bible writers are almost unanimous in relating prophecy to practical issues of life. For them, prophecy and practice are of the same piece. Each complements the other. If one is the warp, the other is the woof of the fabric. Properly understood, the prophetic Scriptures minister to the heart, mind, and will of concerned Christians.

Convinced then of the grandeur and relevance of this study, we approach it with lively anticipation, recognizing that when God speaks, He expects us to listen.

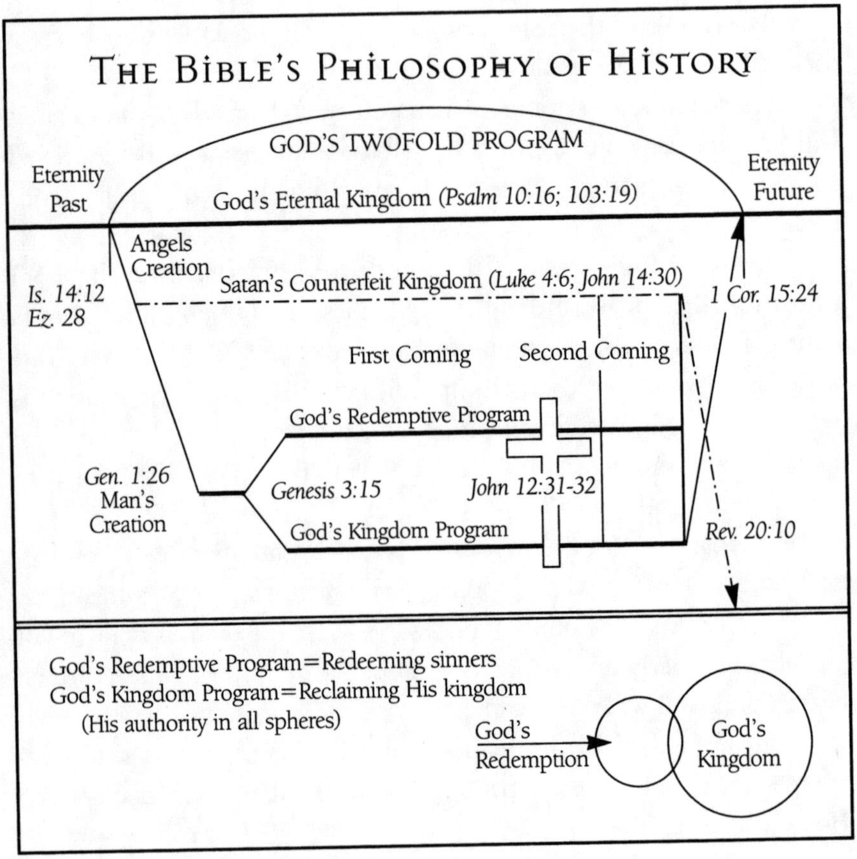
THE BIBLE'S PHILOSOPHY OF HISTORY
GOD'S TWOFOLD PROGRAM
Eternity Past
God's Eternal Kingdom (Psalm 10:16; 103:19)
Eternity Future
Angels Creation
Satan's Counterfeit Kingdom (Luke 4:6; John 14:30)
Is. 14:12
Ez. 28
1 Cor. 15:24
First Coming
Second Coming
God's Redemptive Program
Gen. 1:26
Man's Creation
Genesis 3:15
John 12:31-32
God's Kingdom Program
Rev. 20:10
God's Redemptive Program=Redeeming sinners
God's Kingdom Program=Reclaiming His kingdom
(His authority in all spheres)
God's Redemption
God's Kingdom

CHAPTER TWO

EVERYONE'S QUESTION: WHAT'S GOD TRYING TO DO?

To discern where you're going, you need to know where you've been. The mess we're in has a history; it also has a prophesied finale. Blind chance has no place in the process. God is the first cause, and He is not "biting His nails" wondering how it will all turn out. He has preannounced its final outcome as the result of a detailed series of events.

Before looking ahead we need to check our rearview mirror to the past. The prophecies of the end times, Armageddon, and the Second Coming, for instance, are largely enigmas unless we understand how it all began. Even our minor problems of daily life take on new meaning when we catch this overall perspective. Recognizing these bottom line issues will answer the question many would like to ask: "What's God trying to do?"

GOD'S ETERNAL KINGDOM

The Bible describes God as an eternal king: "The LORD is King forever" (Psalm 10:16). It also declares Him to be sovereign over all things (Psalm 103:19). There is no outpost in His vast universe where He is not in absolute control. Nothing is outside the orbit of His scrutiny. This supreme prerogative of God has never been compromised, for to do so would make Him something less than God. Recognizing His undiminished sovereignty is essential to get a proper view of His kingdom. The work of creation, with all its apparent risks, was the work of His sovereignty. Nothing in the process took Him by surprise.

Before God created man or the material universe, He first created a vast host of angels (Job 38:4–7, NIV). These He made simultaneously, rather than by the procreative process He devised for man. The angels are an innumerable company of spirit beings who were apparently created for eternity. Although not made in the image of God, they were given great intelligence, each having an individual will with freedom of choice. God's purpose for them was to act as His servants in the fulfilling of His kingdom work.

The Centrality of God's Will

In that primordial age, God's will was always done. It was never questioned, much less challenged. Obeying Him and serving His purposes brought personal fulfillment and satisfaction to all His creatures. His will was supreme. The sovereignty of God is basic to His kingdom. It is key to order in the world.

The Meaning of God's Kingdom

As a sovereign King, God obviously has a kingdom. What the term "kingdom" means is often debated by Bible scholars, since it is used in several ways in the Bible. At times it means "authority," as seen in Luke 19:12: "A certain nobleman went to a distant country to receive a kingdom for himself, and then return." Here the term is obviously used in that abstract sense of kingly authority.

On occasion the term simply signifies a "realm" or territory, as noted in Mark 3:24: "And if a kingdom is divided against itself, that kingdom cannot stand." The same meaning is also seen in Matthew 7:21.

A third use of the term "kingdom" is that of the "exercise of kingly authority" over subjects. Jesus spoke of it in this sense in Matthew 12:28: "But if I cast out demons by the Spirit of God, then the kingdom of God has come upon you" (*see also* John 19:36). John Bright stresses this use in his book, *The Kingdom of God:*

> For the Kingdom is no empty domain, so many square miles of territory with geographical frontiers—it is people. Or, to put it otherwise, the Messiah never appears as a lone figure ruling in solitary majesty, but always with corporate qualities. He rules over people; He calls people to rule. (219)

Much theological ink has been spilled over this question. It is generally recognized, however, that these three elements are fundamental to its meaning: its "realm," its "authority," and the "exercise of that authority" over subjects. God's kingdom is the realm over which He rules, exercising sovereign authority over His subjects.

THE PRIMEVAL REBELLION AND COUNTERFEIT KINGDOM

In the operation of His kingdom, God rules by the principle of delegated authority. He is not an "I'd rather do it myself" deity. To accomplish His purposes, He created the angels, organizing them as a hierarchy with different levels of responsibility and spheres of service. To serve as His supreme lieutenant, the Lord endowed a special archangel with striking beauty, wisdom, and power (Ezekiel 28:12–17; Jude 1:9). This one He named "Lucifer" (Day Star) and gave him a throne in the heavens (Isaiah 14:12–14). He made him to be His prime minister over His kingdom.

How long this harmonious arrangement continued in the distant past is not recorded. Endowed with a free will, the crucial test of any creature was his allegiance to the will of God. In the process of time that crucial test came for Lucifer when he shifted his gaze to the grandeur of His God-given splendor and became self-centered in pride. Dazzled by his own greatness, he asserted independence and presumed to be "like the Most High" (Isaiah 14:14). In that moment of self-exaltation, he thrust himself outside the stabilizing axis of God's will and began a swirling catapult into the oblivion of a godless being. That decision was final. He never repented.

Lucifer, however, was not alone in this fatal choice. He had a following of one-third of the angels of heaven (Revelation 12:1–9). With this crowd of minions he formed a kingdom of his own, a counterfeit kingdom of darkness. His name was changed to Satan (adversary) in keeping with his newly assumed devious character.

The fact that so many spirit beings followed him in this revolt suggests that his rebellion constituted the testing point for all angelic beings. Such a test of loyalty had to come. That decision was whether they would follow God implicitly or defect for apparent personal advantage to a tantalizing option. It was their moment of truth. In that watershed test, two-thirds of them made a positive decision for God, confirming themselves forever in the will of God (1 Timothy 5:21). Just as their creation apparently took place all at once, so their eternal decisions also were evidently made and crystallized at the time of Lucifer's rebellion.

Why Didn't God Kill the Devil?

The question is often raised: if God is sovereign, why didn't He immediately destroy this arch rebel? Why didn't He have a mass execution for the whole horde of rebellious angels and be done with them? Or at least, why didn't He lock them up forever in the abyss of hell?

The answer is that God does have such a plan, but in His own time. He is temporarily using these rebels to serve another of His purposes. So deep is His sovereignty that He is able to make the wrath of men to praise Him and all His enemies to serve Him (Psalm 76:10). The devastating irony for them is that they end up serving Him in spite of themselves. Some of the fallen angels He chained until judgment; others He has allowed a limited range of liberty until His further purposes are fulfilled.

The central fact to observe is that God did allow the formation of a kingdom of darkness. It was not a surprise. However, that kingdom formed through voluntary forces led by Satan, not through God's creation. As such, it became an opposite pole to God's kingdom of light and an alluring option for all moral creatures in their exercise of freedom. It became a counterfeit kingdom running concurrently with God's kingdom of righteousness.

This kingdom of God-defiance often appears to dominate in the world. It not only coerces men and women, but also jauntily wins them.

Contrary to many naive notions, the devil is not a green monster with a pitchfork. He is often a do-gooder. His goal in life is not to produce gangsters and drunkards, but to counterfeit the works of God. This has been his ambition ever since he went into business for himself, saying in his preamble: "I will make myself like the Most High" (Isaiah 14:14). The effect of this ploy is that the more closely he imitates God's models in his people, the less likely they are to be inclined to seek God or pursue His will. He is a master imitator of God.

Why then does God allow this counterfeit operation to continue? A part of the answer is to intensify man's spiritual choice and remove it from the arena of mere morality or aesthetics. False religions often have strict morals and beautiful rituals that don't necessarily make them authentic. True faith responds to God's Word, not to the attractions of religious niceties. The net effect is that Satan's kingdom serves as a giant magnet to attract the superficial. He draws off both the chaff and the counterfeit wheat. This polarizing service of Satan is demonstrated in Revelation 20, as he is released to gather the wicked for their final assembly. It also strikingly illustrates the reason for his continued existence.

GOD'S EARTHLY KINGDOM

At some point after the fall of Satan, God began another creation. The man and woman were also endowed with the freedom of choice, dangerous though this second venture might have seemed.

The Need and Peril of Free Choice

Freedom of choice was essential to human personality if they were to be made in God's own image. The grand design of the Lord was to reproduce Himself in human personalities, especially His traits of love and holiness. These divine characteristics can grow only in the soil of moral freedom. True fellowship involves moral choice.

By this moral freedom God sought to establish men and women in a wholesome relationship to His sovereignty. He sought to relate to them by love, not coercion. The bond of love is infinitely stronger than that of fear or mere muscle. For this reason He made Adam and Eve to be partners with Him in His rule. As an initial test they were forbidden to eat of the "tree of the knowledge of good and evil" (Genesis 2:17). They were given a choice of compliance or disobedience, clear and simple. The tree was not put there as a teaser or trap, but as an inevitable test. It gave the couple a choice as to whether they would be loyal to God or submit to an enticing alternative presented by the serpent. Had they turned from his evil suggestion to firm commitment to God, they might have eaten of the "tree of life" and been eternally confirmed in righteousness (Genesis 3:22–24; Revelation 22:2). But they each disobeyed the direct command of God, and the fall of the race took place.

By this deliberate action they declared their independence of the will of God, choosing rather to affiliate with Satan's kingdom of rebels. What could have caused this insanity and disaster? It was not the tree with its luscious fruit, nor was it the serpent or devil using the serpent (Revelation 12:9). These only provided the occasion for the couple to express their freedom of choice. The real cause was their own willful decisions. In this test of allegiance, they failed to trust God's specific word of command and joined the previously fallen host of rebellious angels.

To all outward appearances, this second fall of God's creation was catastrophic. It seemed to dash His high hopes of extending His kingdom through creatures with moral choice. People were given cosmic responsibility to have dominion over the earth—but they couldn't be trusted with a piece of fruit. Was this divine gift of choice to moral beings too risky? Would this endowment be the suicidal undoing of the whole race? It certainly seemed to be counterproductive to God's purpose, for sin appeared to repeatedly come up the victor.

The Two Problems Summarized

In human terms God faced two problems at this point. First, His trusted lieutenant, Lucifer, revolted and began a counter kingdom containing a large contingent of angels. His sovereignty was challenged. Second, man and woman, made in God's image, also defected and fell into a state of sin and personal disintegration. His love was questioned. God's overall kingdom appeared in disarray and its rule was partially usurped.

The question is often raised as to why God bothered with a salvage operation. Why not destroy the whole bunch of rebels and start over? Besides being contrary to His sovereign plan, this would have been no solution. It would have been only an evasion of the deeper problem of sin itself.

Therefore, the Almighty chose to confront and forever resolve the question of sin by addressing two problems: 1) how to reclaim His usurped kingdom, and 2) how to provide redemption for humanity whom He had made in His own image. The solution was not simply asserting the overwhelming power of His divine muscle. Instead He displayed His deepest nature, His attributes of love and grace. Postponing judgment, He began to patiently reveal His grace.

GOD'S KINGDOM AND REDEMPTIVE PROGRAMS

After Adam and Eve sinned in the garden, God first addressed the serpent who had tempted them (Genesis 3:14–15). In judgment, He also gave the *proto-evangel* (first gospel) to the man and woman, announcing His redemptive plan. To the serpent He said, "And I will put enmity between you and the woman, and between your seed and her seed; He shall bruise you on the head, and you shall bruise him on the heel."

This message was obviously for Adam and Eve as well as for Satan. In it God prophesied that following a two-way enmity, two bruising or crushings would take place. The woman's seed would crush the head of the serpent, and the serpent would crush the heel of the woman's seed. The two figures in this conflict are Christ, who was the seed "born of a woman" (Galatians 4:4), and Satan, the "serpent of old" (Revelation 12:9; 20:2).

God's Kingdom Program

By analyzing these two crushings we get a thumbnail sketch of God's twofold program on earth. The first statement, "He shall bruise you on the head," was a declaration that Christ would destroy the devil with a fatal blow. Jesus spoke of His future work of binding Satan the "strong man" of this world system and "casting him out" (Matthew 12:29). His death on the cross was the blow that will eventually destroy Satan. That final judgment of Satan will also include the destruction of his usurped, counterfeit kingdom. Their fulfillment, of course, will occur after Christ's millennial reign. This whole process by which Christ reclaims His authority in all realms and forever squelches rebellion is God's "kingdom program." His kingdom sovereignty will be affirmed.

God's Redemptive Program

The second crushing announced in Genesis 3:15 is the serpent's heel-crushing of the woman's seed. This demonic assault occurred on the cross where Satan was the driving force behind the crucifixion. As a "heel-crushing," it suggests the temporary nature of Christ's death, in contrast to the fatal crushing of the serpent. His death on the cross then became the foundation for God's redemptive program, providing salvation for mankind.

In this proto-evangel, the Lord introduced His twofold program on earth—concerning His kingdom and man's redemption. In its final fulfillment He will reclaim His usurped kingdom in all realms by destroying the devil and his followers, and in the process He will also provide eternal redemption for men.

THE UNFOLDING OF GOD'S TWOFOLD PROGRAM

The progressive development of this divine mission is seen in several ways throughout the Bible.

Two Men of Faith Receive Promises

To inaugurate these programs and set them in motion, God chose two men of faith in ancient times. The first was Abraham who lived about 2100 B.C. With him the Lord made a covenant in which He promised, among other things, a "seed" that would bless all nations (Genesis 12:1–3). This seed Paul identified as Christ, and the blessing which was to come through Him was justification by faith (Genesis 15:6; Galatians 3:8, 16). In that promise God assured Abraham that the blessing of redemption for the race would come through his seed. This one would fulfill God's redemptive program.

To inaugurate His kingdom purpose, God chose David from the same line about 1000 B.C. He also made a covenant with him, promising him a kingdom and a royal seed (2 Samuel 7:12–16). This one would be a King of splendor, bringing peace to the nation. He would eventually rule over the house of Israel forever. Besides ruling Israel, He would extend His rule over the whole world, as noted by the later prophets (Amos 9:12; Zechariah 14:9). This seed of David would fulfill God's kingdom program in the earth by destroying the God-defying rebels and ruling the world in righteousness.

Two Famous Sons Become Types

To impress this point, the Lord gave each of these two men a son that typified or portrayed the seed that was promised. To Abraham God gave Isaac, almost miraculously, and later required him to be offered on Mt. Moriah as a burnt sacrifice. This son beautifully typified Messiah's redemptive work. In a similar way the Lord gave David a son of promise named Solomon (Shalom), to whom He promised a kingdom of universal peace and great glory.

These two sons strikingly portray Messiah as the Son promised to Abraham and David, whom the faithful of the Old Testament looked for with such anticipation. How appropriate it is that the New Testament begins by introducing its central figure as "the son of David, the son of Abraham" (Matthew 1:1). He was born to fulfill both the redemptive and kingdom programs of God.

Two Animals Become Symbols

Two symbolic animals in the Old Testament also portray these two programs of God: the lamb and the lion. The sacrificial lamb of Exodus 12:3 typified Messiah in His redemptive role as the "Lamb of God who takes away the sin of the world!" (John 1:29). Isaiah also spoke of this role of Messiah, seeing Him as the Lord's servant being led "like a lamb...to slaughter" (Isaiah 53:7).

The other animal typifying Messiah is the lion of Genesis 49:9, 10. This metaphor from the Old Testament is borrowed in Revelation 5:5 to describe Christ as "the Lion that is from the tribe of Judah." As the lion represents kingly authority, Christ will come in royal power to rule Israel and the world, thus fulfilling God's kingdom program.

The Two Programs Related

Although these two functions of Christ are inextricably related throughout the Bible, their purposes are distinct. The focus of the kingdom program is on God's authority, reclaiming what was lost or usurped from His kingdom. That of the redemptive program is humanity, providing the basis for our salvation. Though the kingdom purpose is broader, extending to the whole spiritual realm, it could not be accomplished without the redemptive program for people. The two complement each other.

These two programs are seen to converge in John's prophetic vision of Revelation 5, where Christ is seen in the dual roles of lion and lamb. In the wake of this dramatic revelation, the angelic throng loudly acclaims before the throne: "Worthy is the Lamb that was slain to receive power and riches and wisdom and might and honor and glory and blessing" (v. 12). This unique portrayal shows how Christ will have gained His reigning authority, not only by His conquering power as a lion, but also by His gracious worthiness as a lamb, having been slain to redeem. Before He moves in wrath to destroy the kingdom of darkness, He will have walked the fires of judgment salvaging sinners, laying down His life for them. These two roles of Messiah are closely interwoven, but reach in two directions, demonstrating the two supreme qualities of His nature—His love and holiness.

Following Christ's millennial reign and the disposal of Satan, He will then present this reclaimed kingdom back to the Father (1 Corinthians 15:24). That majestic presentation will constitute the fulfillment of His commission from the Father in His role as the seed of the woman. Of supreme importance is the process by which He accomplishes this mission, not by His coercive might, but through His compassionate love. His redemptive grace is really the genius of these programs, and it will also constitute the basis of His eternal fellowship with men and women. That divine-human fellowship will not be built on fear or force, but on grace in a climate of mutual love.

The personal application of this divine program is hard to miss. God's will is not only the central axis around which the world revolves; it is the only center around which anyone can find personal fulfillment. Outside this stabilizing center one finds endless strife and disappointment. Submission to it brings personal release from that strife and freedom to exercise one's God-given energies as they were intended. The old hymn of C. H. Morris beautifully strikes this note, "Sweet Will of God":

My stubborn will at last hath yielded;
I would be Thine, and Thine alone;
And this the prayer my lips are bringing,
"Lord, let in me Thy will be done."

Thy precious will, O Conquering Savior,
Doth now embrace and compass me;
All discords hushed, my peace a river,
My soul a prisoned bird set free.

Such liberation through submission is hardly a popular notion in our day of misconstrued freedom. It is more often denigrated or relegated to eastern or mystic religions. The two, however, are worlds apart. Jesus' prayer instruction for us, as well as His own prayer to the Father, emphasized the importance of submitting to the Father's will (Matthew 6:10; 26:39). Outside that will there is an illusion of freedom, but the stories of Lucifer, and Adam and Eve show its perils. Its consequences are always the opposite of freedom, entangling one in a deeper bondage that denies any real personal fulfillment. True freedom is only found in the center of His will.

SUMMARY

This then is what God is doing on earth, and prophecy is the story of how Christ the "seed of the woman" is carrying it out. It is the real story of Paradise lost and regained. At His first coming He enacted the redemptive program; at His Second Coming He will complete the kingdom program.

His activities today are more directed to saving than to judging. If we wonder why God appears to be oblivious to evil in the world, why He doesn't immediately strike down the wicked, keep in mind His present redemptive purpose. He does not immediately lash out with vengeance as the kingdom lion, but offers saving grace as the redemptive lamb. As we shall see in the unfolding drama of these programs, His kingdom judgment is presently being held in abeyance; but it is not forgotten.

The Bible Covenants

God's Purposes Outlined

GOD'S ETERNAL COVENANT WITH MEN (Hebrews 9:15; 13.20)

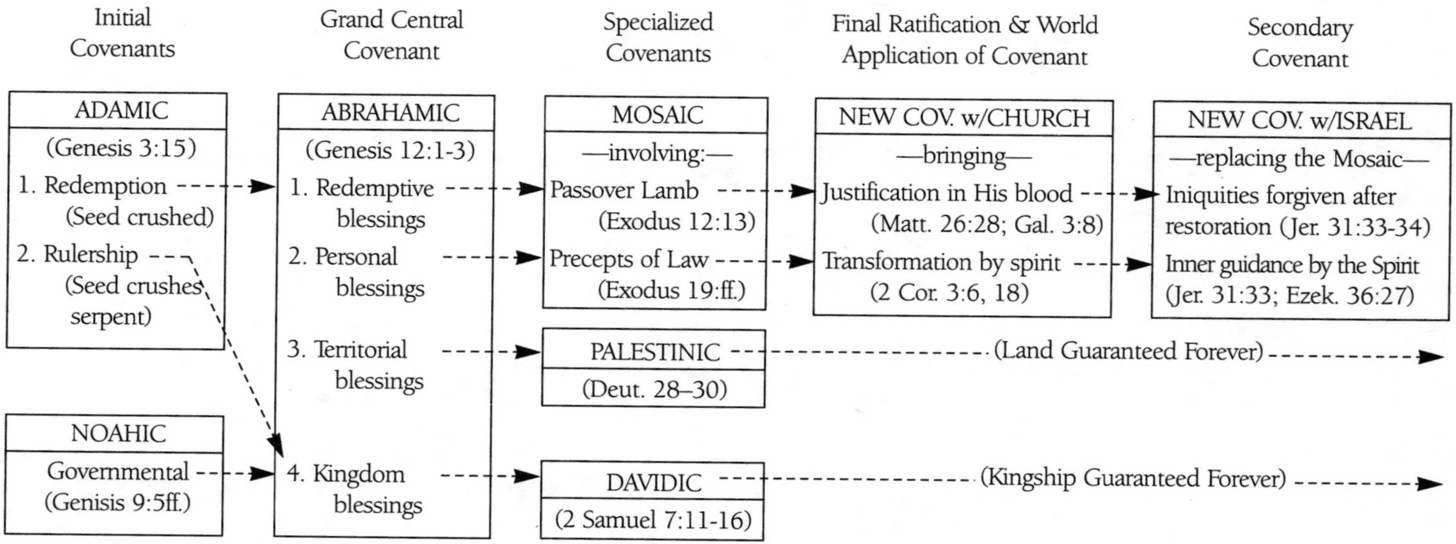

Purpose of the Covenants:

1. To reveal and guarantee God's redemptive purposes in His "Eternal Covenant."
2. To reveal and guarantee God's Kingdom purposes through His chosen nation Israel.
3. To provide a faith basis for personal relationships with God.

CHAPTER THREE

THE COVENANTS: GOD OUTLINES HIS PLAN

Promises, promises. We live in a "hope-so" world of promises. Dreams, hopes, and blithe assurances too often tantalize us with shimmering Utopias. Whether in election-year politics or soap opera enticements, we're deluged with rosy promises. Most of these we recognize as fairyland fantasies, and our best-laid plans often end in disappointment.

There are some things in life, however, that are certain, even more so than time, tide, or taxes. These are the promises of God. His Word cannot be broken and in these pledges God has outlined His program and the place we play in it.

GOD'S COVENANT PROGRAM

To accomplish His purposes God delights to work with people. In this way He builds their faith in Him and reveals His own patience. To introduce His plan and program He made agreements with certain individuals, unfolding His long-range objectives. These agreements are called covenants.

A covenant is basically an agreement. It is a working relationship between two parties about a proposed plan of action. It is, however, more than a plan of action; it's a personal handshake, establishing a mutual relationship of trust. Many human relations like marriage or business contracts involve such pledges.

The Purpose of Covenants

The covenants were given for several purposes. They first announce God's plans (they are predictive); second, they involve individuals to carry them out (they elicit faith). They provided the ground for man's fellowship with God based on trust and respect. The covenants were given to reveal God's purposes, but also to redeem and build grand personalities—God's primary objective with His people.

A third quality of the Bible covenants distinguishes them from mere human agreements. They are guarantees. In this way they are specific and determinative, predicting with certitude what God will eventually bring to pass. Though conditional elements are often involved in their application, their ultimate fulfillment is guaranteed by God's sovereign "I will" (Genesis 12:1–3; Deuteronomy 30:1–10; 2 Samuel 7:10–16). Nothing can alter their final fulfillment.

The Variety of Covenants

These treaties of God with men fall into several groups, all revolving around a central covenant. The first two (Adamic and Noahic) are *seminal* in that they contain the seeds of those that follow. The third (Abrahamic) is the central covenant, containing four promises which summarize the whole of God's future program for humanity. From this central covenant came a group of four specialized pacts, which further elaborate what God will do for His people. Finally, a later, secondary covenant is announced that will replace a previous one that was temporal, broken, and made obsolete.

Recognizing these various guarantees and the special features of each will help us to see God's overall program and how He is developing it throughout the ages.

GOD'S PROMISE TO ADAM

The covenants date back to the Garden of Eden where the initial disaster of sin took place. In this story of creation, the fall, and God's subsequent covenant with Adam and Eve, the name used for God is the "LORD God"

(Genesis 2–3). "LORD" (YHWH) is also the proper name of Israel's God, stressing His eternity and therefore His reliability in keeping His word (Exodus 13:15). This rare combination, LORD God, emphasizes His sovereignty and His covenant-keeping character.

Although the proto-evangel of Genesis 3:15 is not called a covenant, it has the basic features of a covenant. As previously noted, it promised that the "seed of the woman" would destroy Satan and provide for man's redemption. It was the first "gospel," given in the form of a covenant. As later covenants were sealed by blood (Hebrews 9:18), this promise also was accompanied by the shedding of blood, as God provided skins for their covering (Genesis 3:21). It was God's early covenant of redemption and the only mention of a gospel till the time of Abraham.

THE NOAHIC COVENANT

After the great flood, God spoke to Noah and made a promise, establishing a new covenant with him (Genesis 9). It promised that there would never again be a universal flood to destroy the earth. The Lord guaranteed that the seasons of summer and winter would continue and the earth would be preserved from any similar destruction by water. The divine name associated with this covenant is His universal name, God the Almighty, as He gives this assurance to all creation (Genesis 9:12).

Like the one with Adam, this covenant also was unilateral. It guaranteed certain things that God would do. But it also included certain responsibilities for people. They were to be God's partners in governing the earth. Their responsibility was to restrain evil and take vengeance on the wicked, even to the point of capital punishment for murder. Though the Lord would not judge wickedness Himself by another great flood, He appointed people as His adjutant to do this job for Him, promoting righteousness in the earth. As a special reminder of this agreement, the Lord set the sign of the rainbow in the sky (Genesis 9:12–16). (As Josephus described it, it is like a bow pointing upward to God, not downward at man.) As long as the rainbow continues in the clouds, that covenant remains in effect. The Lord called it an "everlasting covenant" (Genesis 9:16).

The essence of this covenant was that God would preserve the earth, and humanity was to preserve righteousness in the earth. It constituted a government franchise for man to rule society for God. This was something new, for God had denied them this responsibility prior to the flood (Genesis 4:15). Having cleansed the earth for a new start, He left human governments in charge of preserving moral order.

THE ABRAHAMIC COVENANT

At the time of Abraham (c. 2000 B.C.), wickedness had again spread over the earth. This continued failure called for divine action. Rather than starting anew by destroying the wicked, however, the Lord called Abram from an idolatrous family in Ur of the Chaldees to be the progenitor of a new nation (Genesis 15:7; Joshua 24:2–3). His first instruction to him was to migrate to Canaan, a land of curse. There He would confirm with him a covenant of blessing (Genesis 9:25; 12:1–3). Obeying this strange command, Abram obeyed and was given a covenant that became the basis of all God's future covenants. It announced what God would do for the world through Abram and his descendants.

The establishing of this covenant is one of the main features of the story of Abram (later named Abraham; Genesis 12–25). It is also foundational to the rest of the Bible. In Genesis 12, the covenant was promised and confirmed; in chapter 13, it was expanded. In chapter 15, it was ratified and guaranteed by the Lord in a special ritual of animal sacrifices. In chapter 17, the physical sign of circumcision was added to symbolize their cleansing as God's people. Finally, in Genesis 22, God added His oath to the covenant in response to Abraham's unstilted devotion to the Lord.

This covenant with Abraham has four parts, each part relates to the following covenants in the Bible. Together they outline God's overall program.

Blessing 1—Personal

Abraham and his seed were promised great personal blessings of prosperity and God's protection. Genesis 13–17 illustrate the significance of this in Abraham's life as he received a new name, great personal wealth, and the Lord's special care. This blessing was evidently conditioned upon each individual's response to God. Jacob, for instance, forfeited much of it because of his resort to fleshly means in pursuing the covenant promises. This he admitted before Pharaoh late in life (Genesis 47:9). His son Joseph, on the other hand, exemplified the fulfillment of this blessing as he lived a godly life in the most difficult circumstances, trusted God's sovereignty, and rose to unprecedented power and glory (Genesis 12:2).

Blessing 2—Territorial

This covenant also promised to Abraham and his descendants a homeland—the land of Canaan (Palestine). Though Abraham lived in parts of this territory, he never actually possessed it as his own (Hebrews 11:13). The land was earmarked for his children to possess. This promise is one of the present-day bases of Israel's claim to the land of Palestine as the children of Abraham, Isaac, and Jacob. Whether they are presently entitled to it is a problem that we will address later (Genesis 12:7; 13:15; 15:18; 17:8).

Blessing 3—National

God promised that He would make of Abraham a great nation, in fact, many nations. This part of the covenant became a severe test for Abraham and Sarah, since both were elderly and she was barren. Though they joked about it, the Lord gave them faith to fulfill the promise quite literally (Hebrews 11:11–12).

The present-day significance of this national promise is seen in that both the Jewish and Arab nations claim Abraham as their father. The specific great nation promised, however, was Israel, as later indicated to Moses and David (Genesis 12:2; 17:4–5).

Blessing 4—Spiritual

Last but not least, this covenant also promised blessing to "all the families of the earth" through Abraham. This extension of the Abrahamic blessing to the Gentiles was designed to meet the spiritual needs of the entire world. As such it relates back to the proto-evangel given to Adam and Eve (concerning the "seed of the woman") and extends also to believers in Christ today. Paul identified this blessing in Galatians 3:6–8 as justification by faith. Christians today partake of the Abrahamic blessing in this special way—they are justified by faith as Abraham was (Genesis 12:3; 15:6; 18:18; 22:18).

This fourfold promise to Abraham unveiled God's future plan for His people, but it also became a test of faith for Abraham. As previously noted, this faith-building process was one of the unique features of the covenants. As Abraham responded to God, his faith grew and his fellowship with the Lord was strengthened. When he first came to Canaan, for instance, he had no wealth, no land, no children, and no human ability to acquire them. He was completely dependent on the Lord. Yet the Lord did not immediately fulfill His promises; He tested Abraham's faith by a long waiting period. The coming of Isaac, for instance, was delayed for nearly twenty-five years. In that time Abraham was not always faithful, but resorted to fleshly means to fulfill the promise. In his impatience, he sought to compromise the covenant by settling for a son through a handmaid. God, however, was not impressed by this generosity, but insisted on fulfilling His word quite literally with a son by aged Sarah.

The lesson impressed in this long-delayed fulfillment was important to God's prophetic program. It demonstrated that, although the time may be long and unfaithfulness may occur on the part of Abraham's children, the Lord would fulfill all aspects of His covenants just as He had spoken. No human actions can nullify or modify His promises (Romans 11:29).

The Lord's giving of this covenant to Abraham illustrates another interesting feature of God's ways with man. Although the covenant was all of God's grace, He developed several aspects of it in response to faith-actions by Abraham. When Abraham left his home in Ur, God gave him a home in Canaan (Genesis 12). After he gave up the Jordan Valley to Lot in the interest of peace, God promised him all the country his eyes could see (Genesis 13). When he later gave up Isaac his son as an offering to the Lord, God added His oath to His word; but He also promised him children as numerous as the stars of heaven. Every sacrifice by Abraham turned out to be an investment with immense dividends. Most importantly, it built a strong faith-relationship between the Lord and Abraham.

THE MOSAIC COVENANT

As Abraham was the father of the Hebrew race, Moses became the founder of the Israeli nation. He came on the scene about 1500 B.C. when the people had multiplied to over two million. Brought up in the house of Pharaoh, Moses received royal training in leadership and was used of God to lead Israel out of Egypt and to establish them as a nation in the wilderness. To function as a nation, they required a constitution of civil, social, and moral laws. Being a theocratic people with covenant relations with Jehovah (YHWH), they also needed spiritual instructions to maintain this proper relationship. Moses was God's man to provide these.

This Mosaic Law became Israel's written constitution as a theocratic nation. It was a guideline for worship and a mandate for service. The question of the time of its termination is often debated: Does it continue today or has it ended? Paul declared several times that the Law ended at the cross (Galatians 3:19; Ephesians 2:15; Colossians 2:14). Yet Jesus, Paul, and others spoke of the Law as being eternal (Matthew 5:18; Romans 3:31). How do we reconcile this apparent contradiction of its being both terminated and eternal?

The answer is that the Law was designed to serve two basic functions in the plan of God. It served as both a covenant system for God's covenant people Israel and as a revelation for all mankind. It was not only a national document for the nation of Israel, but gave the first written expression of God's will for all men. In this way it fulfilled both a narrow and a broad purpose.

The Mosaic Law As a Covenant System

Its first and more specific purpose was that of a written covenant between the Lord and His covenant people Israel. As such, it was a working relationship for the nation with specific instructions, all designed to evoke individual responses to His divine leadership (Exodus 19–24). Keeping the Law meant obeying to the Lord's will and experiencing His favor in their daily lives.

It is essential to recognize that the Mosaic Law was not given as a means of salvation. No one was ever saved by "keeping the law" in any age, though many have tried to do so (Romans 10:3; Galatians 2:16, 21). Salvation is always received by faith in God's Word, whether in Old or New Testament times. That word in the Old Testament was His promise to provide redemption, as seen in the proto-evangel and symbolized by the Passover lamb. The Law was not designed to condition salvation, but to emphasize one's need of salvation (1 Timothy 1:9) while providing God's people with a proper code of conduct. In this sense it served to condition the Lord's blessing on His people while teaching them His ways (Deuteronomy 4:40; 30:9–10).

This covenant aspect of the Mosaic Law, however, came to an end at the cross when the Levitical priesthood ended. The rending of the temple veil at Christ's death dramatized the fact that the old was consummated and the new priesthood of Christ had begun. Caiaphas the high priest, in effect, executed himself out of a job when he had Jesus crucified.

With this change of priesthood, however, came also a change of the law or covenant system: "For when the priesthood is changed, of necessity there takes place a change of law also" (Hebrews 7:12). This was also emphasized by the apostle Paul when he said that the Law was designed to last only until the seed of the Abrahamic covenant (that is, Christ) would arrive (Galatians 3:16, 19). The Mosaic priesthood and covenant system were so intertwined that they expired together, at the cross. Under the new priesthood of Christ, the old motivation of law was superseded by a new motivation of love (Romans 14:9). Before Christ's coming, however, the Mosaic Law functioned as a divine covenant system between the covenant people and the covenant Lord.

The Mosaic Law As a Revelation for All Humanity

Though the Law served this temporary function as a covenant system for Israel, it was also designed as a set of spiritual and moral principles for all men (Matthew 5:18). As such, it was meant to continue forever. Before the Law, no written revelation had been given to delineate God's way of life for all men. The Mosaic Law, however, strikingly filled this need, revealing

God's holiness and love by setting forth an organized code of moral and spiritual behavior for all. It thus served as a mirror by which each could see his or her sins and seek the mercy and grace of God through the sacrificial offerings. The focal point of the Law and offerings was the "suffering servant" of Isaiah 53. That one both fulfilled the Law and made atonement for its breaking. This universal function of the Law has not terminated, as Paul often reminds us (Romans 3:31; 1 Timothy 1:5–9).

Thus the Mosaic Law had a twofold purpose toward Israel and the world. As a covenant system with Israel, it ended at the cross; as a revelation of God's basic principles of holiness and conduct, however, it is as eternal as the heavens. This moral covenant relates to the Abrahamic covenant that promised a seed to bless all nations in that it emphasized the need for that seed.

THE PALESTINIC COVENANT

A further covenant was given to Israel through Moses about thirty-nine years later, detailing their right to the land of Palestine (Deuteronomy 28–30). It was given just before Moses died and Joshua led the nation across the Jordan into the Promised Land. This Palestinic covenant elaborated on a promise that was common to both the Abrahamic and Mosaic covenants—occupying the Promised Land. As related to the Abrahamic, it was unconditional, guaranteeing their final possession of the land. But related to the Mosaic covenant, it was conditional, requiring their observance of the covenant laws. The land would indeed be given to Israel forever, but any generation that refused to comply with the covenant code would be evicted from the covenant land (Deuteronomy 28:58–64). As tenants in the Lord's land, their positive response to His leadership was required to remain in the land.

In the later history of Israel, this blessing was many times forfeited because of their disobedience and straying from the Lord. That failure brought the Lord's discipline through many of their enemies. It finally also brought their eviction and scattering among the nations. The Lord had promised this judgment as the seventh and final chastisement that He would send them for disobedience (Leviticus 26:33; Deuteronomy 28:64).

This covenant, however, did not end with a warning of judgment, but with a promise of final restoration. That regathering, of course, was dependent on their repentance and turning to the Lord (Deuteronomy 30:1–3; cf. 2 Chronicles 7:14). It was grounded on the Abrahamic promise of the land, simply spelling it out. The Lord guaranteed that Israel would finally possess the land forever. Though a partial return of the Jews to Palestine is presently taking place, its final and complete fulfillment awaits the return of Christ to the nation. It is then that their national repentance will take place as they recognize and receive their Messiah, following a time of great national tragedy (Zechariah 12:10–14).

THE DAVIDIC COVENANT

The Lord's "national" promise to Abraham came to fruition about a thousand years later. His promise of a "great nation" included kings and kingdoms and was later specified to come through the tribe of Judah (Genesis 17:6; 49:10). In the crowning of David as King this covenant was partially fulfilled in 1010 B.C. However, the Lord elaborated that promise by giving David a covenant that guaranteed to him and his sons the kingship forever (2 Samuel 7:10–16).

The giving of this Davidic covenant is another instance of the Lord responding to great love and devotion. It was given to David as he grieved over the Lord's ark dwelling in a tent, while he had built for himself a house of cedar. When he then sought to build a house for the Lord, the Lord denied him, but declared rather that He would build a "house" for David. This promise became the Davidic covenant.

In this covenant God promised David and his house permanent throne rights and a permanent kingdom. His house would never be destroyed (as was Saul's). Rather, the throne would always remain in his family, and the kingdom would be established forever. These were divinely guaranteed, even though his sons might prove unfaithful. Four hundred years later when Jerusalem was being destroyed for its sins and the people taken to Babylon, Jeremiah declared, "David shall never lack a man to sit upon the throne of the house of Israel" (Jeremiah 33:17). Through Israel's checkered history, David's sons often proved unfaithful and were sent into exile. But the throne rights remained in his line. Not knowing their genealogies today, modern Israel does not have a king as did ancient Israel; they elect a prime minister, still waiting for their "son of David."

This covenant with David also specified his son Solomon as the heir to the throne (1 Chronicles 22:9–10). No other son of David could claim it. That is why Matthew establishes Jesus' right to the throne by tracing His legal genealogy through Joseph back to Solomon and David. It was through this Solomonic line that Jesus came as king. Mary's lineage through Nathan had no right to the throne. Though Jesus could not be the physical son of Joseph and be our Savior, He had to be the legal son of Joseph to be Israel's king. This Old Testament conundrum is beautifully resolved in the virgin birth.

Jesus' genealogy through Coniah (Jeconiah) is often questioned, since Coniah is thought to have had a curse on his line (Matthew 1:11; Jeremiah 22:30). Nearly all present-day commentaries, in fact, regard the Solomonic line as having ended with Coniah, many suggesting the messianic line switched over to the lineage of Mary, receiving the kingship through Nathan a younger son of David. That, of course, would be unthinkable, as previously noted. Nor did Matthew buy this explanation; rather, he staked Jesus' right to the throne on His coming through Coniah.

That so-called curse on Coniah is better seen as a curse on Zedekiah, the wicked king then reigning. He is the one Jeremiah lectured in Jeremiah 21–22, after the egotistical king had taunted the prophet for a miracle and a good word from the Lord. Very shortly, however, he was captured by Nebuchadnezzar who killed all his sons as he watched, and then blinded him and took him to Babylon. Both the context and a proper reading of the Hebrew grammar suggest that the curse was on wicked Zedekiah, not Jeconiah (Coniah). It is essential to recognize that Jesus' legal genealogy had to come through Solomon and Coniah to be legally designated the "King of Israel."

The Davidic covenant then is the divine guarantee that David's future son through Solomon would reign over Israel forever. The prophet

Zechariah further declared that His rulership would extend over all nations (Zechariah 14:9). He will, in fact, one day be King of kings and Lord of lords (Revelation 19:16).

THE NEW COVENANT IN JEREMIAH

Toward the end of Israel's history as a nation (586 B.C.), Jeremiah the prophet announced a future covenant with both Israel and Judah. This is called the "New Covenant" (Jeremiah 31:31ff.). It is new in that it will take the place of the Mosaic Law received at Sinai that they so grossly violated. The nation was at that time taking the bitter consequence of that violation, but complained that the Lord had let them down. Jeremiah then bluntly enlightened them as to who had let down whom, declaring that their failure to keep the covenant Law had deprived them of the covenant land. He made his point in sledgehammer style.

Jeremiah looked beyond their days of rebellion and captivity to the time of their regathering by the Lord (Jeremiah 31:28). At that time the Lord will replace the Sinaitic covenant with a new one. Like the Mosaic, it will condition blessing; but unlike it, the New Covenant will be an inward ethic, written on the heart, rather than a list of do's and don'ts. All will know the Lord from the least to the greatest.

This New Covenant is generally understood to find its fulfillment in the New Testament gospel, primarily because the writer of Hebrews quotes from it (Hebrews 8:7ff.). The opinion of many throughout history that the Jews lost their covenant rights for slaying Messiah makes this view sound plausible. It certainly has strong similarities to the spiritual life of the church. To apply it primarily to the church, however, requires some impossible allegorizations. The terms do not fit; the timing does not fit; and the guarantee of a final restoration of Israel and Judah to the land becomes sheer deception to the very people with whom it was made (Jeremiah 31:38).

It is best not to foreclose on this promise of a future covenant for Israel. Paul declared that the adoption and covenants belong to Israel (Romans 9:4). The writer of Hebrews simply uses this prophecy of Jeremiah to demonstrate that the Mosaic covenant was not eternal, as many of the Jews thought. The proof he offers is Jeremiah's prediction that the Lord would one day replace it with a new covenant after the two nations are regathered. He sought to shock them into the reality that the old Mosaic covenant with its offering system was obsolete (Hebrews 8:13), not that the Jeremiah covenant was then in force.

To make Jeremiah's covenant the redemptive covenant of the church would then imply that the Mosaic covenant brought salvation, for that is what Jeremiah's covenant was to replace. This Paul vehemently denied (Galatians 3:21). Rather, the church's "new covenant" is the Lord Himself who through His blood in death and resurrection has become our Lord and Guide (Luke 22:20; 2 Corinthians 3:6, 17). As Paul said, He died and rose to be our Lord, not to put us under another system (Matthew 11:28; Romans 14:9).

This New Covenant of Jeremiah then will be established with a new generation of Israel, all of whom will know the Lord and have received His forgiveness. It will begin a new era of spiritual relations when they are regathered from dispersion and have met the Lord Himself. They will have no need for anyone to instruct them by written tablets, for the Lord will dwell among them (Jeremiah 31:33–34). He will then be "the god of all the families of Israel" and institute a new plan of blessing His people (Jeremiah 31:1–6). The prophet declared this future fellowship between the Lord and His ancient people to be as certain as the ordinances of day and night (Jeremiah 31:35–36). The point is that God will not forsake His people whom He foreknew (Romans 11:2).

THE COVENANTS SUMMARIZED

These covenants show the beautiful symmetry of the Lord's program for His people. That program is especially seen in the Abrahamic covenant around which all the others converge. Feeding into it are the Adamic and Noahic pacts, which introduce God's redemptive and kingdom purposes. This central covenant then spells out those purposes by four promises, constituting also an outline of the guarantees given in the following covenants:

1) The Mosaic covenant spelled out personal blessings of prosperity and care, conditioned on individual obedience (Deuteronomy 5:31–33).

2) The Palestinic elaborated the territorial blessings of Canaan, conditional for each generation, but ultimately guaranteed to Israel.

3) The Davidic covenant specified the national blessings of a king and kingdom to come through David and Solomon.

4) The promise of spiritual blessings to all nations is later seen to be fulfilled in Christ's provision of redemption for all people.

5) Finally, the New Covenant announced by Jeremiah is a secondary covenant to be instituted when Israel turns to the Lord and is finally regathered to the land. This covenant will replace the Mosaic code, which was temporal, and will be written on the heart rather than on tables of stone.

All these divine covenants, with the exception of the Mosaic Law, are unconditional, their ultimate fulfillment being dependent on God's sovereign "I will." Each, however, has conditional aspects with respect to individual participation. They were available to Abraham's children as they responded to God and His theocratic rule. Individual blessings were dependent on individual responses. This again points up the fact that the covenants were given to evoke faith-responses on a personal basis and to nurture people in fellowship with God. This is the primary and ultimate purpose of God with men and women (2 Peter 1:4).

Promises, promises, promises. In these God has revealed His divine program of specific goals in human history. Blessings, blessings, blessings. These He has guaranteed by His sovereign "I will," and not one of them shall fail of fulfillment. That is the essence of the covenants and the gospel, all to find fulfillment in Jesus Christ.

The Coming Day of the Lord

(First darkness, then light)

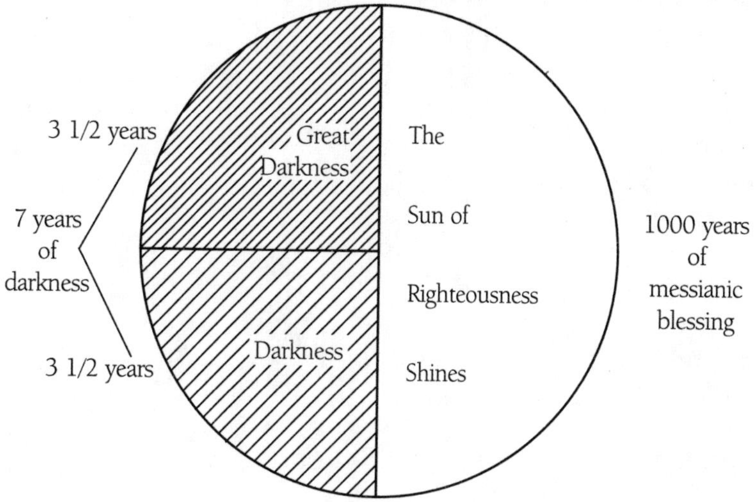

Messiah's Work as the Servant of the Lord

(His threefold ministry)

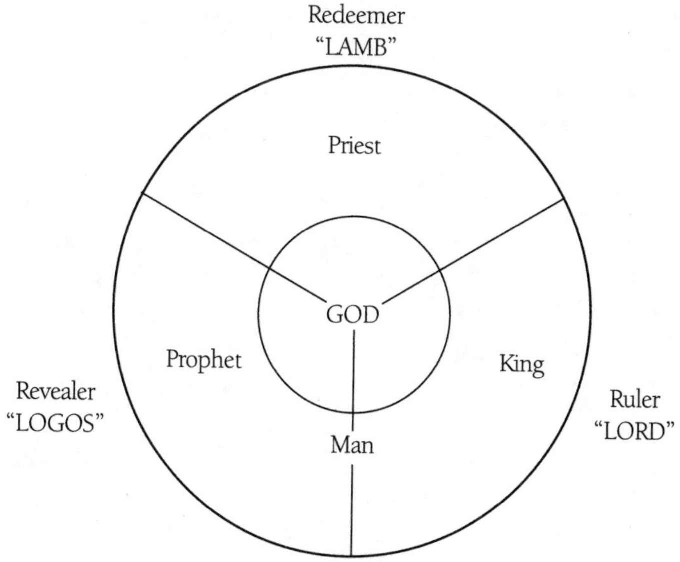

CHAPTER FOUR

THE PROPHETS: GOD DETAILS HIS PLAN

Most human predictions change with the seasons. We can't see around the corner, let alone into the future. However, God's foresight is as sharp as His hindsight; He is Lord of the future. Individuals may dabble in general prognoses of guess and hope, but God specializes in specific details of the future. As we have noted, He has claimed a monopoly in the field. To demonstrate this aspect of His sovereignty, the Lord endowed certain men with the ability to "sightsee" the future. These men were called prophets in the Old Testament, and forecasting the future became their badge of authenticity (Isaiah 41:21–23; Daniel 2:28).

THE WORK OF THE PROPHETS

The prophets of Israel go back to the founding fathers, Abraham, Moses, and Samuel (Genesis 20:7; Deuteronomy 18:15; 1 Samuel 3:20). Unlike the offices of priest and king, however, they were not restricted to specific families or tribes. Prophetesses were also raised up for this emergency service, commanding the attention of the nation. These prophets of Israel can be listed in two general groups, the "speaking prophets" and the "writing" prophets. Most of the "writing prophets" came on the scene after the "speaking prophets," recording specific messages from the Lord.

The times of the writing prophets of Israel were mainly in the latter stages of Israel's history. They were raised up as special heralds in times of great national crises. Most of them came on the scene when idolatry and degeneration were rampant and judgment was about to fall. Their tenure was often when the kings and priests had departed from God's Law and the covenant of blessing. They spoke to the people long after the covenants had been established. Their mission was to call the nation to repentance and righteousness that the covenant promises might be fulfilled. In the process they were used by God to fill in many of the details of that prophetic program. What the covenants had outlined, the writing prophets detailed in many specific ways.

These prophets of Israel came to be an institution in themselves. A rugged and stern breed of individuals, they were called to fulfill an assignment that was anything but popular. Coming from outside the system, they spoke with thundering power to the whole society of kings, priests, and people. In a sense, they constituted the nagging conscience of the nation. Preachers they were, but not mere finger-pointers or ritualists. Their appearance was often a solemn omen: God was about to speak in judgment or deliverance. Though frequently reviled as they spoke, they were later exonerated and revered as their judgments came to pass. They left the people no doubt that a mighty prophet had been among them.

It was through these doughty saints that God chose to unveil many details of His future program. As the covenants provided the skeleton of that program, the prophets boldly described details of its life and substance.

The content of the prophets' messages touched many aspects of life, but we can summarize them under the two concepts of judgment and blessing. They warned of judgment for sin and promised blessing for repentance and obedience. Many of their words were historically fulfilled, but many others concerned things to come. They both addressed the needs of their own generations and envisioned what God would do in the distant future. Their prophetic binoculars often had both close-range and telescopic lenses.

Our concern in this survey, however, is with the end-time program when God will culminate His purposes in the earth. By looking through their telescopic lenses we can get a broad perspective of the prophetic end times by highlighting their emphasis on judgment and blessing. These can be seen by reviewing two of their central themes: "the judgment of the coming Day of the Lord," and "the blessing of the coming of Messiah."

THE JUDGMENTS OF THE COMING DAY OF THE LORD

This first prophetic theme of "judgment" in the Day of the Lord, brings up a concept that is anything but popular today. To many it is downright contemptible and incompatible with Christian love. Religion, we are told, should be attractive, soothing, and appealing. If God is both loving and almighty, why all this talk about judgment?

The popular view of God as an indulgent grandfather may be folksy and "Good Ol' Charlie Brown" theology, but it is not found in the Bible. Though the Bible does have much to say of God's love in Christ, it also reveals His anger and coming wrath on sin. It has more to say about judgment, in fact, than about any other subject (as seen in the Old Testament prophets and the words of Jesus).

Several kinds of judgment are described, but the one most frequently spoken of in the Old Testament is that of the Day of the Lord. Franz Delitzsch, the great Old Testament scholar of Germany, called this term the "watchword of prophecy." It is used twenty times in the Hebrew Bible and alluded to countless other times (some seventy-five as "that day"). Though it concludes with the great age of messianic blessings, the prophets especially emphasized this coming day of judgment or world accounting. Since the judgments of that day loom so large in their view of the future, it is essential that we grasp their overall meaning as they related it to future events.

The Day of the Lord Identified

The Day of the Lord in its simplest form means "God's day," in contrast to "man's day." It can be thought of as a special time when God steps into human affairs to assume direct control, whether in judgment or blessing. It does not necessarily mean a single day of twenty-four hours, but rather a specific time period. Such, for instance, was the time of the great flood of Genesis which lasted over a year; the judgment of the locust plague in Joel 1; and the destruction of Jerusalem by Nebuchadnezzar who is said to have wielded the "sword of the Lord" (Zephaniah 1).

More specifically, however, the Lord will grab the reins of world affairs to fulfill His covenant promises of judgment and blessing. In this more technical sense the prophets spoke of it as a specific time in the future when God will bring the nations of the world to account. This divine accounting seems to relate especially to the Noahic covenant, as we shall presently note.

The time limits of that future period can be seen more precisely from its use in the New Testament. In 2 Thessalonians 2:3, Paul declares that the Day of the Lord will begin when the Antichrist appears. His appearance will mark the commencement of that period when God will use this wicked king to polarize all anti-God forces shortly before their destruction. Its end will come after the millennial age and God's renewing of heaven and earth, as Peter notes in his final epistle (2 Peter 3:10). These references indicate that the entire period of the Day of the Lord will extend over a thousand years from the beginning of the tribulation period to the final purging of the earth for the eternal state.

The preponderant usage of this term, however, concerns that time of world judgment just prior to Christ's return, known as the "tribulation period." This is evidently the same period referred to by Daniel as the "seventieth week" of Israel. It is basically that end-time period, often described in the Bible, when God will bring judgment and wrath on the nations as they unite in rebellion against Him. That time of judgment, however, will relate to both Israel and the world at large.

Judgment on the World

The Prophets consistently proclaimed that judgment must precede blessing. Before the earth can experience the reign of Messiah, it must be purged of its sin and lawlessness. David in his second Psalm portrayed this coming judgment as a time of God's wrath poured out on a raging world, whose leaders formed a conspiracy against God's "Anointed" (Psalm 2). Joel, one of the first writing prophets, also described it as a day of darkness unparalleled in human history (Joel 2:1–2). He described it as a time of destruction from the Almighty, the "fireworks" of which would reach to the starry heavens (Joel 1:15; 2:30f.).

Isaiah, a prophet of the late eighth century, emphasized world judgment. In his "Little Apocalypse" of chapter 24, for instance, he envisioned the earth as being utterly spoiled as a result of man's transgression of God's laws. The desolation will be so great that few inhabitants of the earth will survive (v. 6). He saw the earth as reeling to and fro and the sun and moon as being ashamed. The specific reason for this divine judgment Isaiah attributed to the nations' failure to keep the everlasting covenant (Isaiah 24:5). This is obviously the Noahic covenant, the only everlasting covenant given to the nations as such (Genesis 9:5–11). The implication is that God will judge the nations for their failure to restrain evil and maintain moral righteousness.

Daniel the prophet in exile also speaks of this intense period of God's wrath on the nations. He described it as a "time of distress such as never occurred since there was a nation until that time" (Daniel 12:1). His prophecy especially emphasized the part Antichrist will play in the final drama. He saw this dark figure as the human agent especially responsible for igniting the international horror. Following a meteoric rise to power after which he coerces the world to satanic idolatry, this fierce, godless, world dictator will assemble the nations of the world against Jerusalem in vengeance against God. Except for the supernatural help of Michael the archangel, even the elect of God would be destroyed in this holocaust (Daniel 12:1; cf. Matthew 24:21–22).

The climactic event of the period, as the prophets portray it, will be the coming of Messiah Himself. Isaiah 63 describes His coming in the role of a "man of war," treading down His enemies in anger and fury. His coming will make the earth to tremble (Isaiah 2:21). Of this the New

Testament has much to say in the consummation book of Revelation. Although the Lord will personally orchestrate this entire judgment on the nations from heaven, He will finally descend Himself to the place of judgment to complete the job—to "thoroughly purge his floor." Of that much more will be described in a later chapter.

These Old Testament passages stress the fact that God has set a day in which He will judge the nations. He will call them to account for perpetuating wickedness in the earth. Though He is long-suffering, He has not forgotten the wickedness of the unrepentant. He has not watered down His standards of righteousness or declared some kind of universal amnesty as a compromise with man's penchant to sin. His hatred for sin has not assuaged. The Day of the Lord will demonstrate His wrath against those who despise both His law and His grace.

Judgment on the Nation Israel

This warning of coming wrath on the nations should have struck fear and awe in the most callused hearts of Israel. The irony is that the opposite took place. They rejoiced at this condemnation of the heathen. The self-righteous of the nation saw it as their day of vengeance on their adversaries. To them it was just recompense for their voracious onslaughts against them. This attitude is especially reflected in the book of Jonah where even the prophet hoped for their destruction rather than their salvation.

Many of the prophets however, condemned this attitude and warned the nation of it (that was the point of Jonah's message). In staccato words of warning they sought to arouse the nation: "Alas, you who are longing for the day of the LORD," said Amos. "For what purpose will the day of the LORD be to you? It will be darkness and not light" (Amos 5:18). Far from being exempt from that judgment, they declared that Israel will actually be the vortex or focal point of much of that terror. Most of the prophets speak of this final purging of the nation.

The Bible references to this period of intense trial for Israel date back to Moses and the covenants. As he spoke his final words to Israel, he lamented that in the distant future they would be scattered among the nations. The covenants did not immune them from judgment. The later prophets also emphasized this theme as they came to warn both kingdoms in their times of national apostasy. Joel in the south, for instance, decried the drunkenness and dead ritualism of Judah and Jerusalem, pleading for repentance. Amos in the north, eloquently pleaded for their return to righteousness, condemning their blatant carnality as the nation plunged toward destruction. As they basked in the prosperity and pleasure of the golden age of Jeroboam II, this shepherd-prophet scored them with his bony finger of condemnation. Though he included the heathen in his roster of judgment, he saved his most explosive salvos for Israel. The nation, he declared, would bear the brunt of that judgment, for she had more than her share of sinners, most of whom knew better, but willfully disdained that knowledge.

As Amos spoke to the North prior to its captivity, so Jeremiah spoke to the South as it also careened to destruction in the following century (625–586). His prophecy, however, envisioned also a distant judgment for both nations. While announcing immediate judgment at the hands of Babylon, he foresaw also a day of travail in the distant future for both Israel and Judah. "Alas! for that day is great, there is none like it; and it is the time of Jacob's distress" (Jeremiah 30:7). Following this time of final tribulation, however, the prophet declared that a remnant would be saved, after which both nations would be regathered in peace and spiritual unification. This prophecy spoken while Judah was on the skids, obviously refers to the time of Israel's final regathering at Christ's return. Then "David their king, whom I will raise up for them," will reign over the whole nation as he serves under Christ the King of kings (Jeremiah 30:9).

The Great and Terrible Day of the Lord

Several prophets refer to the Day of the Lord as the "great and terrible [dreadful] day of the Lord" (Joel 2:31; Zephaniah 1:14; Malachi 4:5). They suggest that part of that period will be of special intensity, a fact also noted by the New Testament. Interestingly, these three prophets spoke at the beginning, middle, and end of the prophetic era, about two hundred years apart (830; 630; 430). Joel, one of the first writing prophets, noted that this intense wrath would begin with certain heavenly signs and disturbances. The sun will "be turned into darkness and the moon into blood" before the great and terrible Day of the Lord (Joel 2:31). This is similar to Zephaniah's description (1:14ff.). and almost identical to that of the apostle John in Revelation 6:12–17.

Malachi also reminded the nation of this divine day of judgment in his final message of the Old Testament. His last words alerted them to a special sign the Lord would send to commence that day (Malachi 4:5–6). That sign will be the return of Elijah the prophet for a special ministry to the nation. As with other judgments, God's wrath is often preceded by warnings. Malachi saw the Lord's "smiting the land with a curse" as contingent on their response to Elijah's coming and powerful ministry. This appears to be what John also refers to in Revelation 11, as he describes the two witnesses in the end times. Their "power to shut heaven so that no rain falls in the days of their prophecy" (three and a half years), almost certainly alludes to this return of Elijah who began his judgment ministry in the time of idolatrous Ahab by calling for a drought (1 Kings 17:1).

This time of great and terrible distress for Israel Jesus called the "great tribulation" (Matthew 24:21). It will be a brief period of unprecedented trial followed by His own return in glory. Though the people of Israel have known unrelieved suffering through much of their history, Jesus said their greatest crucible lies ahead. For reasons not entirely of their own making, they have certainly not yet recognized Jesus as their Messiah. Doubtless the church bears part of the blame for alienating them, but there is yet little sign of a turnaround. However, at the conclusion of this final purge, the whole nation will mourn for Him as they see His wounded hands and side (Zechariah 12). Though traumatic for all involved, it will accomplish its divine purpose of salvaging a purified remnant for the new society of Israel in the messianic kingdom.

These passages reveal the great concern of the prophets for the coming Day of the Lord. They saw it as a future period in world history when the sovereign Lord will call the world to account. He will judge them for their nonresponse to His sovereignty as Lord of the nations. This judgment will serve several salutary purposes in the divine plan. It will first demonstrate the natural consequences of sin in a world raging with passions and independence of God. In that short period it will show what a horrible holocaust sin can bring on a world when briefly allowed to go unrestrained.

Second, it will give an ominous demonstration of God's solemn view of lawlessness and rebellion. It will show that His patience with sin in the world does have an end. The Bible's portrayal of God's wrath against sin will be seen to be more than just a pious myth of divine fuming. It will confirm that His long-suffering, though long, is not endless.

Finally, the judgment of that day will cleanse the earth to prepare it for Messiah's kingdom of righteousness. As the world of Noah's time was scrubbed by water, so the earth will again be cleansed for a new beginning of peace and righteousness. That will usher in the blessing era of the Day of the Lord. As the Hebrew day began with a period of darkness followed by a period of sunshine, so the darkness of the Day of the Lord will be followed by the sunshine of Messiah's coming. He will come as "the sun of righteousness...with healing in its wings" (Malachi 4:2).

THE BLESSING OF MESSIAH'S COMING

The second grand theme of the prophets is that of the coming of Messiah, often called "the servant of the Lord." His Person and coming, of course, are central to the whole of Scripture, but are especially prominent in the Prophets. Though they often begin their prophecies with warnings of the Day of the Lord, they almost invariably conclude by alluding to the coming of Messiah and His kingdom. His coming is the stream of hope and joy in their messages. To get a taste of this content, let's recall the meaning of the name "Messiah," and then look at the person and work of Messiah as described by the prophets.

Messiah means the "Anointed One" (translated "Christ" in the New Testament). In Old Testament times, Israel's leaders were usually anointed for service. This gave them distinction among the people and divine power to execute their work. Their being anointed with oil spoke of the Spirit's presence and power working in them. Whether as prophet, priest, or king, they were acknowledged as the Lord's servant-leaders by this anointing.

There was, however, a unique person that the prophets looked for who was to be the supreme servant of the Lord, anointed as Messiah. Though only Daniel used this title (9:25–26), the other descriptions of Him assume this special anointing. His coming was the central hope of the Old Testament, for it was He who would deliver His people. Since so many myths and legends later grew up around this messianic concept, it is important to identify Him from the prophets themselves.

Messiah, the Servant of the Lord

The prophet Isaiah is often called the messianic prophet, though the Psalms and Zechariah also have this emphasis. Prominent in Isaiah is the designation, "servant of the Lord." This title suggests that this coming one would be both human and divine, the Son of David and the Son of God. Isaiah 9:6 describes Him as both a child born and Almighty God. His name, in fact, would be Immanuel, "God with us."

This twofold portrayal of Messiah is also drawn by Zechariah who described Him as being pierced as a man and as the Lord (YHWH) Himself (12:10; 14:3–4). The blending of these two natures by the prophets is quite common in the Psalms, and is, of course, explained and expanded in the New Testament. John the Apostle, for instance, referred to this hypostatic union of God and man in Messiah by showing Him as both the eternal Creator and yet made flesh to dwell among us (John 1; Isaiah 40:28).

This title, servant of the Lord, then suggests His coming to do God's service. As such, He would accomplish God's work, fulfilling His kingdom and redemptive purposes in the earth. This work of Messiah may be reviewed by recalling the three offices He was to fulfill: prophet, priest, and king. As a fulfillment of these sacred offices, Messiah was to be the final Prophet, Priest, and King. He would far outrank Moses the first prophet, Melchizedec the first priest, and David the first king.

To appreciate His servant work, it will help to review these Old Testament offices and how they served as types of this great antitype. They portray Messiah as the final Revealer, final Redeemer, and final Ruler for God in the earth.

Messiah the Prophet

The prophetic work of Messiah was first introduced by Moses the first prophet (Deuteronomy 18:15). This he did as he was preparing to leave Israel under Joshua's leadership. Stressing the importance of giving heed to God's Word through the appointed leaders, he also announced that another Prophet would one day arise, to whom they had better give earnest heed.

For what purpose, we might ask, was Messiah to come as a prophet? The special work of a prophet's was to speak for God. They were His special ombudsmen, whether as forth-tellers or foretellers. Often their messages were accompanied by miraculous credentials, especially in the presence of strong resistance. Moses, for instance, performed many miracles in Egypt where he had to convince the people that he spoke from God. Likewise, Elijah and Elisha wrought mighty miracles as they denounced the idolatry of Baal in Israel. Miracles were signs from heaven to command attention and underscore their divine authority as they confronted unbelief.

Those miracles of the prophets were a kind of foretaste of what the Prophet Messiah would do. His miracles, however, would be far more numerous. They would, in fact, constitute His credentials as the final prophet from God. Like the prophets of old, He would do His mighty works in the power of the Holy Spirit (Isaiah 11:2; 42:1; 61:1). In this power He would heal the sick and judge the wicked in the presence of great opposition (Isaiah 35:4–6; 42:1–4).

The preeminent work of the Old Testament prophets, however, was not performing miracles, but proclaiming God's message. Moses was famous for his miraculous works, but he was far more distinguished for his mighty words. He was especially known as the lawgiver. Likewise, this final Prophet, whom he introduced, was to be preeminently known for His mighty words (Deuteronomy 18:18). He would, in fact, be the outstanding revelation of God, far superseding Moses as the voice and Word of God. John in the New Testament constantly identifies Jesus in this way. As the living Word, He came to reveal both the character of the Father and His final message to men (Hebrews 1:1–2).

The Old Testament, then, saw the coming of Messiah as God's prophet par excellence. His prophetic ministry would be backed up with the staccato power of miracles, arousing all to the fact that God had again spoken to His people, this time by one far greater than Moses (Hebrews 1:2). This prophetic work was the first important aspect of Messiah's ministry as the servant of the Lord.

Messiah the Priest

Israel, however, needed more than a prophet; she needed a priest. Besides revelation, she needed redemption. Though in covenant relation with the Lord, her most basic need was atonement for sin. To fill this need for Israel and all mankind, Messiah would come not only as a prophet but also as a priest. He would, in fact, be the ultimate and final High Priest. David made this point in Psalm 110:4: "The Lord has sworn and will not change His mind, 'Thou art a priest forever according to the order of Melchizedek.'" Later writers also elaborated on this high priestly work of Messiah.

His Priestly Functions

To appreciate the significance of Messiah's priestly work, we need to recall the primary functions of the Old Testament priests. Their work involved two basic functions: making atonement for sin and making intercession for sinners. At the brazen altar of the temple they offered sacrifices for sin; on the basis of that offering they then offered incense in the holy place and made intercession for sinners. The prophet Isaiah nicely summarized this work as he applied it to the coming Messiah: "He Himself bore the sin of many, and interceded for the transgressors"

(Isaiah 53:12). In contrast to the work of a prophet who spoke to men for God, the priest spoke to God for men. He was God's ordained channel of approach to Himself on the basis of the atoning blood (Leviticus 17:11). The priest was the divinely appointed mediator between God and man.

His Qualifications

To perform this work the priest had to have special qualifications. Not just anyone could assume the office. The New Testament book of Hebrews summarizes the Levitical code by noting two basic requirements for a priest (Hebrews 5:1–4). First, he had to be "taken from among men"—that is, a genuine representative of man. As man's attorney before God, he had to understand the human dilemma by walking in the sandals of men.

Second, he had to be ordained by God—that is, he could not just take up the vocation on his own. A special anointing or approval by God was required for him to stand before the Almighty. Likewise, Jesus "became to all those who obey him the source of eternal salvation" (Hebrews 5:9). These two basic qualifications of a priest in the Old Testament were supremely fulfilled in Christ.

Isaiah 53 gives a classic portrayal of the servant of the Lord fulfilling these high priestly functions. This passage is really the high point of the Old Testament in describing Messiah's atoning work. Isaiah, the "prince of prophets," constructs a beautiful symmetry around this imperial chapter, as well as within it. The twenty-seven chapters of the second half of the book (40–66) are divided into three sections of nine chapters each, with a similar conclusion in each, "There is no peace for the wicked" (the last chapter describing it). Also the central chapter of each section highlights the theme of that section and they all converge around chapter 53. This symmetry may be seen in a pyramidal outline that builds up to and flows from the majestic peak of this central chapter.

ISAIAH 40–66

I. THE GREATNESS OF GOD AS SOVEREIGN CREATOR 40–48

40. His greatness as a sovereign Shepherd
41. His greatness to deliver Israel
42. His greatness as a "Servant"
43. His greatness to save the undeserving
44. His greatness contrasted with idols
45. His greatness to unshackle through Cyrus
46. His greatness over Babylon's idols
47. His greatness to judge proud Babylon
48. His greatness to purge obstinate Israel

II. THE GRACE OF GOD AS SUFFERING SAVIOR 49–57

49. The Lord's Servant as a worldwide Savior
50. The Lord's Servant deplores Israel's divorce
51. The Lord's Servant to save in righteousness
52. The Lord's Servant prepares to bring salvation as "Lamb"
53. The Lord's Servant offers Himself as atonement for sin
54. His salvation extended to Israel in remarriage
55. His salvation extended to all the world
56. His salvation extended to the responsive
57. His salvation extended to the worst of sinners

III. THE GLORY OF GOD AS ROYAL RESTORER 58–66

58. Israel's religious depravity deplored
59. Israel's social depravity declared
60. Israel's future righteousness and glory
61. Israel's Bridegroom coming with jewels
62. Israel's royal remarriage in righteousness
63. Israel's great revenge at the Lord's return
64. Israel's remnant in deep penitence
65. Israel's purging for millennial glory
66. Israel's rebirth in humility and joy

This symmetry is further seen in that the central chapter of each section (44; 53; 62) epitomizes the emphasis of that section, and all the chapters converge on the "unbelievable report" of 53. Also the central four verses of 53 (5–8) constitute the heart of the gospel: after being rejected and pierced by men, the Suffering Servant bore our sins as "the Lord laid on Him the iniquities of us all." And amazingly, the central word of this central chapter in the Greek Septuagint text (144th of 290) is the identification of this servant as the "lamb" (53:7). Messiah's work as the Lamb of God is central to Isaiah's theme, as it is also to the whole Bible.

Isaiah concludes this chapter on the Suffering Servant with a succinct summary of the work of a priest. Though rejected and numbered with transgressors, the prophet says of this one that He "bore the sins of many and made intercession for the transgressors." That, of course, was the twofold work of the Old Testament priest who beautifully typified the high priestly work of Messiah.

An Old Testament Mystery Resolved

Though His priesthood is amply stated in the Old Testament, it is not left without problems. Unresolved is the mystery of how He could be a priest if He came from the wrong tribe—the tribe of Judah, rather than the priestly tribe of Levi. This problem is not answered, in fact, until the New Testament Book of Hebrews where the writer addresses this lingering dilemma. There he makes the point three times that Christ's priesthood was not of the Levitical order of Aaron, but of the superior order of Melchizedec (Hebrews 5:6–10; 6:20; 7:1–17). It was superior in that even Abraham paid homage to Melchizedec. Like Melchizedec, this priest would be one of a kind, without predecessor or successor. He would be the final and ultimate priest before God. This is so important to the Hebrew writer that he turns the whole argument of his book on this point. The obsolescence of the old covenant with its ritual system rested on this accession of Christ as the final priest for both Israel and the Church (Hebrews 7:12). Only in Christ could this Old Testament mystery of Messiah's priesthood be resolved.

Messiah the King

The most heralded function of Messiah, as prophesied in the Old Testament, was doubtless His coming as king. He was to be king of Israel and of the world. Not only would He reveal truth as Prophet and redeem men as Priest, but would also rule the earth as King. This reigning role of a glorious king, of course, became the beatific vision of the nation. It buoyed their spirits with hope, especially in later times as they groveled under the heel of Gentile oppressors.

PROMISED IN THE COVENANTS

The basis of this vision of Messiah as king derives originally from Jacob's blessing on his son Judah (Genesis 49). That blessing, however, was based on the Abrahamic covenant (2 Samuel 7:12–16; Psalm 2:6), which was further elaborated in the Davidic covenant. To David the Lord promised a son that would reign over Israel forever. Isaiah also referred to this when he spoke of Messiah's coming from the royal house of David (Isaiah 11:1). David evidently cogitated much over this promise, for his Psalms make frequent mention of such a coming king (e.g., Psalm 2:2, 6–12; 24:7–10; 89:3–4, 34–37; 110:1, 5–6).

PORTRAYED BY THE PROPHETS

The prophet Zechariah, however, gives the most explicit portrayal of this coming king. His vivid description is progressively developed throughout his book. In his final chapter he shows how He will come in judgment following a massive confrontation of nations against Jerusalem. This picture is not pretty, detailing a great slaughter of Israel and the nations, climaxed by the descent of Messiah to avenge His people. As He comes He trounces all His enemies. The prophet's final portrayal depicts Messiah as "king over all the earth," receiving homage from all nations who come to Jerusalem to worship (Zechariah 14:9, 16).

Zechariah's description of Messiah's coming, however, appears to be somewhat paradoxical, if not contradictory. Before picturing Him coming as a mighty king, he sketches Him coming in meekness and humility. Rather than riding a monarch's white steed, He comes riding a lowly burro (Zechariah 9:9). To complicate it further, he later portrays Him as one who has been pierced in the house of His friends (Zechariah 12:10; 13:6). This shepherd of Israel, he declared, would be smitten and the sheep scattered. What kind of Messiah is this?

This anomaly is difficult to harmonize apart from the New Testament. Its unexplained tension is seen in many of the prophets, but never entirely relieved. Nor could it have been by the very nature of events that would bring it about. Jewish commentaries even today are nonplused by it, many regarding the book of Zechariah an insoluble enigma. Some have sought to explain it by the idea that two different messiahs were promised in the Old Testament, a suffering servant and a conquering prince. One they identify as "son of Joseph," and the other as "son of David" (Edersheim, *Jesus the Messiah,* II, 434–35). This notion, however, is not derived from the Old Testament, but was a later concoction of the second century A.D. They used it to explain the Roman slaying of Bar Kokhba who claimed to be Messiah.

This problem, of course, dissolves in the New Testament after the actual crucifixion of Christ. He Himself explained that His Second Coming in glory would be entirely different from His first coming in humility, as we will note in a later chapter. Though He came the first time as the Suffering Servant to atone for sin, He will come the second time as the conquering king to judge and rule the world.

In retrospect we recall that David had a similar experience in becoming king, in many ways typifying Christ. Before he gained his throne, he suffered many injustices from jealous King Saul and went through a long period of exile. He gave a living portrayal of Messiah, his greater son. The promised Messiah would experience both of these roles in infinite degree to fulfill His mission of both redeemer and ruling sovereign over the earth.

Messiah's Kingdom

In describing a king and his work it would be unthinkable not to refer also to his kingdom. Likewise, the Old Testament has much to say of the messianic kingdom. King Messiah will not be an abstract king, but will reign over a kingdom. As we previously noted, that rule will involve not only His authority, but also a territory and people over which He reigns. Most of the prophets speak of this Old Testament portrayal of His kingdom, but especially those of Isaiah and Ezekiel.

ISAIAH'S VISION OF THE KINGDOM

The prophecy of Isaiah is most unique in its emphasis on salvation, but he also had much to say of the coming kingdom of Messiah. His predictions cover many aspects of Israel's life, both historic and prophetic. Concerning that coming kingdom, he spoke of its spiritual, social, political, and physical features. Though he thoroughly rebuked their increasing depravity, he also envisioned a bright future beyond their final purging with many changes occurring in their national life.

A sampling of these might be noted: a small righteous remnant will be preserved and regathered from all parts of the world. The land itself will be rejuvenated to blossom and fill the earth with fruit. Righteousness will cover the earth; health and productivity will flourish; and even the animal kingdom will be at peace (Isaiah 11; 25; 27; 35; 65). He notes also that Israel under Messiah will be the superpower among the nations, Jerusalem will be the world capital, and universal peace will cover the earth. All this the prophet envisioned as coming to pass by virtue of Messiah's redemptive work and His personal presence among His people.

This first major prophet paints this glowing picture of a reunited nation, but he frankly discerns it as a distant hope for the faithful, beyond their present morass of sin and depravity.

JEREMIAH'S VISION

Jeremiah followed Isaiah nearly one hundred years later but gave comparatively little space to the future kingdom. This weeping prophet was so overwhelmed by Judah's mounting rebellion, he spent most of his time warning of impending disaster. In the midst of that, however, he did provide a glimmer of light in the distant future concerning their broken covenant. As previously noted, chapters 30–33 speak of Israel's final restoration as guaranteed by the Abrahamic and Davidic covenants. Having declared in chapter 11 that they would experience God's curse for having broken the Mosaic covenant, he here announced that the Lord will one day institute a new covenant to replace the old. This new agreement will embrace both kingdoms when they are regathered in the land and regenerated. Jeremiah was careful to emphasize that these spiritual blessings would come after their final period of tribulation which he called "Jacob's trouble" (Jeremiah 30:7).

Ezekiel's Vision

This third major prophet was also a priest, but he ministered to the captive Jews in faraway Babylon. As a godly cleric, he gave the priestly version of their captivity in Babylon, showing its cause to be their sins of idolatry and temple defilement. For this he saw the Lord write "Ichabod" over the land, portraying the "glory" making a reluctant departure from the temple (Ezekiel 11:22f.).

In his final chapters (40–48), however, he pictured the return of that glory in the distant future along with the restoration of Israel's worship system. Not only will Jerusalem be rebuilt, but the temple also will be reconstructed with entirely new dimensions. Though similar to previous sanctuaries, that future temple will have some striking differences. Absent will be the ark of the covenant, the lampstand, the table of showbread, the mercy seat, the cherubim, the altar of incense, and the veil. A most amazing omission is the absence of a high priest, though other priests are mentioned.

These apparent errors are not explained and seem unconscionable for this priest turned architect—unless he had a special reason for leaving them out. On further reflection, however, that reason becomes obvious. The fact that Messiah Himself will be there in person is reason enough. He will be there as the true essence of the law, the lampstand, the showbread, the mercy seat, etc. In that future kingdom, He will not only be the king on the throne, but also the recognized high priest of Israel. His personal presence there explains those missing parts and serves also to confirm the actual rebuilding of that future temple. It is consistent, as well with Ezekiel's earlier prophecies, all of which were fulfilled historically in a quite literal way, almost with a vengeance.

A more difficult problem arises, however, in the reinstitution of the sacrificial ritual. Ezekiel describes many details of that renewed system, including animal sacrifices. How do we reconcile this resumption of bloody offerings with the New Testament declaration that Christ was the final sacrifice for sin (Hebrews 9:25–28)? Was one of them mistaken?

To properly answer that, we need the perspective of the New Testament and especially the basic argument of the book of Hebrews. We will address this problem in a later chapter after we acquire that broader perspective.

SUMMARY OF THE PROPHETS

As the covenants were given to outline and guarantee God's program, the prophets later came to fill in the details. They came as God's special envoys in times of spiritual declension, calling the people back from disaster. As they rebuked the nation for sin, they also alerted them to the grandeur of a fantastic future promised to God's people.

Central to all their prophecies was the coming of the divine servant of the Lord, later called Messiah. This one would minister to the nation as the true prophet, priest, and king. His coming, however, always presented a bit of a mystery, for He was to come as both a suffering servant and a conquering king. Though these roles were not clearly sorted out, the prophets described His mission as bringing both spiritual deliverance from sin and national deliverance from their enemies.

From Abraham to John the Baptist, His coming was longingly anticipated, especially in times of exile and foreign oppression. That coming, however, came to tantalize different people in different ways, depending on their spiritual outlook. Some looked for spiritual redemption and a deliverer from sin; others were more concerned for national deliverance and economic welfare. The prophets, however, nowhere suggested that they could have the second without the first. The spiritual had to precede the material and political.

The further questions of when and how these events were to occur, however, remained enigmas to most of the prophets. Not that these were foolish and impious questions, but they were just not discussed. In God's good time, He did address the timing of both the coming of Messiah and His kingdom. To provide such a calendar the Lord prepared one of the wisest men of unblemished character in the Old Testament. His name, of course, was Daniel, and it is to His unique contribution to Old Testament prophecy that we must now turn.

God's Two Prophetic Timeclocks

The Times of the Gentiles and the Seventy Weeks for Israel

THE TIMES OF THE GENTILES							THE SEVENTY WEEKS FOR ISRAEL
Date	Empire	Daniel 2	7	8	11–12		Daniel 9
606 B.C.	Babylon		Lion				
536	Media-Persia		Bear	Ram (With 2 horns)	Named "Persia"	444 B.C.	Command to rebuild wall of Jerusalem
333	Greece		Leopard	He-Goat (Alexander the Great)	Named "Greece" Then Syria		69 "Sevens" (483 Years)
63	Rome		Dreadful Beast				
A.D. 33			Indefinite Gap (Church Age)			A.D. 33	Indefinite Gap
???	Revived Rome		10 Horns Little Horn	Little Horn	Willful King	???	One Seven: 3 1/2 Years / 3 1/2 Years
Messianic Kingdom		GOD'S KINGDOM Set Up	Saints to Rule		Saints Raised		Time of everlasting righteousness

CHAPTER FIVE

DANIEL'S PROPHECIES: GOD SETS HIS TIME CLOCK

Though the Bible is not a "Farmer's Almanac," it is not just a hodgepodge of apocalyptic drama either. Its prophecies have a neatly programmed calendar, set on a countdown schedule. God is not nervously watching the cycles of history, hoping to somehow slip in His predicted agenda. His calendar for the future is precise, worked out before the world began.

This divine timetable, however, is not open for public inspection. It is more like a family secret, made known to those in the family who can be trusted with it. That presumption may irk the unbelieving world, but His program is with people of faith, not those who reject His Word.

THE UNIQUENESS OF DANIEL

Such a man of mettle was Daniel the prophet. He was one of the finest men of sterling character in the Old Testament. Only Joseph parallels him in moral fiber and spiritual resolve. Both were disciplined by severe trials in foreign lands, and both learned to stand alone with God. The Lord seldom uses anyone who is not willing to purify his life, and these were outstanding examples of that principle. Like Joseph, Daniel rose to a pinnacle of power in world empires. Several times he served as prime minister, both over Babylon and Persia, thus exerting immense influence in world affairs.

Daniel's most significant role, of course, was that of a prophet. In line with his royal genealogy and background, his prophecies deal with Gentile kings and empires, primarily as they relate to Israel. The events of those empires took on great importance in prophecy, for God used them to peg significant points in His future program for both Israel and the world. On God's prophetic time clock, these Gentile nations serve as hour hands, indicating to Israel and all God's people the time and progress of His program.

Daniel's prophecy is different from the other major prophets in that he has very little to say of Messiah. On only two occasions does he refer to Messiah, once as being "cut off" (9:25–26), and once as a crushing "stone" that comes to set up an everlasting kingdom (2:44–45). But his emphasis is more on Antichrist, who stalks as a shadowy figure throughout the book and whose demonic agents seek to control empires (Daniel 10:13, 20). Daniel's concern is to trace the movement of empires and international affairs. He seeks to alert the godly of Israel to an awareness of God's sovereignty in world affairs, recording the repeated testimony of stubborn King Nebuchadnezzar that God reigns supreme in the kingdoms of men (Daniel 2:47; 3:29; 4:35).

His main concern is with the movement of Gentile kings and kingdoms that inadvertently serve God's purposes, in spite of themselves. Daniel outlines those movements, showing also the coming role of Antichrist who will epitomize ungodly kings. Isaiah as a prophet emphasized redemptive history; Daniel as a royal statesman gives the structure of kingdom history till Messiah sets up His world kingdom.

Daniel then develops his prophetic chronology along two basic lines which are parallel at many points: The "times of the Gentiles" and the "seventy weeks for Israel." These two structures concern events on the international scene that relate to Israel, all leading to the eventual coming of God's kingdom on earth.

THE TIMES OF THE GENTILES

The "times of the Gentiles" is that period of time in which the Gentiles have dominion over Israel, especially Jerusalem. It does not mean the whole history of Gentile kingdoms, but a specific series. Though the term is not used by Daniel, it was coined by our Lord as He referred to Daniel's prophecy in Luke 21:24. Jesus declared that Jerusalem would be "trampled underfoot by the Gentiles, until the times of the Gentiles be fulfilled." Therefore, this period began when Jerusalem was captured by Nebuchadnezzar in 605 B.C., and will be completed when Christ comes to set up His everlasting kingdom on earth (Daniel 1:1–2; 2:44; Luke 21:27).

Before further identifying this period, we should note what Daniel has to say about Gentile kingdoms, one of the basic themes of his book. He introduces them in chapter 2 by noting Nebuchadnezzar's dream of a great statue, representing five successive Gentile kingdoms. Through chapter 6 he elaborates on the theme of their subservience to God. In chapter 7 Daniel himself has a vision which restates the same structure of the times of the Gentiles, but from a different viewpoint. As King Nebuchadnezzar saw it in chapter 2 as a brilliant statue from the human view, Daniel the prophet saw it from the divine view as a menagerie of wild animals. Daniel then elaborates that vicious character under demonic influences through chapter 11. The last chapter culminates his theme by showing the divine rescue and assessment. Let's look more closely at these two pictures.

The Human View of the Times of the Gentiles

Nebuchadnezzar's dream of a great metallic statue in Daniel 2 gives a picturesque description of the times of the Gentiles. The statue's five body parts indicate five successive world empires from its head of gold to its toes of iron and clay:

1) The head of gold . . . . identified as Babylon;
2) The breast and arms of silver . . . . . Persia;
3) The belly and thighs of bronze . . . . Greece (and four divisions);
4) The legs of iron . . . . Rome;
5) The feet and toes of iron and clay . . revived Rome.

These five kingdoms were foreseen as dominating Israel during her time of disfranchisement. They would be her overlords until Messiah's rule would come. Daniel elaborates on the first and last kingdoms, especially the last. This will be a confederacy of ten kingdoms in power when Messiah comes to crush all authority and set up His everlasting kingdom. Its character of iron and clay suggests great strength, but little cohesion. The dream ends with the entire statue of Gentile empires being destroyed by a supernatural "stone" falling on its feet, that is, on the final form of Gentile rule.

The various metals used to symbolize these successive empires suggest two progressions. The first is a progressive deterioration or lessening value and specific gravity of the metals. Gold is more valuable and heavier than silver, and so on down the line from the head of the statue to the toes. Similarly, the power of Babylon was concentrated in the head; that of Medo-Persia was divided; and likewise Greece and Rome more distributed. The senate and the army, the emperor being chosen from one of these groups, in fact, ruled Rome. In the final kingdom of iron and clay that deterioration is so wide spread as to suggest fierce independence and heterogeneity.

The second progression is that of the increased strength of the metals from gold to iron. The probable implication is that the overall strength of each succeeding empire progressively increases. Babylon, for instance, was strong, but small and insignificant compared with the universal power of Rome. Thus each of the four empires had a progressively wider rule and lasted a longer time.

The principle lesson of the great statue, however, concerns the beginning and end of the times of the Gentiles. That period began with the reign of Nebuchadnezzar, the "head of gold," and it will come to an end when the God of heaven comes to destroy Gentile rule and set up His everlasting kingdom on earth. Gentile kings rule only at the behest of God and are governmentally responsible to Him.

The Divine View of the Times of the Gentiles

The last half of Daniel (7–12) is almost entirely prophetic, giving an increasingly concentrated picture of the end-time period. That final period will bring the times of the Gentiles to a close and usher in the everlasting kingdom of Messiah. Note how these chapters progressively focus on the end times. Chapter 7 gives the broad outline; 8 emphasizes the rise of the middle kingdoms of Medo-Persia and Greece to develop the details of the little horn of the end times; 9 brings Israel into the picture to show the relation of Israel's future to the times of the Gentiles; and 10–12 conclude the prophecy by highlighting the character and activities of the increasingly emerging figure of Antichrist in relation to Israel. The focus is on the end-time period when God will bring all nations to account as to how they have used or misused their authority, especially with relation to Israel.

The broad outline of chapter 7 is similar to that of chapter 2, but with some striking differences and additions. Here Daniel has the vision and the times of the Gentiles are seen from the divine view in the imagery of four scrapping beasts. All are carnivorous and prey on victims around the great sea, that is, the Mediterranean. The description of each beast suggests something of the character of the kingdom it represents. One is a lion with wings; the second, a bear standing higher on one side; the third, a leopard with four wings and heads; and the last a vicious nondescript beast with iron teeth. This last beast is seen to have ten horns, out of which an eleventh (little horn) arises to dominate all.

Daniel's focus in this vision is on the little horn, a detail not included in chapter 2. After inquiring about it, he is informed that the little horn is a final king who will arise out of a small kingdom to assume world control. Special note is made of his anti-God character and violence against the saints for a period of three and a half years (7:20–25). This blasphemous tyrant is finally broken by the coming of the "Most High," who with the saints sets up an everlasting kingdom. The whole prophecy has a storybook ending of triumph, but the intervening period of Gentile domination is portrayed as one of much grief for the saints, especially in its final form.

The Divine Purpose of the Times of the Gentiles

To recognize the divine purpose of this extended period of Gentile rule over Israel, it will help to recall the background that brought it about.

Before Israel became a nation, many Gentile kingdoms had flourished for centuries. Most of them were idolatrous and quite independent of God (Genesis 10–11). When the Lord called Abraham and the patriarchs, He proposed to set up a national theocracy that would rule the world for God. Israel became that chosen nation, being called out of Egypt and organized to be a theocratic society. As such, Israel was responsible to bring the knowledge of God to all the world, as Solomon declared in his inaugural prayer and blessing (1 Kings 8:43, 60). Had they done so, they would have been given an extended theocratic rule over the earth.

Israel, however, failed miserably in this responsibility. Besides that, she refused to subject herself to the Lord's leadership. Therefore, God sent them many chastisements as He had promised in Leviticus 26. Instead of being warned by these, they only increased in callousness, the South failing to take heed even after the destruction of the North (Isaiah 5:4; Ezekiel 23:9–11; Hosea 6:4f.). They degenerated downward and became even worse than the heathen. In the end, contempt for God's Word came to characterize the whole nation, prophets, priests, princes, and people alike (Jeremiah 36:23–24; Ezekiel 22:25–30).

God's final response to this contempt for His authority was sharp and decisive. He sent them into exile and ended the nation's theocratic authority. Refusing to submit to God's authority, Israel was relieved of her own kingdom authority. The Lord sent Nebuchadnezzar in 605 B.C. to take Jerusalem, and Israel's king was shortly taken to Babylon in chains. The last two reigns were only caretaker roles, ending in further defiance.

This subjugation began the period known as the times of the Gentiles. It is the time in which God rules Israel through the Gentiles, rather than using Israel to extend His rule over the world. This change in the divine economy concerning Israel and Jerusalem characterizes the entire period of the Gentiles. The first six chapters of Daniel emphasize the fact that, although Gentile rulers are on the throne, they have that authority only under the sovereign rulership of God. This point was hard for some to accept, but Nebuchadnezzar, the first king of these Gentiles, gave it as his final recorded testimony. He traumatically got the message, though it took a seven-year insanity for him to finally pass the test (Daniel 4:32–33).

Our Relation to the Times of the Gentiles

Having looked at the prominent features of this period, we might ask whether we are today living in the "times of the Gentiles." Jesus declared that "Jerusalem will be trampled underfoot by the Gentiles, until the times of the Gentiles be fulfilled" (Luke 21:24). Did that period come to a close when modern Israel recaptured Jerusalem in 1967?

Probably not. The end of that period, as noted by Daniel, is marked by Christ's coming as the "stone" to destroy Gentile rule and set up His everlasting kingdom. That is undoubtedly a future event. Furthermore, Jerusalem and its holy places are not totally under Israel's control, though they claim the city as their capital. For them to presume to occupy the temple square would quickly incite international jihad by the Muslims. Their claim to Jerusalem today is precarious at best.

It might also be noted that Israel's kingdom is nonexistent in the divine economy during the church age. As Paul declares, there is "no difference" between Jews and Greeks, but all are regarded as one herd of sinners and candidates for salvation in the body of Christ (Romans 3:22; 11:32; Galatians 3:28). Although the Jews are still a chosen people, God recognizes no "kingdom" of Israel under covenant relations today. They have neither their old covenant kingdom status nor its ritual system, as symbolized by the rent veil at Jesus' death.

The divine purpose of this Gentile calendar was to alert all to the fact that the Lord is sovereign in all the affairs of men, even those of the Gentiles. He is not just a casual or uncommitted observer. His covenant plans to establish an everlasting kingdom of righteousness on the earth are doing fine. They have not gone awry, Israel's infidelity and the Gentiles seeming upset of the divine apple cart notwithstanding. In His time each Gentile empire dutifully played its role, and that final empire of Antichrist is waiting in the wings to do likewise.

THE SEVENTY WEEKS OF ISRAEL: GOD'S JEWISH TIME CLOCK

The Lord has given us more than one way to tell time. Another measurement of the progress of His program is the time cycle known as the "seventy weeks of Israel." This was also given by vision and is recorded in Daniel 9, a chapter that is peculiarly Jewish. It is the only chapter in Daniel that uses the covenant name LORD (YHWH; 8 times) or deals primarily with Israel. This time clock has a Jewish accent, describing events on the local landscape of Israel rather than on the international scene. Though running on the current of Israel's life, it does have some similar features to the times of the Gentiles. It begins at a specific historic point, involves a series of national events, and concludes by fulfilling several important divine purposes. This time clock constitutes the basic framework of prophecy for the nation Israel.

The Background of This Prophecy

As with the vision concerning the Gentiles, this prophecy was given out of a background of national stress. The scene, again, was Babylon. Jerusalem had been destroyed and the people had been in captivity for nearly seventy years. The prophets attributed this captivity to the fact that Israel had cheated the Lord out of seventy sabbatical years and jubilees. That amounted to about 490 years of disobedience, dating back to the beginning of the nation (2 Chronicles 36:21). As they were being taken to Babylon, Jeremiah had predicted they would be there for seventy years, after which they would be returned (Jeremiah 25:11; 29:10). Their time of discipline in the divine woodshed was nearly finished.

Many of the Jews in Babylon, however, had settled down and taken on the style of the "good life" in that prosperous river valley. Still others, such as Daniel, had their eyes on Mt. Zion in Jerusalem and God's promise to bring about a return. The high positions Daniel attained in Babylon had not spoiled his spiritual vision. As he studied Jeremiah's prophecy of return in 537, he sensed the urgency of the time and sought the Lord in confession and supplication. This, by the way, was shortly after his being cast into the lion's den for his faithfulness in prayer in chapter 6.

Far from demanding that God fulfill His promises to return His people, Daniel recognized that God works only through repentant people; He responds to those who humbly seek His mercies (Daniel 9:18).

The prophet perceived that God rarely does anything without first moving His people to desperate prayer. He moves people before moving mountains—or empires. Accordingly, Daniel's study of Scripture moved him to pray, and his prayer moved God to act.

The Lord's response at this time, however, was not what might have been expected. Instead of dispatching the archangel Michael to fetch all the strays back to Jerusalem, He sent Gabriel on a prophecy mission. God was about to enact a fresh program in Israel before He would fulfill His covenant promises. With Israel's seventy years captivity drawing to a close, there would indeed be a return to the homeland. But another period of "seventy" lay before the nation—not seventy years, but seventy "weeks," that is seventy "sevens" or 490 years. Those 490 would also be divided into three divisions: seven sevens (49), sixty-two sevens (434), and one seven (7) (Daniel 9:24–27) to fulfill the cycle.

The Purpose of the Seventy Weeks for Israel

The evidence is that Daniel and others of the Jewish captives looked for more than just a hike back to Jerusalem. Many were concerned for their spiritual needs and God's promises. They looked for Messiah and the inauguration of His messianic kingdom, as foretold in the Scriptures. Those anticipations are implied in Daniel 9:24, and they constitute the major divine purposes which the Lord will fulfill at the conclusion of the seventy weeks. These may be summarized in seven points:

1) The overall purpose:	to fulfill the covenants with Israel
2) The social purpose:	to end Israel's transgression of the Law
3) The redemptive purpose:	to make final atonement for sin
4) The reconciling purpose:	to achieve reconciliation with God
5) The kingdom purpose:	to establish the kingdom of righteousness
6) The prophetic purpose:	to seal or complete prophecy
7) The glory purpose:	to anoint the "most holy" (i.e., prepare the temple for the return of the "glory")

Whether all these things were understood or even anticipated, they were promised by the prophets and are listed here by Gabriel as things that should have been expected (Daniel 9:21–24). The angel declared that, after a period of seventy sevens, all these divine purposes would be fulfilled.

For Daniel and the faithful of Israel this vision provided an answer to two baffling mysteries that would concern them in the coming centuries. The first was the question of when Messiah would come to deal with sin and when He would set up His kingdom on earth. This showed that those events were yet in the distant future. The second was the question of how the changes of world empires would relate to Israel and her future. This prophecy showed that God's time clock is geared to both the international scene and to specific events in Israel. They also showed their relation to the prophecies of Isaiah and the other prophets.

The Beginning of the Seventy Weeks

This Jewish time schedule is much more precise than that of the "times of the Gentiles." It is almost a digital clock. Its purpose was to mark off specific segments of time and events to instruct those anticipating God's program. As a time device, it had specific markings to indicate its starting point so that the projected time schedule would not be in doubt. Its starting point was the time of "the issuing of a decree to restore and rebuild Jerusalem" (Daniel 9:25). That rebuilding is further delineated to be the building of the street and wall of Jerusalem.

This starting point is often debated, however, inasmuch as several decrees were issued by Gentile rulers relative to the exiles' return (Ezra 1:1–2; 6:3, 13; Nehemiah 2:1–6). Only one, however, answers the description of this prophecy concerning rebuilding the city wall. That is the decree of the Persian emperor, Artaxerxes Longimanus, who sent Nehemiah back to Jerusalem specifically to rebuild the city wall (Nehemiah 2:1–6). For the remnant of Israel, that date was most memorable, for that decree allowed them finally to gain a semblance of independence and protection against the continued onslaughts of their neighbors (Nehemiah 6:15). Nehemiah's record of this date is also quite precise (Nisan 1, 444 B.C.), establishing a firm point of beginning for this Jewish calendar of seventy weeks.

The Sixty-Nine Weeks until Messiah

The first focal point of this prophecy is the coming of "Messiah the prince." The time span till that event is given as 483 years, or two segments of seven sevens and sixty-two sevens. The first seven (49 years) evidently spoke of the "troublous times" of rebuilding Jerusalem from 444 to 395 B.C. That period also saw the conclusion of the Old Testament prophets, which was the start of the 400 years of prophetic silence till the coming of John the Baptist.

The question is often asked: By what interpretive hocus-pocus do we get seven years out of one "week"? The answer is that the term "week" (Hebrew *shavua;* Greek *heptad*) simply means "seven"; whether it speaks of days or years is determined by the context. That same term is used in Genesis 29:27 of Jacob's seven years service to obtain Rachel. In the context of Daniel 9, the prophet had just studied Jeremiah's prophecy of Israel's seventy years captivity, a punishment for failing to keep sabbatical and jubilee years for 490 years (2 Chronicles 36:21). Thus this additional period of 490 years of trial under the Gentiles fits the context. The "sixty-nine weeks" then designates a total of 483 years till "Messiah the prince," beginning with the command to rebuild Jerusalem in Nisan 1, 444 B.C.

The Time of Messiah's Coming

The point at which the sixty-nine weeks (483 years) ended has also been a matter of controversy among interpreters. Various methods of calculating that span have been used. Perhaps the most precise is that of adding up the number of Bible years and days (360 days to a year, Genesis 7:11, 24; 8:4; Revelation 11:3; 12:6; 13:5), and then measuring them out on the actual calendar of solar years (a solar year being 365.24217 days, or 365 days, 5 hours, 48 min. and 46 sec.). This may be outlined as follows:

1) Total Bible days: 69 x 7 = 483 years x 360 days = 173,880 days
2) Actual solar years: 173,880 – 365.24217 days = 476.0677 years
3) Total time span: Nisan 1, 444 B.C. + 476.0677 years = March 30, A.D. 33
4) Check: Nisan 1, 444 B.C. to Nisan 1 (Mar. 5), 33 A.D.= 476 years
   Add .0677 years x 365.24217 = 24.726 days = March 30, A.D. 33

That date, March 30, A.D. 33, was Palm Sunday, the day Jesus entered Jerusalem as the "the King who comes in the name of the LORD" (Psalm 118:26; Luke 19:38). The prophet Zechariah had also referred to it as the day "your King is coming to you…riding on a donkey" (Zechariah 9:9). Later that day Jesus wept over the city, announcing its coming destruction. The reason He gave: "because you did not recognize the time of your visitation" (Luke 19:42, 44). He sharply rebuked them for not knowing the prophetic significance of Messiah's coming on that day, the day Daniel's prophecy of the sixty-nine weeks came to an end.

If these calculations are correct, the scientific accuracy of this prophecy is remarkable, and for many, unbelievable. But why should we think it incredible that "God should raise the dead" or demonstrate His sovereign accuracy? Although He does not give us prophecy to entertain our curiosity, He does give it to strengthen our sense of His sovereignty in all things.

Events Following the Sixty-Nine Weeks

Besides the good news of Messiah's coming, the angel Gabriel had some jolting news for Israel. Two tragedies would follow Messiah's arrival. The first was that this Anointed One would be cut off after His initial appearance. Far from receiving His kingdom and establishing world rule, He would be struck down, not receiving His due. This, of course, accords with Isaiah's revelation of the Suffering Servant in Isaiah 53, and Zechariah's mention of His piercing (12:10). That they fully understood it is doubtful, but the Lord intimated that they should have had some awareness of it.

The second tragedy revealed to Daniel was the consequent destruction of the holy city and the desecration of the temple. With the city and temple not even rebuilt following its first destruction, the angel predicted another destruction, followed by an extended period of war and desolation. Jesus likewise foretold this destruction, with an added announcement: the Jewish people would soon be all but decimated, and those remaining would be taken captive into all the world (Luke 21:24). That destruction we know took place in A.D. 70 in the aftermath of a Jewish revolt and two-year siege of the city by the Romans. So devastating was this leveling of the city, there was little more than ashes and corpses that remained. An exception was part of the Western Wall (Wailing Wall), which was spared as a warning to any future rebels who might challenge the power of Rome. Furthermore, the plight of the surviving Jews became even worse than slavery as they were humiliated and used for lion fodder in the arenas of dispersion throughout the world. The enormity of these two tragedies for the nation are beyond calculation.

Is There a Gap in the Seventy Weeks?

The fact that these two tragedies were to take place after Messiah's appearance suggests the need to recognize a gap between the sixty-ninth and seventieth weeks. Not that Daniel's prediction made such a gap necessary, but the events of history show that a gap was, in fact, introduced. Though there are many who deny this, several considerations make such an extended hiatus obvious. The first is that there was a gap of nearly forty years between Jesus' death and the destruction of Jerusalem, as predicted by Gabriel. If a short gap did indeed take place, what would militate against a longer one?

Second, Jesus Himself saw the seventieth week as future, declaring that the "abomination of desolation" spoken of by Daniel would occur shortly before His Second Coming (Daniel 9:27; 12:11; Matthew 24:15). That event would, in fact, be a sign of His soon return. He thus evidently assumed a giant gap between the sixty-ninth and seventieth weeks.

Finally, if the seventieth week did follow immediately after the sixty-ninth and no gap was intended, where then are the things that should have been fulfilled at the end of the seventy weeks? Where are the "finish of transgressions" by the people and the kingdom of "everlasting righteousness" that should have followed?

It is therefore evident that a gap did occur after the sixty-ninth week and that this Jewish time clock stopped when Messiah was cut off. In God's good time it will be reactivated to fulfill the seventieth week. That future resumption will take place after the present age of the church is finished and the Lord again begins to deal with Israel as His covenant people. Until that time, that covenant clock has lost its tick, and although repairmen are busy clearing out the cobwebs today, it is still idle as a timepiece.

The Beginning of the Seventieth Week for Israel

Daniel's prophecy gave a specific time when that clock would again be plugged in to measure off the final seven years. That will be when the "coming prince" makes a covenant with the nation Israel (Daniel 9:27). This alliance will be made for a period of seven years, though the pact will be broken at midpoint by a change of character in the coming prince.

We immediately ask: "Who is this prince, and how is he a prince?" Also, why would he make a covenant with Israel?

He is identified here simply as one that comes from the same origin as the people who would later destroy Jerusalem (Daniel 9:26). Since that was Rome, this unnamed prince evidently comes from some section of the old Roman Empire. Daniel's reference to him as "the prince that shall come," also implies that he is a figure already referred to in his prophecies. In chapter 7 this mysterious bogeyman is seen as the "little horn," and in chapter 8, as the "king of fierce countenance." He was to appear in the latter time and would oppose the "Prince of princes" (Daniel 8:23–25). The one he describes is doubtless the Antichrist who will arise in the end time as the destroyer of God's people. His being the fierce king of Syria and also from the Roman Empire does not constitute a problem, for Syria was part of the old Roman Empire. The term "prince" means a ruler or leader, not just the son of a sovereign.

The second question is why Antichrist would make a covenant with Israel. That query will be confronted in a later discussion on the end times, but some suggestive clues are here given as to the content of that covenant. The fact that it is broken at the midpoint, halting the "sacrifice and oblation" is really the key. This implies that Israel's old ritual system will have been reinstituted prior to this time, before it is suddenly stopped. Evidently the Antichrist will have made a seven-year treaty with Israel, allowing her to reinstitute and carry on her sacrificial system.

For that to happen further implies that a temple of sorts will have been built on the old Temple Mount (perhaps north of the present Dome of the Rock which archeologists now believe is misplaced some 340 feet south of the original altar). Israel's offerings and rituals cannot be resumed without such a temple on that spot. That, however, would incur worldwide Muslim wrath, since that is part of Islam's Haram es Sherif or "noble sanctuary." It is therefore evident that the Antichrist will begin with some kind of concessions to allow Israel to set up her ritual system.

The Time of Abomination and Desolation

For some reason, however, this whimsical dictator will break that alliance with Israel after the first three and a half years, calling a halt to their sacrificial rites. This will be a turning point event that will commence a period of great trial for the Jews, unprecedented in the history of mankind (Daniel 12:1). Daniel describes it as a time of abomination and desolation, the altar abominated and the people desolated. He later reveals that the Antichrist will magnify himself in the place of God and reign supreme for three and a half years. Only by the help of the archangel Michael will the remnant of Israel be preserved through this holocaust. Many will be tried and purified, Daniel declares, but the wicked will only become more wicked.

The reason this covenant is broken at the midpoint is not revealed by Daniel, but is strongly suggested in other passages. Ezekiel 38–39 gives the political reasons, for instance, and John in Revelation 12–13 shows the supernatural causes. Most of these details we will assemble later when we survey the end-time period and focus on the world's buildup for Armageddon. The significance of this broken covenant and its aftermath will be seen to be cataclysmic for the nation, but essential to God's program to bring in everlasting righteousness.

SUMMARY

This brief review of Daniel shows the importance of his two major themes, the times of the Gentiles and the seventy weeks of Israel. Those prophecies put God's program on a careful time schedule, pegging future events for both world empires and the people of Israel. It alerted the faithful of Israel to the fact that the covenant Lord was still sovereign in world affairs, though wickedness seemed to rule.

That vision was most important to the buffeted remnant in the coming centuries when evil empires governed the land and the cause of righteousness seemed all but lost. Though silent and incognito, the Lord still ruled "within the shadows, keeping watch above His own." "Behold, He that keeps Israel will neither slumber nor sleep" (Psalm 121:4). The covenant Lord would not desert His chosen heritage, even in dispersion.

When Messiah did come in the passage of time, He came to fulfill those covenant promises and prophecies. He came as the long-anticipated Deliverer. Nonplused, we naturally ask: Why were those many promises of messianic glory not fulfilled? What went wrong at Messiah's first coming to His people? And what went right?

That brings us to the watershed point of human history and also of Bible prophecy—the mystery of the divine Incarnation at Bethlehem.

CHAPTER SIX

THE PROPHETIC DRAMA AT BETHLEHEM: WHAT WENT WRONG?

In Bethlehem, earth's highest drama began to unfold. Orchestrated by God Himself, its setting and stage stretched from heaven to earth. A more diverse cast could hardly be found. Prominently featured were angels and devils, shepherds and wise men, peasants and potentates, saints and sinners. All were conscripted to star in the unforgettable drama. Involved in its astounding plot were heroes and villains, suspense and bravery, and tragedy and triumph, highlighting the glory of daring virtue and divine trust. The curtains opened at lowly Bethlehem.

All these, however, were incidental and mere props to the central drama of the Incarnation. In this event the eternal God "broke into history," cradled initially in a manger, but crucified later on a cross. The inconceivable took place. Here earth's calendar found its focal point, making all else peripheral to this incarnational event.

MESSIAH'S WELCOME BY ISRAEL

Jesus was born into a humble and godly home. His coming to this home of Mary and Joseph was most significant. To qualify as king of Israel, He had to be the son of David through Solomon (1 Chronicles 22:9–10). There was but one royal line. Matthew begins His story by tracing this important lineage to David and Abraham (Matthew 1:1). Jesus could not be Israel's king without being the legal son of Joseph, for Joseph was heir to the throne. Presuming kingship through Mary would not stand, for her line (through David's son Nathan) had no right to the throne. Jesus had to be the eldest son of Joseph legally (which is one reason why Joseph could not have had children by a previous marriage).

On the other hand, Jesus was not fathered by Joseph, but by the Holy Spirit (Matthew 1:20). To be man's Savior, He could not be the physical son of Joseph, for He would then have partaken of the sin nature (Romans 5:12). The enigma was that He had to be Joseph's legal son to be king, but could not be his physical son and be Savior. Thus He was born into this lowly home as the Son of God, conceived of the Holy Spirit, and as the Son of Man, born of the Virgin Mary. That enigma was resolved by the virgin birth.

Scores of Old Testament predictions were fulfilled in His birth. Though most in Israel were not aware of all these fulfillments, many were alerted to their significance. Supernatural witness was given in a variety of ways. Angels were again pressed into messenger service, and even heavenly constellations got into the act. Through these witnesses, gentile magi journeyed from the East to arouse Israel's leaders, and lowly shepherds spread the news up and down the Judean hillsides.

In light of the grandeur of this event, we might ask how this heavenly visitor was received. Not knowing the facts, we would think that surely silver trumpets blared and Jewish shofars sounded throughout the land. Doubtless kings and priests left their courts to welcome Him, suspending all secular activities for a national holiday. Surely the day of His birth was indelibly imprinted on the pages of history.

Such, we know, was not the case. On both the secular and religious scenes of Israel, the event scarcely caused a ripple. His celebration was limited to a band of shepherds, a group of astrologers from the east, and some elderly saints who rejoiced at his first appearance in the temple. Otherwise, little excitement or enthusiasm was evident, and even the date of His birth has been lost. Doubtless this was providential to prevent the worshiping of days. Ironically, the only firm evidence we have for dating His birth is the death date of the Edomite king who tried to destroy Him. Slashing out in jealousy at this heralded King from heaven King Herod himself died a few weeks later and was buried in Bethlehem, the place of his baby slaughter. From this date, April, 4 B.C., we calculate Jesus' birth as taking place sometime during the previous year, 5 B.C.

As His birth was largely unnoticed by the world, so also was the major part of His life. Except for a trip to Jerusalem at age twelve, His maturing years at Nazareth are completely passed over in the records. He made no headlines as a precocious child, nor did His hometown guess that He was anything but an ordinary carpenter. The first sermon He preached at the local synagogue surprised everyone (Luke 4:22). Not until John baptized Him in the river Jordan, did Jesus begin a public ministry. The fictitious stories of His fashioning clay pigeons and making them fly may have a mystic appeal, but they have no basis in fact. His youth and young manhood were evidently rather ordinary.

The climax of this irony, however, was that His ministry also was largely unreceived. His "altar calls" were not responded to like Billy Graham's or even John the Baptist's. As obscurity characterized His early years, general rejection came to characterize His later ministry. He ended up, in fact, with a price on His head as a common nuisance.

In light of the glorious expectations painted by the Old Testament, this paradox of rejection is hard to believe. Before we pursue its causes, let's briefly review some of the background of His ministry that contributed to this nonresponse and rejection.

The Kind of Messiah Israel Sought

Israel's anticipations of Messiah were grounded in what the prophets had foretold. Their predictions had portrayed Messiah as one who would come to save them from their sins and from their enemies. They pictured Him as a suffering servant and as a conquering king. Why then did the nation not receive Him when He came? Were their expectations too literal and fleshly? Were they wrong in anticipating a national king and kingdom like that of David? Or did Jesus fail to live up to the promises of the prophets?

Their Preconditioning for Rejection

During the 400 years of prophetic silence from the time of Malachi, many changes occurred in Israel. World superpowers had changed several times, and the Jewish people had often been a political football on the international scene. In the lingo of blacksmiths, they were continuously caught between the hammer and anvil of Syria and Egypt.

During this time a great struggle of cultures was also being fought. Hellenism had spread over the Roman Empire, and Israel was caught in the middle of that cultural revolution. Some Jews elected to adapt, but many others adamantly resisted, condemning anything that violated their traditions. It was a matter of religion with them. This bullheaded resistance by the faithful finally brought the diabolic plot of Antiochus Epiphanes, the Syrian king, who vowed to purge the land of Jehovah worship itself. He substituted Zeus worship in the temple and killed thousands of Jews.

This in time ignited the fierce response of Israel's faithful, led by courageous Mattathias, the priest of Modin. In the armed struggles that followed, supernatural help was many times evident and great exploits were done under the leadership of the Maccabees. A semblance of independence was finally achieved after several years and the temple was rededicated on December 25, 164 B.C. These were fierce and desperate days of trials for Israel's remnant, but they doubtless had a purifying effect. They forced the people to defend their faith, both philosophically and physically against the onslaughts of paganism.

Out of the fray, however, came several religious parties, representing different philosophies in Israel. One was the "Sadducees," a high priestly class who adopted a simple theology restricted to the Torah (Pentateuch). Rejecting any notions of a spirit world, they developed a "this-world" attitude of life and became basically a political party. They also controlled the lucrative affairs of the temple and dominated the Sanhedrin and chief priesthood. Their number, however, was quite small, being limited to the aristocratic class.

In opposition to this liberal party, there developed the more conservative party of the "Pharisees." They were first known as the Hasidim or Puritans, but later came to be called the Pharisees (separatists).

Conservative in doctrine and practice, they rejected the encroachments of Hellenism. This became the party of the common people, centering their activities around the local synagogues. In their struggle to maintain purity of life and doctrine, they not only preserved the Scriptures, but also collected the interpretations of the elders. These memorized opinions came to be called the "Traditions of the Elders" and constituted their common rule of faith and practice.

These two parties then dominated the religious life of Israel when Jesus came and formed much of the background of His life and ministry. That background was not so much a climate of liberalism or cultism, but basically one of conservatism. It was conservatism with a vengeance.

Their View of a Conquering Messiah

This vengeful conservatism played an important part in developing their view of Messiah. It taught them to watch for His coming, to be sure; but their yearning for national vengeance blurred their vision of what to expect. Having fought the encroachments of paganism, both religious and political, they saw themselves as valiant champions of godliness and true religion. When Messiah would come, He would surely dash to their side and vindicate their cause. Like David, He would slay "Goliath" and rout the "Philistines." As a Jewish Alexander the Great, He would destroy their enemies and catapult them into international prominence. The prophets certainly confirmed this "conquering prince" expectation; but it became a political fixation with them, blurring their view of the spiritual work of Messiah.

The Suffering Servant Forgotten

Granting the validity of this expectation that Messiah would be a great national "David," we are still surprised at what they overlooked. How could they possibly forget Isaiah's vision of the servant of the Lord, coming in humility and suffering? David, Daniel, and Zechariah were also quite explicit in portraying these messianic sufferings. How could Israel's religious leaders develop such tunnel vision as to block out this essential work of Messiah?

Part of the answer is that they saw themselves as the "servant" of the Lord, not without some scriptural support (Isaiah 41:8; 44:21). And for many, the suffering servant of Isaiah 53 was a mystery and largely a moot question. The Ethiopian proselyte of Acts 8:34 reflected this uncertainty as he studied the passage. (The dual Messiah concept of a suffering son of Joseph and a reigning son of David, was a concoction of the third century A.D., to explain the Roman slaying of Bar Kokhba who claimed to be Messiah.) In the minds of many Jews of Jesus' time, however, Israel herself eminently filled the role of the suffering servant. Her continued trials in the fiery furnace through history have certainly not diminished the grounds for that misconception for many Jews today.

It is thus evident that the remnant of Israel saw their political need for national deliverance as paramount and overriding any spiritual need of repentance. Seeing themselves as the righteous of the earth, they were outraged at the thought that they were the ones needing repentance.

This then was the mindset of Israel as Jesus came to present Himself and the claims of God before them. Their distorted view of both the Scripture and their spiritual need preconditioned them for their skewed view of Messiah when He came.

Messiah's Presentation to Israel

Out of the mass of materials presented by the Gospels, we can survey the prophetic movement of Jesus' ministry by several key events. Failure to see this movement misses the real impact of both His ministry to Israel and His outreach to individuals. Several major events should be noted.

John's Judgment Ministry

Jesus' forerunner, of course, was John the Baptist as the prophets had foretold (Isaiah 40:3ff.; Malachi 3:1). He came for the primary purpose of preparing Israel for the coming of the Lord. Messiah's work was first of all to bring salvation and purification to His people. To prepare the nation for this, God groomed this man of rock, a prophet of heroic character, to preach and denounce sin with a fire and force unprecedented in Israel. His cudgel of judgment fell on the lives of all from the lowly peasants and soldiers to the king in his bedroom. He came as the burning conscience of the nation, and no one escaped the flaming vehemence of his judgment. He called the nation to its knees.

John's ministry, however, was also unique in that he did not seek reform from within the establishment or religious system. Not that he was an outsider, for he was the son of Zacharias the priest and thoroughly familiar with the inner corruption of the system. As such he could have instituted revival at the temple or synagogues. Instead, he preached in the wilderness near the Jordan and started a "come out" movement. God's ax, he warned, lay at the root of the trees and He was about to cull His orchard of deadwood (Luke 3:8–9). Religious profession or pedigree were no substitute for genuine heart repentance. "Bring forth fruit worthy of repentance," he cried.

John baptized those who responded. This ritual of baptism was an outward identification of the righteous remnant, signifying that they were preparing themselves for Messiah's coming. John's purpose was twofold, to prepare the people for Messiah and to introduce Messiah as the "Lamb of God" for salvation (John 1:29, 36).

The response? His immediate response was immense. From Jerusalem and all Judea they came, as well as from as far away as Syria. Word spread like wildfire across the hills of Palestine that a prophet indeed had arisen in Israel. His preaching became the talk of the nation. To journey to the Jordan to hear him preach was to hear "Elijah." An unprecedented ground swell of excitement and expectation developed that shook the nation from religious citadels to the political throne.

Whether all this response was genuine and spiritual, however, is doubtful. For many it was superficial, just a religious shot in the arm as a "seasonal thing" (John 5:35). The time soon came, in fact, when most of them were conspicuous by their absence, having jumped the bandwagon when the road got bumpy.

The response of the religious leaders was wary from the beginning and soon crystallized into a vote of rejection. Though they came to hear him, they were agitated by his aloofness to them and presumption (Luke 7:30). Nor did the prophet spare these men of the cloth as they stood before him. He branded them a generation of vipers and denounced their false hope in the trappings of Jewish pedigrees (Matthew 3:7–10). To them his pronouncements were rantings and smacked of the foulest heresies. They feared this rugged reformer from the beginning, and their initial aversions were only the start of a giant rift that was to divide them as Messiah Himself later came on the scene.

This judgment ministry of John was divisive, to be sure, but it was an essential prelude to Jesus' ministry. Though the Savior came to bless His people, judgment had to precede blessing. Their shallow response to the forerunner forced Jesus to take up the same cudgel Himself: "Repent, for the kingdom of heaven is at hand" (Matthew 3:2; 4:17). Although His ministry was basically one of joy, His purpose of seeking repentance was not diminished. In the process, however, He, like John, also received a meager response. Repentance was hard to come by in Israel.

Jesus' Miracle Ministry

In contrast to John, Jesus peppered His ministry with miracles. These He did in great variety and abundance. He healed the sick, raised the dead, and commanded the world of nature. In His presence the physical world did obeisance, bowing to its Creator.

Jesus' miracles, however, signified something more than His divine presence. They constituted His messianic credentials (Matthew 11:2ff.). Isaiah the prophet had foretold that Messiah would do miraculous works after being anointed by the Holy Spirit (Isaiah 35:4–7; 42:1–7). Though these would characterize the messianic age, they would also alert the nation to Messiah's presence.

Miracle-working, of course, was not an innovation of Jesus. Many of the prophets had performed miracles, confirming their message from God. This was the primary purpose of miracles, to confirm the Word of God. The first miracle worker, for instance, was Moses who was also the first to record God's Word. In the New Testament the apostles performed miracles also until the Word had been given and confirmed. But Jesus was Himself the unique Word of God, and His abundant miracles gave testimony that Messiah was on the scene as the unique Prophet of God.

The Response of the Leaders to Jesus' Miracles

With such a display of the supernatural, we might wonder how the people responded. As with John's early ministry, their response was immense and contagious. From all over Palestine and Syria they came for healing, acclaiming Him as a great prophet. The common people especially received Him gladly.

That eager reception, however, was not to last long—especially with the leaders. They were strangely unimpressed by His miracles. Because of this, Jesus used the healing of a leper to command their attention. After healing the leper, He sent him to witness to the priests at the temple (Mark 1:40–44); healing a leper was recognized as the work of Messiah. At His next recorded miracle, Jesus saw that the Jerusalem leaders had come as a committee to investigate Him (Luke 5:17). He then proceeded to give them a lesson in theology by healing in an unusual way: before healing a paralytic, He first forgave his sins. To the aghast leaders He drove home the point that He was not just a healer; He was God Himself (Luke 5:20–24). As Isaiah 53 had foretold, Messiah was to come as our healer, but more importantly, as the one who would bear our sins.

The leaders' response to this revelation was characteristic of their final response. They called it blasphemy. Their problem, however, was that miracles are hard to argue with. How do you answer the healing of a paralytic? opening blind eyes? or raising the dead? The answer is that a person can rationalize anything once he has closed his mind to reality. It took the leaders a little while to do it, but they finally came up with their insidious answer to His miracles: He does them in the power of Beelzebub, that is, the devil (Matthew 12:24). With this charge they dogged Him to the cross and shouted down any attempt to prove His messiahship by His miracles.

The Response of the Common People

If the leaders were not impressed by miracles, the common people were. They loved His magic and goodies. It soon became apparent, in fact, that they loved them too much. They wanted what He had more than who He was. He decided to test them. One day after He fed the 5000, they almost forced Him to become king. This offer He declined. Why? Why didn't He take advantage of this grass-roots movement to acquire the kingship of Israel?

The next day told the story. As He spoke to the same crowd across the lake at Capernaum, they asked for more of that magic manna. But instead of hustling more handouts, He offered Himself as the "bread of life" (John 6:35). When they finally realized, after more begging, that He was not going to merely play chef, they deserted Him en mass (John 6:66). This desertion showed that they loved Him as a "burger king," but not as a spiritual King. When the dust settled, only His twelve disciples were left, and even they were edgy.

This "bread" test took place at the midpoint of His ministry, at the time of Passover. It was perhaps six months after the leaders had blasphemed His miracles as satanic. Its importance lay in the fact that it showed that the nation's rejection of Him was not limited to the leaders, but had spread to the common people as well. This event was most disappointing, being an ominous sign of the general bent of the nation. It demonstrated their desire for material and political relief, but not for spiritual. The messiah they sought was Santa Claus, not the Savior.

Jesus' Kingdom Message

The purpose of Jesus' miracles was to call attention to Himself and His message. He usually followed His powerful works with powerful words. As the unique Word of God Himself, Jesus came with a special message from God. To appreciate the prophetic import of that message, we need to briefly review its highlights.

The Call for Repentance

Jesus' initial message to the nation was a call to repentance: "Repent and believe in the gospel" (Mark 1:15). This He continued throughout the first year. When the leaders took counsel to destroy Him at the beginning of the second year, He changed His approach. It was then He called the twelve disciples and began their intensive training (Mark 3:6, 13). This was after John was thrown into prison and Jesus' own kingdom offer had been rejected by many. Disdain for the King constituted disdain for His kingdom. The trend and mood of the people at the end of that first year gave an ominous barometric reading of their cooling attitude and final rebuff at the cross.

The Sermon on the Mount

In the summer of His second year of ministry, Jesus gave His most famous discourse, the Sermon on the Mount. This was after many elements of rejection had set in. We might challenge whether this delightful sermon on virtue had any relation to His rejection and His changed approach to ministry.

Broadly speaking, Jesus pursued two prophetic purposes in this discourse as He instructed a variety of disciples. It was really an introduction to His intensive training program. First, He sought to clarify true righteousness. To a people enmeshed in religious rigmarole, He stressed that the righteousness of God's kingdom begins with the heart. To think evil is tantamount to doing it, in His view. God is not just concerned with the actions of the hand, but looks beneath to the heart. In this sermon, Jesus simply elaborated the classic principles that Micah had long ago proclaimed: the offering of thousands of rams means nothing to God, if justice, mercy, and humility are missing (Micah 6:6–8).

This first purpose was most important in clarifying God's way of life. It was a primer for people of all ages, especially for those in doubt about the true character of life in God's economy. As related to the Old Testament, it pointed out the internal principles of the Mosaic Law. As related to the New Testament, it applied these eternal precepts to men and women of all time (Matthew 5:18). It is essential to note that it was not meant to be a plan of salvation (by any stretch of theology), but a description of the true character of God's children (Galatians 2:16). Its contingencies were not designed as requirements to enter God's kingdom, but as conditions for receiving blessings in His kingdom.

A second purpose of Jesus in the Sermon on the Mount was to declare war on false religion (Matthew 5:20). He solemnly enunciated that the Pharisaic system of legalism was foreign to God's kingdom. The best righteousness of the scribes and Pharisees, He said, would only land them in hell. Notice the progression in Matthew 5–7. In chapter 5, He denounced their external system of doctrine: they majored on minors and forgot the essentials. In chapter 6, He denounced their external religious practices as mere pretension for the praise of men. Finally, He denounced their whole way of life in chapter 7 as self-centered and built on sand. In proclaiming the gospel, He also denounced their counterfeit system that substituted man-made traditions for the God-given principles of the Prophets.

Jesus' New Program Introduced by Parables

The parables were by no means an invention of Jesus, but He made them famous as a literary form. This He did when the leaders' rejection of Him began to crystallize, first by parabolic sayings and later by longer stories. In rejecting Him, they inadvertently rejected also the messianic kingdom. Jesus then began to withdraw from the nation as such, and enunciated a new kingdom program soon to be inaugurated. Jesus used the parables as the ideal vehicle for introducing this new program. They enabled Him to reveal new truths to the receptive, while concealing them from the rejecters.

The first group of major parables are those of Matthew 13, which were spoken shortly after the leaders blasphemed His miracles (Matthew 12:24). They introduce the basic principles of His new program. Jesus' purpose here was to clarify for the disciples the new direction of the kingdom in consequence of the nation's rejection. The question before the frightened band was how the kingdom could proceed with the King rejected by the nation. How would God now pursue His kingdom program in the world?

This series of eight parables unveiled truths not revealed in the Old Testament. They were "hidden since the foundation of the world" (Matthew 13:35). In these stories Jesus told how He was planting this New Kingdom, how it would grow, the value of pursuing its program, and the responsibilities of stewards in its affairs. After planted, it would grow by an internal power, not by external politics or military force.

Though it would start small with a handful of uneducated fishermen, it would inevitably grow to encompass the globe and shake the world. There would indeed be counterfeits, but not to worry; God will allow them to grow and be discarded in His own time. Scaffolding is necessary for any building. The order of the day is to sow, reap, and watch God give the increase.

As noted, this was a brand new message. It diverted from the Davidic kingdom that was initially offered by John and Jesus, which had been rebuffed by the leaders (Luke 1:32–33; 19:11–15). That rejected program would simply sit on the sideline for an indefinite time. Rather than physical and political, its dynamics would be basically internal and spiritual. This new kingdom is not the church, as such, but its major purposes for this age are being carried out in the church. It is rather an "interadvent kingdom program," fulfilling God's purposes in the earth between the two advents of Christ.

THE KINGDOM EXPLAINED IN THE OLIVET DISCOURSE

Before going to the cross, Jesus gave the disciples a special discourse on the future of the kingdom (Matthew 24–25). When the disciples finally realized that Jesus was going to leave, they asked about His plan to return to resume His covenant program. To this Jesus replied that the tragic events spoken of by Daniel would take place just prior to His coming. Antichrist would again desecrate the holy place and great tribulation would follow to decimate the earth. But immediately after this, Christ would return with power and great glory to gather His elect and cleanse the earth for His everlasting kingdom (Matthew 24:29–31). His purpose in this revelation was to assure them that those coming trials would be but the birth pangs of a new age, not their final destruction. They would signalize His soon return.

This assurance was also given to indicate that the Old Testament kingdom program outlined by Daniel was not forgotten. Though Messiah was rejected by Israel and an interadvent program was interposed during this age, God had not reneged on His solemn oaths to the fathers (Romans 11:29). No rejection on their part could negate His promises.

After Israel's final purge, Christ would return to set up that long-promised, everlasting kingdom on earth.

WHY ISRAEL REJECTED MESSIAH

In reviewing Israel's history, we have noted that the nation was preconditioned to failure. Their rejection of Messiah was almost inevitable because of their barren soil. Though the Pharisaic movement in Israel had had a great history of purging the nation, it had stagnated and lost its spiritual life. It was now an empty shell of legal religiosity. Though they had served as God's firebrands for reform, they became a "generation of vipers" (Matthew 3:7; 23:33). How could such a drastic transformation take place in these pillars of the chosen people of God? To appreciate what happened, we need to observe some of the specific causes that brought that change.

Israel's False Religious System

With all their trappings of true religion, Israel had formed a colossal counterfeit system. This was especially tragic in light of God's great promises and investment in them. They were God's chosen instrument and had become the depository of His truth. Their ritual system was designed to lead the people to God through sacrifices pointing to the Christ. But unwittingly it became a tool of the devil by which the whole nation was made allergic to Messiah when He came. It became in reality a man-made system of religion. How such a diabolic transformation could take place in something so good is explained by two distortions.

Their Distortion of Scripture

In seeking to preserve the truth of God and apply it to life, the scribes and rabbis developed an ethical code called the "oral law." This was a collection of rabbinic opinions, long thought too sacred to write down. They were later compiled and organized for the Jews in dispersion by Rabbi Judah Hanasi in A.D. 199 and were called the *Mishnah* (repetition). The *Mishnah* codified the Mosaic Law into 613 precepts—365 prohibitions and 248 commands—each having hundreds of nuances. Max Dimont remarks that much of this was trivia that made Jewish life "resemble a madhouse of obsessive rituals attributed to Moses and God." Their collection is known as *The Talmud* ("learning," Palestinian and Babylonian), which includes the *Mishnah* (repetitions of the Mosaic Law) and the *Gemera* ("supplements," or explanations and applications of the rabbis).

These grew out of what was known in Jesus' time as the "Traditions of the Elders." Though human opinions, they came to assume more authority in practice than the Law itself (Matthew 15:6). It was with respect to these minutiae of the traditions that Jesus unleashed His most devastating missiles at the scribes and Pharisees. When they complained that His disciples failed to wash before eating, He denounced their washing ritual as a camouflage to cover up their godlessness (Mark 7:1–7). He called them hypocrites and went on to show how they had used their traditions to undercut God's commandments. The Law, for instance, commanded them to honor their parents; but they had devised a slick trick of interpretation to avoid caring for needy parents by pronouncing their own goods as "corban" (Mark 7:11). This meant it was dedicated to God and therefore too sacred to use for parental support. With religion like this, who needs atheism. Having failed to destroy Israel by the Syrians, the devil was doing a more thorough job through the religious leaders.

In Jesus' final lecture to the religious leaders, His greatest condemnation was leveled against their man-made traditions (Matthew 23). By them, He declared, they were keeping people out of the kingdom. While making eloquent prayers, they were devouring the widows and orphans. By their traditions they so distorted true religion as to make it an impossible burden to bear and a thing of contempt (Matthew 23:4). His most severe condemnation was not against criminals or drunkards, but against those who twist and confuse God's Truth. Jesus, in fact, condemned their whole system in this final word to the leaders. They had made the Word of God into a grotesque contortion of man-made traditions.

Their Distorted Plan of Salvation

Having developed a man-made revelation, it was only natural that they should evolve also a man-made system of salvation. The nation was blessed with all the beautiful accouterments of religion to manufacture their own approach to God. They had the miracles and prophecies of the fathers to build on; they could thus appeal to God's authority. For their superstructure, they built a system of merit through works, not unlike the Mosaic code (which was not meant to bring salvation, Galatians 3:21). It distorted that divine code. God's way of salvation in the Old Testament required faith as the decisive element, being demonstrated by obedience to the Word. In the Pharisees' reconstruction, they used clever revisions of these to come up with an ingenious contrivance of legal salvation (Romans 10:3). Meritorious to the core, it was hardly conducive to the graces of true religion. The justice, mercy, and humility of which Micah 6:8 spoke were almost obscured in the system, as they preened the proud and mighty and despised the meek and lowly.

Preeminent among its observances was Sabbath-keeping. Having been given originally as a sign of the Mosaic covenant, Sabbath observance had practically become a fetish with them (Exodus 31:13). They remembered that its breaking had been the reason God evicted them from the land in 586 B.C. (2 Chronicles 36:21). Thus its observance was an article of faith which they meticulously kept with almost nonsensical strictness.

Jesus saw this slavish devotion to Sabbath-keeping as idolatry and went out of His way to challenge it (Mark 2:23–28). He purposely performed miracles on the Sabbath to confront the issue. They had made an idol of its observance, worshiping and serving the "creature" more than the Creator. To this challenge they responded with righteous indignation and made it the primary issue in their decision to destroy Him (Mark 3:6). To tamper with the Sabbath was to strike a blow at the heart of their religion. Though Jesus clearly demonstrated His messiahship and lordship over the Sabbath while breaking it, they saw it as an intolerable sacrilege and worthy of death.

For smashing these two idols—their traditions and their Sabbath—Jesus was condemned by the nation. Such iconoclasm could not be condoned, for it jeopardized their whole religious structure; it eroded their legal foundation. Thus they had no place for this Galilean maverick in their system, and He had no place for their Satan-inspired system in His kingdom program.

Israel's False Religious Leaders

Jesus, however, was not rejected by a system. People, especially the religious leaders, rejected him. "As go the leaders, so goes the nation." Shepherds are responsible to lead the sheep. For this reason, Jesus condemned Israel's leaders for leading the nation down the slippery slope of unbelief and rejection (Matthew 23).

Humanly speaking, the leaders had their logical reasons for disdaining Jesus. He came as an outsider to their system. He contradicted many of their notions and violated traditions they held dear. To them He was like a bull in a china shop, overturning sacred relics. Also He came from the despised town of Nazareth, hardly the environment from which Messiah should come (John 1:46). He was self-educated rather than schooled in their seminaries. He had little use for their traditions and practically snubbed their scribal authorities. On the other hand, His cronies were fishermen and tax collectors, often consorting with lowly outcasts. His life style was out of step with theirs and His philosophy, unchecked, would constitute their death knell. For this assortment of "crimes," they had to reject Him as a counterfeit messiah.

We should recognize, however, that their rejection of Him was not the whole story; He also rejected them. This was evident as early as the Sermon on the Mount when He pronounced the scribes and Pharisees unfit for the kingdom of heaven (Matthew 5:20). He often returned to this theme in His later ministry. In the parable of John 10, for instance, Jesus portrayed a pastoral scene in which a good shepherd came to his fold seeking his sheep. Instead of finding them under worthy shepherds, he found them taken over by thieves and robbers who were fleecing, bleeding, and devouring them. Jesus then identified Himself as the Good Shepherd and Israel's leaders as thieves and robbers. He saw them as the main "fly in the ointment" of Israel's spiritual medicine.

This gloves-off indictment of the religious leaders brought again their fiery declamation. His assessment of them had been a devastating call. To use another figure, Jesus charged that the ship of Israel had been commandeered by a band of pirates who were making off with both the ship and the sheep. He saw them as henchmen of Satan: "You are of your father the devil" (John 8:44). This, of course, was no surprise to Jesus, but it is instructive to us. It shows the utter impossibility of His accepting them or adapting to a leadership orchestrated by the devil. The final upshot was that He declared them disfranchised of any leadership in God's kingdom (Matthew 21:43).

SUMMARY

This parable of the false shepherds taking over the flock of Israel unveils the true setting of Jesus' coming to the nation. He came according to prophecy to save them from their sins and from their enemies. But with rose-tinted glasses they failed to see their need of spiritual salvation and wanted only a political messiah. They forgot that Messiah's prophesied kingdom of glory had to begin with judgment and purging. For this reason many saw Jesus as an unwelcome nuisance and an enemy to be purged. He failed to live up to their entrepreneurial vision.

The more basic reason for this rift and lack of admiration between Israel and Messiah was the diabolic leadership of the nation. Prior to Christ's coming, an evil transformation had taken place in their religious life. Though their leadership had risen to great heights of godly courage less than 200 years earlier in battling the inroads of Hellenism, it had since then drastically changed. The devil had installed his henchmen at both the political and religious helms of the nation. Not only was there no room for Messiah at the inn or on the throne; He was even less welcome at the temple and synagogues. In confronting these religious pawns, Jesus unmasked them for what they were before the people. They were satanic cover agents attempting a coup d'etat of God's kingdom. Other reasons for their mutual rejection are really subsidiary to this fundamental gulf between Messiah and the degenerate leadership of Israel.

It was in this setting, however, that God sovereignly brought about His redemptive program. The wrath and whims of men do not frustrate the purposes of God in the final analysis. Yet, in accord with prophecy,

God offered His Son, Messiah, to His people in a most genuine way. He allowed them the free exercise of their wills in the process: "He came to His own, and those who were His did not receive Him. But as many as received Him, to them He gave the right to become children of God" (John 1:11–12).

Out of this apparent tragedy, God brought the spiritual triumph of the cross and the offer of salvation to all people. The immediate fruit of Messiah's rejection then was the present age of the Church. Before turning to the subject of Christ's return, we need to briefly review the prophetic mystery of the present age.

CHAPTER SEVEN

THE PRESENT AGE: ARE WE FULFILLING PROPHECY TODAY?

Armageddon fever strikes whenever war looms on the horizon. Each world crisis seems to rumble more ominously. This has probably been true ever since Jesus predicted wars and rumors of war in the end times.

PROPHETIC SYMPTOMS OR ILLUSIONS

Our generation, in fact, is more volatile, more wired for demolition. Secular writers recognize this and often wax apocalyptic in describing the awesomeness of nuclear weaponry. Recent world events certainly justify this, the demise of the Soviet bloc notwithstanding. The evening news almost daily uncovers new evidence of the world as a massive munitions dump ready to explode. We should remind ourselves that that fear is not restricted to foreign war zones. It is daily felt in many local communities where families are often their own worst enemies, and even children arm themselves for survival against violence at school and in the streets.

Also significant for the prophecy watcher is the fact that the nation Israel is now a factor in the international community. Her presence on the world scene is an alarm in itself, as well as that of Egypt and the Arab states. The recent Gulf War served to emphasize this by riveting world attention on the Middle East and the lands of Bible prophecy.

On the other hand, prophecy has a fairyland flavor for many. They regard it as a pious myth of fantasy. Aside from the tensions in the Middle East and the rash of racial wars throughout the world, we have difficulty finding ourselves in the prophetic picture. The world has always had wars of greater or lesser intensity. On the final reel of prophecy, Rome and her ten-state revision were to be the dominant kingpins. Without resorting to imaginary reconstructions, we search in vain for such today, for there simply is no Roman Empire in existence.

How then does our age fit into the prophetic landscape? We should recall that God's prophetic time clock has stopped. Both the "times of the Gentiles" and the "seventy weeks of Israel" are time periods that stopped before their completion when Messiah's death took place. That clock will not resume its ticking until God is through with His program for this age. His covenant program for Israel is on standby, while the Lord deals in mercy with all the world. It is foolish to allegorize ourselves as the "lost tribes of Israel," "mystery Babylon," or some other mystic designation to shoehorn ourselves into the apocalyptic picture. Should we feel a chill of loneliness because we can't find our names in the prophetic handbook? God's interadvent program for this age was not detailed chronologically as a clock to be watched. We simply live by faith.

There certainly are many movements stirring on the international horizon to suggest that this program is nearly complete. The rustling of fig leaves can be heard in many ways. But by and large, we do not take our bearings today on the almanac of world events. Attempting to stretch the prophetic tape of years and days onto our time has wrought all kinds of confusion and precipitated a flock of heretic movements. Such self-centered searches are futile in the study of prophecy.

Our age, therefore, is primarily a signless age. To properly adapt ourselves to this signlessness, we should be aware of what God is doing during this extended period of the church. That program is elaborated in the New Testament, especially in the epistles. Let's note several features of this interadvent age to observe the prophetic significance of God's program in the church today.

THE CONSEQUENCES OF CHRIST'S REJECTION

The church age, of course, is a direct consequence of Israel's rejection of Messiah. Christ came as the prophets had foretold, but found a spiritually unreceptive people. Though deeply grieved by this, the Lord was not frustrated in the outworking of His program. He simply introduced a new phase of it that He could not announce in the Old Testament prior to the time the rejection took place. It was definitely not an afterthought, but simply a later revelation.

This divine strategy of interposing an unannounced program because of rejection by unbelievers is certainly not new in God's economy. The Old Testament is full of it. For instance, He introduced plan "B" for Adam and Eve when they rejected plan "A." He did likewise with Israel when they refused to enter Canaan under Moses. There He simply held plan "A" in abeyance, postponing it for a later, believing generation. Likewise, in Israel's rejection at the cross, such a change took place resulting in both judgment and blessing: judgment on the rejecting nation and blessing for the world. Let's look at these results as they relate to our age.

God's Program for Israel on the Sidetrack

Although the nation Israel was once something special in God's program (the "apple of his eye"), she is not that today. God sees no difference today between the Jews and the Gentiles, as far as privilege is concerned (Romans 3:9, 22). We are all integrated together as one flock of sinners, none better, none worse (Romans 11:31–32). Though still God's chosen people to whom the covenant promises were given, Israel lost her place of covenant favor in God's current program because of her rejection of Messiah.

In Paul's description of this changed relation of Israel to the Lord (YHWH), he spoke of both her "condition" and her "position." Her condition was that of spiritual blindness; her position that of being cut off from God's "olive tree" (Romans 11:17–24). We should note, however, that he qualified this blindness in two ways: it was partial, rather than total; and it was temporary, rather than permanent.

ISRAEL'S BLINDNESS WAS PARTIAL, NOT TOTAL

This blindness was a subjective judgment that came upon Israel as a result of rejecting Jesus. They developed a "spirit of stupor, eyes to see not" (Romans 11:8). Having gazed into the "shechinah glory" of Messiah's person and yet refusing to respond, they became blind to spiritual truth. As a subjective judgment, it affected those who refused to respond, not the entire race. Paul used himself as exhibit "A" to show that Jews are being saved during this age by turning to Jesus as Savior. Today also, there are estimated to be several hundred thousand Hebrew Christians in America, plus many in Israel and other parts of the world. These demonstrate that Israel's blindness was partial, certainly not to every individual.

This declaration of Israel's blindness is quite evident even today. Her contempt and disdain for Jesus as Messiah is like a national mania, almost an article of faith. They admittedly have an increasing interest in Him as a teacher and as an outstanding Jew, but not as Messiah. Israel will allow nearly every deviation from Jewish orthodoxy in their policy of toleration and pluralism, even atheism; but not Jewish Christianity. This issue has come to the Knesset of the State of Israel several times. On December 25, 1989, the Israeli Supreme Court ruled that messianic Jews "do not belong to the Jewish nation and have no right to force themselves on it. Those who believe in Jesus are, in fact, Christians." Their self-proclaimed toleration and pluralism doesn't include Christianity.

Though this blindness was self-imposed by the Jews, the church has inadvertently contributed to it through much of history. Many Christian leaders saw the Jews as a cursed race and maligned them for slaying Messiah. They forgot that Jews and Gentiles were equally involved in both Jesus' trial and crucifixion. This malicious charge of deicide and the church's militant evangelism toward the Jews, created a giant rift that continues to this day. And ironically, the person of Jesus became the focal point of that malice. Thus their messianic blindness has not been lessened, but has almost become an issue of racial loyalty.

Israel's Blindness Was Temporary

In discussing Israel's fate in Romans 11, Paul asks whether God has permanently repudiated His chosen people. His answer is an emphatic "No!" The promises God made to the fathers were made in full anticipation of their failures (Deuteronomy 31:16–29). Yet He guaranteed them with His oath. Those covenants were not dependent on human faithfulness, but God's, and were therefore irrevocable (Romans 11:29).

To show the logic of this postponement, Paul likened Israel to the branch of an olive tree (Romans 11:17). He used the olive tree to symbolize God's tree of blessing through which He blesses the world. As olives supply food for energy and oil for light, Israel was God's instrument to bring sustenance and light to the world. But because of her failure to produce either of these, the nation was cut from the olive tree as a withered branch (cf. Matthew 3:10). In her place God grafted a "wild" branch of Gentiles which basically makes up the church. During this age God is channeling His blessing of spiritual food and light to the world through the church.

This arrangement, however, is not God's permanent way of blessing the world (Romans 11:24). Though entirely adequate for His present purposes, it is not His ideal. Rather, He vows to graft Israel back into the tree of blessing when "the fullness of the Gentiles has come in" (Romans 11:25). Her conversion may seem impossible today, but Paul declares it will be as natural an operation for God as when a farmer grafts a natural branch back into a tree.

The coming regrafting of Israel is pictured as a grand anticipation for all the world. Paul states it this way: if God could bring blessing on the world through Israel's rejection, how infinitely much more blessing will He bring through Israel's reception of Messiah (Romans 11:12, 15). It will be like life from the dead. Our society today is dead by comparison to that coming age of Israel's glory. War, poverty, and disease will be banished and even nature itself will be changed. The implication is that there can be no real peace and prosperity in the world until Israel is grafted back into her God ordained place of blessing. No wonder the psalmist admonished us to pray for the peace of Jerusalem (Psalm 122:6)!

The Divine Lesson for Us Today

Although Israel was made the recipient of God's mercy, that mercy was not to be presumed upon. Sin inevitably exacts its judgment. Israel's being set aside demonstrates that God's covenants were not meant to immune anyone from judgment where His grace is presumed upon. He does not cast His pearls before swine (Matthew 7:6). As with rebellious Israel in the wilderness, God can slough off a whole generation and fulfill His program when He is good and ready in a people who are also "good and ready." He's in no hurry. This setting aside of Israel was an awesome demonstration of that principle.

That lesson is especially pertinent for our generation. God's goodness was meant to lead us to repentance (Romans 2:4). Where the spiritual fiber of a people deteriorates by neglect and willful rejection of the truth, the faith of our fathers will not deter judgment. It will only increase it. Affluent America is not a charmed people, immune from judgment, but is even more liable for judgment because of its unprecedented blessings. Though God is slow to wrath, His wheels of judgment inexorably grind to consume those that persist in disregard for His law and His grace.

For instance—our national problems have assumed monumental proportions when we take time to look: political corruption, rampant immorality and sexual perversion, a widening gap between the haves and have-nots, growing insensitivity to destruction of the unborn, domestic violence, gang terrorism and racism, drug addiction and alcoholism, and family disintegration at every level—all under the awesome cloud of an immense national debt that threatens to collapse our whole way of life. And the answer to these snowballing problems has seemingly escaped everyone, except to pass them on to our children—with interest.

The reality is that these are but symptoms of deeper problems—just the tip of the iceberg. They have a spiritual base. Their deeper roots are in our skewed value system: putting pleasure and passions above piety; making material gain more important than morality; constantly stressing the physical, rather than the spiritual; emphasizing sophisticated weaponry more than trust in God; living for the pressing present, rather than the future; and substituting humanistic thinking for the wisdom of God's Word.

This is frankly an agenda for divine judgment. To persist in these is to follow the path of Israel in her downfall from immense blessing to disintegration. As she was cut down for rejecting God's Word, the great societies of our time can also expect such a felling, if they fail to take heed. God held Israel especially accountable because of her abundant revelation. How much more our generation with not only the lessons of Israel, but the massive revelation of the New Testament as well!

God's Program of Salvation through Messiah's Death

The second result of Messiah's rejection was that Christ died on the cross to atone for sin. That event brought the immeasurable blessing of spiritual life for all to receive. We might ask how such a grand result could come out of an act of deicide. Was Israel's rejection of Messiah necessary for our salvation? If so, why then was it so bad?

These are some of the questions the Jews of Paul's time threw at him (Romans 3:8; 6:1). They were, of course, an effort to discount his gospel of grace. However, they reflect a basic misunderstanding of what was involved in the atonement, a misunderstanding shared by many today. How could God bring man's greatest blessing out of his most horrendous crime? Does God employ evil means to accomplish good ends?

WAS ISRAEL'S REJECTION NECESSARY?

The Scriptures often assert that Christ made atonement for sin as He died on the cross. This was prophesied by Isaiah and is many times stated in the New Testament (Isaiah 53; 1 Corinthians 15:3; 1 Peter 2:24; etc.). He "bore our sins in His body on the cross." Without that death, there could be no salvation. We are then driven to ask what part Israel's rejection had in producing our salvation. If her rejection contributed to man's salvation, isn't God unjust in condemning Israel? This was the retort of Paul's Jewish antagonists in Romans 3:5–8, as they argued that this would mean that evil is good because it produces good results. On the surface, the argument sounds logical.

The German theologian Karl Barth pursued a similar line of argument in developing his doctrine of election (*Church Dogmatics*, II:2, 470ff.). He argued that since Judas Iscariot aided in the process (albeit in unbelief and infamy), he performed a necessary, gruesome task and became "the most important figure in the New Testament apart from Jesus" (Ibid., 502). Both Judas and Israel, in his view, performed tasks necessary to our salvation. Their actions typified man's rejection, he said, and they constitute an example of how God elects a person who rejects Him.

This argument, of course, leads inevitably to the doctrine of universalism, that all sinners will finally be saved in spite of themselves. The sins of all people drove Christ to the cross and thus allowed Him to display His infinite grace. As the shrewd Jews of Paul's day suggested, this would mean that sinners are not to be condemned, but rather applauded. The whole concept makes a mockery of righteousness and piously puts a premium on evil, making the end justify the means.

How Did Christ's Death Atone for Sin?

In establishing how Christ's death brought salvation, we need to be more precise to avoid error. Although He atoned for sin on the cross, it was not because of what men did to Him there. Their crucifying Him was in no way redemptive. Nor was it primarily Jesus' suffering at the hands of men that brought salvation. If the nails, cross, and other elements of physical suffering purchased salvation, the two thieves would have saved themselves, for they suffered similar deaths alongside Jesus. It would also suggest that others who suffer similarly might purchase their own salvation.

The physical suffering of Christ, however, was not the whole story. He suffered not only at the hands of men, but also at the hands of God. Though He was wounded and bruised by men; it was not they who "laid on him the iniquity of us all" (Isaiah 53:6); it was God. His life was not taken from Him; He "gave himself a ransom for all" (1 Timothy 2:6; cf. John 10:18).

It is interesting to note that Christ's time on the cross was divided in two parts: three hours' suffering in daylight, and three hours' suffering in darkness. The first three hours are described in some detail; the last three in near silence, as if incapable of human description. During this time He cried, "My God, my God, why hast Thou forsaken Me?" (Matthew 27:46).

The impenetrable mystery of how God dealt with sin in the person of His Son during those hours of darkness is passed over by all the Gospel writers. How do you describe the spiritual suffering of bearing the sins of the world? There He made complete satisfaction to God's outraged holiness concerning the issue of sin. This He did alone. No one participated with Him in the sense of contributing to it.

The hypothetical question is sometimes asked as to how Jesus would have died for sin if Israel had not rejected Him. The implication is that He needed Israel's rejection to bring about salvation. It also implies that a divine coercion forced Israel to reject Jesus so He could die for sin. In this view, Christ did not come to offer Himself as King, but to provoke men to slay Him.

This is an "iffy" question, but it helps us see more clearly the significant point of the atonement. Christ's condemnation and death at the hands of Israel and the Romans was not the essential point of salvation. He could have died at the hands of Egyptians, Greeks, or other people, as far as the human perpetrators were concerned. Had Israel been repentant and received Him as Messiah, He would still have had to die for sin. His priestly work of making atonement was inescapable if salvation was to be accomplished. The ironic thing is that the very ones He came to save condemned him. This, of course, was prophesied and in the plan of God (Zechariah 12:10). In the process, it served also to highlight the greatness of God's love and the depths of man's sins. While men did their worst in treachery, God gave His best in love.

THE FORMATION OF THE CHURCH

We have noted that the rejection of Israel had a twofold effect. It put Israel's covenant program on the sideline for an extended period, and became the occasion for Christ's atoning work on the cross. This then lay the groundwork for His interadvent program of building the church. It is a program unrelated to Israel's covenants and is built on the foundation of Christ's work on the cross. To see its significance, let's trace its development as unfolded by Christ and the apostles. When was it begun? what is its purpose? and how long does it continue?

The Church Age Introduced

In the final year of Jesus' ministry, He announced His plan to build the church (Matthew 16:18). Having been rejected by His own people, He pledged to build a new organism on a new foundation. This foundation would be a new quarry of stones (meaning of *petra*), later identified as the "foundation of the apostles and prophets, Christ Jesus Himself being the corner stone" (Ephesians 2:20). It would not be a reconstruction of Israel, but a new spiritual body through which God would fulfill His interadvent purposes.

Prior to this announcement, Jesus had introduced the interadvent age as a period that would extend till His return in glory. This period is mainly the church age, though not entirely. As previously noted, He introduced these truths by parables so as to break the news gently to the disciples, who had looked for an immediate messianic kingdom. The parables always moved in the realm of reality, showing the naturalness of the change that would take place. He compared it to a farmer planting seed, a woman making bread, a merchant searching gems, and a fisherman catching fish (Matthew 13). All were true to reality and therefore hard to argue with. By these analogies He taught that Israel did not overthrow God's true kingdom program's recalcitrance. It was really unscathed by that rejection, but would simply revert to another instrument of God for an extended period of time.

These parables were powerful introductions to this new program. In the parable of the sower, Christ pictured Himself as a sower. Though He planted generously, only a small part of the seeds found good soil. These, however, would produce an abundant harvest (Matthew 13:23). In the parable of the tares, He alerted them to the fact that false or counterfeit seeds would also spring up, planted by the devil. This warned them that many phony pretenders would show up among them, putting on a good act of piety, whom God would attend to in His time.

His story of the mustard seed was given to encourage the little band that the kingdom would eventually experience great growth. It would grow all out of proportion to its small beginning. To further explain that growth, Jesus told the parable of the leavening process to show the dynamics by which it would operate. Its growth would not come by outward schemes of human manipulations or ecclesiastical dictates, which methods proved devastating to Israel. Rather, it would forge ahead and attain worldwide influence by an internal dynamic, like leaven within meal. That power was later revealed to be the Holy Spirit. Opposition (or kneading), far from hindering its growth, would only stimulate its growth in every part. In these provocative stories, Jesus taught foundational truths about how God would work through the church during the interadvent period.

These truths of the church age were further elaborated by the Lord the night before He went to the cross. In the Upper Room Discourse (John 13–17), He described the new relationships of believers in the body of Christ. Special emphasis was given to their spiritual relations: to the Father, to Christ, to other believers, to the world, and to the Holy Spirit. He described a new agenda for them.

Jesus spoke of the church age as a time of serving God in a hostile world. Though He Himself would be absent, the Holy Spirit would be their constant companion. This new companion would give comfort for times of distress, wisdom for understanding God's Word, and strength to accomplish God's work. Utilizing His power, believers would do even greater works than the miracle works of Christ (John 14:12); they would be involved in transforming personalities for eternity. In this they would be coworkers with the Holy Spirit (John 15:26–27). Employing His power, no work would be too hard and no obstacle too great.

The Lord stressed in this final counsel that the key to effective service would be love. This He exemplified by washing their feet. It was not optional, but essential—a command to the will, not an appeal to the emotions. Though they differed in gifts and responsibilities, they were to strive for unity of mind and purpose in Christ (John 13:1; 17:26). With Christ absent from the earthly scene, they were to constitute His "body" and be His witnesses in the world.

Formation of the Church at Pentecost

The actual formation of the church, however, did not take place until after Christ ascended to heaven. The divine builder did not come on the scene till ten days later. It was at the Jewish Feast of Pentecost that the

Holy Spirit descended on the gathered believers, baptizing or placing them into one body and taking up His residence in each individual. This event became the official beginning of the church, to which Christ pointed forward at His ascension (Acts 1:5–8). In constructing the church, Christ is the divine architect and the Holy Spirit is the divine builder (1 Corinthians 12:11–13; Ephesians 2:22). Although the Holy Spirit is omnipresent in all ages, He indwells believers during the church age in a special way to accomplish His work of building the church.

The Divine Purpose of the Church

To appreciate the place of the church in the interadvent age, we should note several divine purposes it fulfills. As Israel was called to special service in the Old Testament, the church likewise has a divine mission. These may be seen in several figures that describe her.

The Church As the Body of Christ on Earth

In His absence, the Lord appointed His body of believers to be His representatives. They are to do His work on earth while He is absent. To accomplish this, the Holy Spirit seeks to mold each believer into the image of Christ and then places each in a specific place of service. The goal is to mature each one "to the measure of the stature which belongs to the fulness of Christ" (Ephesians 4:13). This He does as each one makes Christ the center of his or her life.

The Spirit not only works "in" believers, but also "through" them to fulfill God's program. To do this, He endows each one with certain gifts or abilities as He sees fit (1 Corinthians 12:7). In accord with God's program, the Holy Spirit does not work alone, but equips each member with service abilities so that all may be involved. No one's gifts are insignificant. Though some may be more glamorous or showy, all are to be used with humility and as a divine stewardship. Those with seemingly insignificant abilities are to use them with diligence, recognizing their service will be rewarded according to faithfulness, not the amount of "splash" they make in the kingdom. Nor are the gifts to be selfishly exploited, but used for the benefit of all. With such diversity of gifts, it is essential to have unity. Such can only be achieved through a healthy love relationship. The Spirit works through the machinery of the believer's gifts only as they operate in the oil base of love.

The practical outworking of these purposes is achieved through local assemblies of believers. The "local church" is the primary meaning of church in the New Testament. Such an assembly is a group of believers who have associated themselves together for mutual edification, to glorify the Lord, observe the ordinances, and to carry out the great commission of discipling all nations. Organized as a democracy, it has members, leaders, and a mutually adopted standard of conduct and discipline. Such a democratic organization makes each member responsible. It also gives opportunity for each to be involved. There is little evidence in the New Testament that the work of God in this age can be accomplished in any other way. Thus they represent Christ in the world and are workers together with the Holy Spirit in proclaiming the gospel to all nations.

The Church As the Bride of Christ

Though the Church is now called the "body of Christ," it will one day be called the "bride of Christ" (1 Corinthians 12:27; 2 Corinthians 11:2; Ephesians 5:25–27; Revelation 19:7). The church age is especially unique in that during this time the eternal God is securing a bride for His Son. No event was so important to a father in the Old Testament, and the analogy doubtless applies to God as well (Genesis 24). Like Abraham, God sent the Holy Spirit into a far country to seek a bride for His Son.

The immense significance of this union to both the Father and the Son can scarcely be overdrawn. Nor should the divine anticipation of it be pared down because of His sovereignty. But for believers to be involved as the bride in the drama is the epitome of Cinderella stories. No fiction writer ever came up with so daring a plot as this rags-to-riches episode. As the bride of Christ, the Church will one day share His riches and honor, reigning together with Him. More will be developed on this theme in a later chapter, but we here note it as one of the greatest events on the divine calendar—the marriage of God's Son to His bride, the church.

The Church As a Display of God's Wisdom and Grace

The apostle Paul portrayed God as a divine artist and not above displaying His handiwork. This is Paul's point in Ephesians 2:10 as he describes the church as God's work of art. The divine sculptor is deftly forming it as one of His grandest showpieces. His purpose in this display is to reveal to all the rational universe the multifaceted wisdom of God (Ephesians 3:10). Though creation is a display of His power and glory, the church is a singular display of His unique wisdom. As in creation He started with nothing, in forming the church He started with less than nothing—degenerate sinners—and infuses them with the qualities of His divine nature (Ephesians 2:1f.; 1 Peter 1:4). That has to be the product of unfathomable wisdom!

Besides displaying His wisdom, the church will also be a window display of His grace. It will be the special object of His affection. Paul declares that it is God's purpose in the ages to come to shower the church with the "surpassing riches of His grace in kindness toward us in Christ Jesus" (Ephesians 2:7). That grace is necessarily restricted today because of the issues of sin. But in the ages to come, those issues will be removed and the Lord will lavish on the church the fullness of His grace. This is not to demean what He will do for Israel, but to emphasize what He will do for those of this age who respond to His grace. The Lord has determined to display in the church the deepest qualities of His nature, His love and grace.

SUMMARY OF THE PRESENT AGE IN PROPHECY

As related to Old Testament prophecy, the church age is a kind of parenthesis in which God has diverted from His covenant program with Israel. The Israeli time clock has been put on "hold." Far from being an "afterthought" with God, the church age could not have been made known till the actual rejection took place. Paul described it as a "mystery...hidden in God" from creation, unrevealed in the Old Testament (Ephesians 3:9). After that rejection took place, God moved to show His special favor to all men in a unique outpouring of His grace (Ephesians 3:2, 5). He has commanded "affirmative action" for all, with any discrimination a thing of the past. All nations are counted equal, both as sinners and as candidates for His mercy.

Reflecting on the ingenuity and grandeur of this overall program, the apostle Paul hilariously exclaimed: "Oh, the depth of the riches both of the wisdom and knowledge of God! How unsearchable are His judgments, and unfathomable His ways!" (Romans 11:33). While remaining true to His covenant program with Israel, He is also reaching out in grace to all the world. Who but God could conceive such a plan, and who but God could carry it out!

CHAPTER EIGHT

THE MYSTERY OF THE RAPTURE

How will it all end? Will life as we now know it soon terminate? Visions or apprehensions of the end of the world are rather common in the thinking of rational men. A mysterious anticipation of a summons for all to gather at a great judgment morning, perhaps accompanied by a cosmic blast, is quite general. We look for some kind of consummation of the present order.

The source of this assumption is not only the Bible. It is also an ontological concept, seemingly ingrained in the human psyche, of an eventual accounting or squaring of all inequities. Life with all its injustices is hardly rational without it. Such a climactic, disjunctive moment of history is envisioned in most cultures.

Of this the Bible has much to say. It is, in fact, the primary and only definitive text on the subject of future events in all literature. This call to account is the moral imperative underlying the entire biblical text.

HOW TO INTERPRET THE PROPHETIC SCRIPTURES

Serious study of the Bible, however, reveals a far more detailed picture of the consummation. As we turn our attention to the details of that future program, we need to clarify again what we believe to be the most reliable method of interpretation. This is especially important in the area of prophecy where every commentator seems to do what is right in his own eyes.

As previously noted, both the Bible and history substantiate the *grammatical-historical* method, sometimes called *literal*, as the most consistent method of interpretation. This method assumes that the Bible was written to be understood in the normal way of understanding all literature. Its basic contrast is with the subjective, *allegorical* method of the medieval church that wrought so much havoc in multilevel interpretations in the Dark Ages. It does not overlook figurative language (which obviously abounds in the Bible), but puts a brake on fanciful speculation and humanistic thinking, forcing the reader to ask why any specific statement should not be understood in the normal way.

This method admittedly narrows one's approach to the subject of prophecy and especially the book of Revelation. It takes seriously Jesus' final warning that His words are not to be tampered with by adding to or subtracting from their message (Revelation 22:18–19). In the history of interpreting Revelation, the church has often forgotten this warning in its efforts to make the book conform to progressive history. This can be seen by noting the three basic views of the coming Millennium ("thousand years," Revelation 20:2–7): 1) amillennialism, 2) post-millennialism, and 3) premillennialism. One's view of this Millennium largely affects one's understanding of Revelation, as well as one's overall view of Bible prophecy. We need to review them briefly.

Amillennialism

The amillennial view, perhaps the most popular today, either denies a literal millennium or sees it as a figurative picture of the church age (or of heaven itself). It was developed by the church fathers about the time of Augustine, as the church began to experience popularity in the empire. At that time it appeared that a figurative reign of Christ through the church was just around the corner.

Postmillennialism

The postmillennial view developed some time later during the time of the Reformation. It assumed that the church age would evolve into a millennial period of glory through the preaching of the gospel. Christ would then return after this triumphal "Millennium." Though that position has taken various forms, it has but few adherents today, inasmuch the world appears less millennial all the time. Global wars and racial skirmishes seem to be multiplying on every front.

Premillennialism

The premillennial view maintains that Christ will personally return to set up His messianic kingdom on earth over which He will reign for a thousand years. The validity of this position is that it accepts the texts that describe the millennium in a normative way, without resort to allegorism (Revelation 20:1–7). It allows the book to speak as true "revelation" in describing things hitherto unrevealed. It also takes seriously the Old Testament prophecies of a great messianic age for Israel and relates them to this millennial reign of Christ. By contrast, the first two positions are forced to practically ignore those Old Testament promises or remodel them as allegories. This resort to allegorization jeopardizes prophecy itself, making it subjective to anyone's bias. The premillennial position interprets those passages in a strictly contextual way, the normative way of interpreting all parts of the Bible.

Consistently applied, this method unfolds an amazing symmetry and consistency in the understanding of both history and prophecy. Nearly all the fulfilled prophecies of both Testaments were understood and fulfilled in this way. It is hard to think of any exceptions. This method reduces the subjective element and allows the biblical text to speak for itself. It would be futile, indeed, to approach Bible prophecy in any other way.

What then is the next projected event on the prophetic calendar? Is it Christ's return to the earth? Or is it the coming of Antichrist? What about the specter of economic collapse, the possibility of nuclear disaster or ozone failure? Does the Bible have anything to say of these ominous clouds gathering on the world scene? What is its prophetic word of hope for our confused and suicidal generation?

THE NEW TESTAMENT REVELATION OF THE RAPTURE

Since the end-time calendar is so loaded with both bright and dark spots, we need to clarify its key events and understand their purposes. Its major events will be the resurrection and rapture of the church, the rise of Antichrist, the ensuing great tribulation, the diabolic challenge at Armageddon, and the return of Christ to the earth. All of these precede the millennial reign of Christ on earth and, in an oblique way, make preparation for it (Revelation 20:1–6). The order in which they occur, of course, is a matter of debate, but becomes fairly clear as we note the character and purpose of each.

The subject of Christ's return is prominent throughout the New Testament, but especially detailed by Jesus and Paul. Both describe His coming to rapture the saints and later to reign over Israel and the world. At times these comings appear as one event and at other times as quite distinct. Let's first note Jesus' instruction in the Gospels and then Paul's teaching on His return in the epistles.

Jesus' Instruction on His Second Coming

This area of instruction by Jesus may be summarized by reference to two classic passages in the Gospels. Both were given during passion week as He prepared the disciples for His coming absence. They were given, however, under entirely different circumstances.

JESUS' OLIVET DISCOURSE

The first of these passages is the Olivet Discourse, given to the disciples in the middle of passion week. This discussion was precipitated by the disciples' query as to when He would return and what sign would announce His coming. In reply, He first warned of false messiahs that would arise deceiving many nations (Matthew 24:4–5). This is similar to the deception Daniel had predicted when Antichrist comes to make a false covenant with Israel (Daniel 9:27). That, of course, is Jesus' point, and the parallels are most striking.

Jesus then reminded them of the "abomination of desolation" of which Daniel had also spoken (Daniel 9:27; 12:11). This abomination, Jesus said, will begin a period of extreme tribulation for Israel that will continue until He returns in glory. This Lord identified this calamity as an outstanding sign that will announce His return to Israel. According to Daniel, it will occur at the middle of that seven-year period.

In summary then, just before that abomination by Antichrist, there will be a great deception of many in Israel; after it, there will be a great destruction of many in Israel (Matthew 24:10–24). Jesus thus tied His return solidly into the end-time prophecies of Daniel. He also related it to the prophecies of Israel's final tribulation, describing how the true remnant of that time will fare.

Jesus refers to the disciples as the faithful remnant of Israel. No one else could possibly represent this group, least of all the religious leaders. But speaking as Israelites, the disciples asked for a sign that would herald His return to the nation. In reply, He declared that after Israel's final purging, He will return with judgment for the rebels and deliverance for His people. Far from giving up His covenant program for Israel, He assured them that He will come again with salvation and healing to regather the remnant for millennial blessings (Matthew 24:31; Isaiah 27:13). That coming, however, will be preceded by a series of cataclysmic events, preparing both Israel and the earth for His messianic kingdom.

Jesus' Upper Room Discourse

The second classic passage describing His return is John 14. This is part of a larger address known as the Upper Room Discourse which He gave on the eve of the crucifixion. In this final caucus with them before the cross, Jesus announced the coming of another "companion," the Holy Spirit, who would take His place. But He also assured them that He Himself would later come to receive them to Himself (John 14:1–3). Though this coming could speak of His receiving them individually at death, the contextual evidence is that He spoke of His final coming to bring them to the Father's house. As He Himself was going to the Father in bodily form, He would return to take them also in bodily form to those "abiding places" that He will prepare for them in the Father's house.

There is a striking resemblance, as J. B. Smith has noted, between this statement of Jesus and that of Paul's description of the Rapture in 1 Thessalonians 4:13–18:

John 14:1–3		*1 Thessalonians 4:13–18*	
trouble	v. 1	sorrow	v. 13
believe	1	believe	14
God, Me	1	Jesus, God	14
told you	2	say to you	15
come again	3	coming of the Lord	15
receive you	3	caught up	17
to Myself	3	to meet the Lord	17
be where I am	3	always be with the Lord	17

The two passages are remarkably similar, even to the exact order of words and phrases. In the context of John, Jesus is here announcing the Rapture of the church which Paul will later discuss in greater detail. In contrast to Matthew 24, Jesus in the upper room does not deal with Israel and her trials, but with the new body of believers whom the Holy Spirit would direct and empower until Jesus comes to take them home.

It is thus evident that Jesus spoke of two different events in Matthew 24 and John 14. One concerned the faithful of Israel who would be on earth in those final days before His return. The other concerned the body of believers who would sojourn in the world under the guidance and tutelage of the Holy Spirit during much of the period of Christ's absence. To this body of church believers He will come to take them to the Father's house; to Israel He will later return to deliver and unite them on earth. Whereas His word to Israel was a restatement and clarification of Daniel's prophecy, His word to the church was a fresh announcement of things that the Holy Spirit would later enlarge upon (John 14:26; 16:13–14).

There appears to be little similarity between these two events, strongly suggesting that His coming will be in two stages: first to receive the church out of the world, and later to regather and refine Israel in the world to fulfill the Lord's covenant promises.

Paul's Instruction on the Coming of Christ

It was through the apostle Paul that the Holy Spirit later revealed many of the New Testament truths concerning the church age. He was specifically appointed as the apostle to the Gentiles (2 Timothy 1:11). Though he often spoke of Christ's return, two classic passages were given to clarify the subject of the Rapture (1 Thessalonians 4–5 and 1 Corinthians 15). Both of these enlarge on Jesus' instruction concerning His return in John 14. One dealt with the question of who would be included; the other described the resurrection of the church and problem of how dead bodies could be raised. As 1 Thessalonians spoke of the church's "transportation" to be with the Lord, 1 Corinthians spoke of the church's "transformation" to be like the Lord. Let's note how Paul develops each.

THE TRANSPORTATION OF THE CHURCH IN RAPTURE (1 THESSALONIANS 4)

The first recorded epistle of Paul was to the Thessalonians, and it stressed the need for holy living. This he did with many reminders of the Lord's coming; he was not averse to feeding this young church on the prophetic Scriptures. In his previous stay with them, he had emphasized these truths in relation to the coming "Day of the Lord." This, of course, made them quite Rapture-conscious. After he left them, however, some of their group had died, giving rise to the question as to whether the dead would miss out on the Rapture. Would saints who die miss this glorious "meeting in the air"? Had they believed in a simultaneous rapture and return of Christ to the earth, the question obviously would not have been raised.

Paul's response was a clear and resounding declaration that all believers in Christ will take part in the Rapture:

> For the Lord Himself will descend from heaven with a shout, with the voice of the archangel, and with the trumpet of God; and the dead in Christ shall rise first. Then we who are alive and

> remain shall be caught up together with them in the clouds, to meet the Lord in the air, and thus we shall always be with the Lord. (1 Thessalonians 4:16–17)

His point was that deceased saints will definitely join that throng that rises to meet the Lord in the air. Far from being excluded, the dead will, in fact, rise first. This did not mean they would meet the Lord first, but that they would resurrect first to join living saints in their ascent to glory. His point was that all believers of the church age will join together in this grand ascent to meet the Lord in the air. It will be their first stop on the way to the Father's house (John 14:2).

The "Transformation" of the Church in Resurrection (1 Corinthians 15)

The problem Paul dealt with in 1 Corinthians 15 was a bit different. The Corinthians had come out of a background of Platonic philosophy, a view that did acknowledge some kind of spiritual resurrection. However, because they considered "matter" to be evil, they denied the possibility of a bodily resurrection. This challenged a central doctrine of the church.

To these people Paul wrote his classic passage on the resurrection of the church and how it will take place. Arguing first from the fact of Christ's bodily resurrection, to which there were many living witnesses, he proceeded to show the logic of physical resurrection. The problem he confronted was how a decomposed body could be recomposed and raised to life. That problem is further complicated where cremation has taken place and one's ashes are strewn in the ocean. Will God be able to reassemble all the pieces, and put "Humpty-Dumpty" together again? The apostle then gave one of the strongest statements on this doctrine, defending the future resurrection of the body.

To display its logic, Paul used an illustration from nature. A new sprout can only grow as the old seed is sown in the ground and dies (1 Corinthians 15:36). Like that sprout, the believer's body will one day arise out of death in a new and glorified form. While retaining many recognizable features of the old, the new body will also be different. It will be incorruptible, glorious, and powerful. It will, in fact, be similar to Christ's resurrection body in which He entered rooms without opening doors and ate food, though He didn't need to (1 John 3:2).

This description suggests several things about that new body. Being incorruptible, it will never be subject to sin, disease, or decay. As a body of power, it will be equipped—far beyond our fancied "Superman"—to participate in an eternal adventure yet unrevealed, requiring immense power (1 Corinthians 15:43). As a spirit body (in contrast to a soul body), it will enable one to associate in normal relations with spirit- beings (God and angels), as well as with physical beings on earth (1 Corinthians 6:3). It will, in other words, be a body fully equipped for the "rigors of heaven" and its endless pleasures.

The "Mystery" of How Living Saints Will Be Transformed

With this explanation, however, Paul had a further word of revelation. The principle that death is necessary to bring about the rising of a new sprout (or body) will have an outstanding exception. That exception Paul called a "mystery," that is, a truth previously unrevealed, but now made known (1 Corinthians 15:51ff.). That is how he described many truths about the church (Ephesians 3:3–5, 9). This mystery dealt with the problem of how living believers will be raptured if death is necessary to produce a resurrection body. Will they have to undergo a quick death to resurrect? Or, will they just be caught up in their corruptible bodies?

Paul's answer is that those still living when Christ returns will experience instant transformation. Since "flesh and blood" cannot inhabit God's kingdom, they must receive incorruptible and immortal bodies. Only such could cope with the challenges and enjoy the delights of heaven's glories (1 Corinthians 15:50). Besides a glorious "transportation" to heaven as revealed in 1 Thessalonians 4, they will also experience a grand "transformation" for heaven. But instead of passing through the death process, they will be transformed in an "atom" of time, that is, the smallest fraction of a second. By a special miracle, living believers will be changed "in a twinkling of an eye," their bodily makeup metamorphosed as they rise to meet the Lord in the air. Though not resurrected from the dead, they will be completely transformed to prepare them for that eternal relationship. Instant glorification will be their unique experience.

The Seven-Year End-Time Period

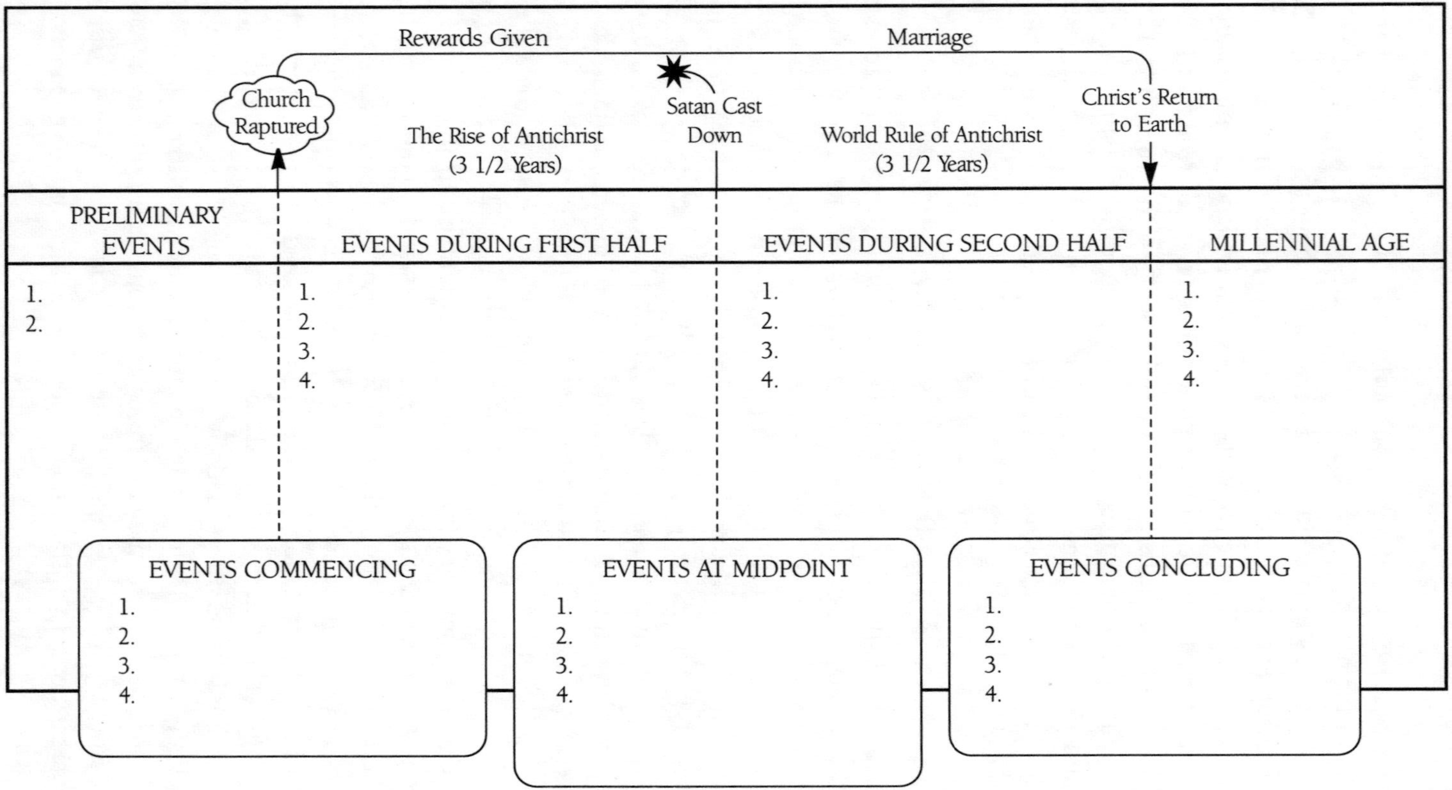

Rewards Given
Marriage
Church Raptured
The Rise of Antichrist (3 1/2 Years)
Satan Cast Down
World Rule of Antichrist (3 1/2 Years)
Christ's Return to Earth
PRELIMINARY EVENTS
1.
2.
EVENTS DURING FIRST HALF
1.
2.
3.
4.
EVENTS DURING SECOND HALF
1.
2.
3.
4.
MILLENNIAL AGE
1.
2.
3.
4.
EVENTS COMMENCING
1.
2.
3.
4.
EVENTS AT MIDPOINT
1.
2.
3.
4.
EVENTS CONCLUDING
1.
2.
3.
4.

CHAPTER NINE

THE METEORIC RISE OF ANTICHRIST

Can the world be united? Can it long survive in a nuclear age without a semblance of unity? The massive consequences of rejecting divine counsel seem even now ready to exact judgment. Their threats are ominous and multiply daily: almost ubiquitous sexual revolt; seemingly unstoppable AIDS disaster; terrorism of mob rule; disregard for human life; racial clashes the world over; nuclear and ecological menaces; and a widening economic gap between the haves and have-nots. Can these rumbles of apocalyptic horsemen be sedated to defuse their explosive threats? Or is disaster ahead?

Unity is admittedly a spiritual amalgam, the basics of which are not currently in large supply. The truth is that, while our age has spawned scientific and technological giants, it has produced spiritual pygmies. This spiritual retardation is apparent everywhere. An ungluing process is at work in our domestic, social, and political life, affecting everything from religion to economics. Even the haven of the home has fallen prey to disintegration. These trends do not augur well for unity. The question is whether these rising forces of divisiveness and human destruction can be diverted from their seemingly inevitable goal. Or will our spiritual bankruptcy plunge us over the brink?

THE WORLD SETTING FOR ANTICHRIST

The need for a solution is accelerated by our nuclear, computerized age. Few generations have glared into the jaws of holocaust as has ours. Even ungodly pragmatists see the need for some kind of unity to stifle the ravages of greed and degeneration.

The Need for a Charismatic World Leader

That need is ripening in many ways. Nationalism is becoming more militant and racism is raising its ugly head in every quarter. These only emphasize the need for racial equality, economic balance, removal of class barriers, and religious tolerance. Global awareness and interdependence are ballyhooed as solutions to divisiveness and provincialism. The recent Gulf War illustrated the need for such cooperative effort. Yet unity is largely effervescent in an increasingly volatile world.

Our own democracy inadvertently contributes to this malaise. Social tensions and cries for equality are part of its growing pains as it sues for liberation. It is easily forgotten, however, that democracy and liberation, carried to extremes, end in anarchy leading to despotism. They carry the seeds of their own destruction. As Sir Robert Anderson once noted, the tendency of history has been, "first the revolution; then the plebiscite; then the despot. The Caesar often owes his scepter to the mob" (*The Coming Prince,* 191). Extremities of mob rule always spawn a dictator with surrender of personal liberties almost inevitable. In other words, democracy is no guarantee against dictatorship. Its abuse can produce the social chemistry ideal for the rise of a dictator.

However he arrives, such a world dictator is predicted and is in the making. The Bible has more to say about this coming potentate than of any other figure of prophecy, aside from the Lord Jesus Himself. When will he appear? Where will he arise? What will he be like? How will he rule?

These questions have long been pondered from prophecies in both the Old and New Testaments. While it is useless to speculate where Scripture is silent, it is essential to listen when it speaks. What it says about this giant figure of prophecy is important to properly understand God's end-time program. Under the leadership of this political opportunist and shrewd military strategist, a new world will be carved out.

The Saintless Earth

This carving will take place in the wake of one of history's most devastating events. The Lord's retrieval of the church at the Rapture will leave a world devoid of genuine believers. For all their "sweet orneriness," their presence has a salutary affect. Their swift and silent departure will be a sledgehammer blow to much of the world. It will leave a frenzy of confusion, despair, and massive destruction (worse than Israel's exodus from Egypt). Planes may suddenly be without pilots, speeding trains without engineers, and many cars without drivers. (A friend of mine has a sign on his dashboard: "If you hear a trumpet, grab the wheel!") Every community will grieve the loss of friends and loved ones. The wake of the Rapture will inevitably leave a monumental devastation.

Following this excruciating debacle, however, the world will pick up the pieces and carry on as it has in the aftermath of other catastrophes. Though millions will be stung with initial despair at having missed an offer of salvation, that despair will not last. It will soon give way to a strange complacency and strong delusion (2 Thessalonians 2:11). No massive dash to repentance will be evident. Rather, a sense of relief and lustful joy may be prevalent with the restraints of the church removed. Though the repressive atmosphere of a sin-dominated world will soon be felt, it will be taken in stride as the spirit of sin and sinister selfishness flourish in the hothouse of Antichrist.

Business as usual will soon resume after "the saints go marching in" and the initial looting is quelled. World industry, politics, social enterprises, and even much religion will recoup and carry on. It is doubtful that earthquakes, world wars, pestilence, or famines will immediately follow. These may, in fact, be totally missing, as world culture and humanistic dreams get a new jump-start and even intensify.

Antichrist Emerges As a World Mediator

Out of this confused milieu will arise a new world leader—a suave individual with political savvy and personal charm. He will come at an opportune time to make international proposals for peace and prosperity. Though he will later show his teeth as a "beast," he will begin as the epitome of genteelness. Far from being Mr. Hyde, he will come as a healing Dr. Jekyll.

Where does this fascinating fellow come from, and how does he attain his position of power? Since he appears as a friend of the Jews, is he himself a Hebrew?

His Nationality

Answers to these questions are not given, but some interesting clues are suggested. The principal sources on Antichrist are the books of Daniel and Revelation, with brief references from other prophets and apostles. Daniel indicates that he will be a Roman or from a section of the Roman Empire, coming from the same people that destroyed Jerusalem in A.D. 70. This is suggested in Daniel 7:8, 24, where the little horn arises out of the Roman Empire to become dominant over "ten horns" or nations.

This shadowy figure is further identified in Daniel 8:19, 24, where "the final period of indignation" is described. Although the Syrian King Antiochus Epiphanes partially fulfilled this prophecy in 167 B.C., it looks beyond him to one he typified. That final king will operate in a power not his own; he will destroy many Jews after being at peace with them; he will oppose the "prince of princes"; and he will himself be destroyed in a supernatural way (Daniel 8:23–25). This prophecy then suggests that he may be from the Syrian north as was Antiochus Epiphanes. In Daniel's portrayal of him in 11:36–45, he calls him "the king" of the end times, as if well known from previous references.

In summary, these passages identify him as from the Roman Empire, the Grecian Empire, and the Syrian north. Since these succeeded or overlapped each other, the identifying prophecies simply move from the broad area of the Roman Empire to the more specific area of eastern Asia Minor.

The Kingdom of Antichrist

It is evident, however, that he will not begin as a great international somebody, but as a "little horn," a lesser ruler. His rise will begin as he subdues three kingdoms by military prowess in successive drives. With this leverage and momentum, he will acquire dominance over an empire of ten kingdoms through intrigue and political brokerage. He will be a diplomat par excellence.

The nations thus amalgamated will be basically European. Their areas will be so contiguous with the old Roman Empire that they are said to be a "ten-toe" development of it, perhaps grouped around the Mediterranean as was the Roman Empire. That area today would include Spain, France, Italy, Yugoslavia, Greece, Turkey, Syria, Israel, Egypt, and several smaller states. Since there seems to be animosity between this coming Antichrist and the Arab nations, it may be that Egypt and her satellites will not be in his orbit of power, but aligned with the great northern bloc.

This idea of a united Europe, of course, is certainly not new. From the time of Charlemagne to Adolf Hitler, many leaders have attempted to reconstruct such an empire over which to rule. Even today the formidable economic structure in Europe known as the common market is designed to control and regulate European economics. This group is not the one that will constitute the empire of Antichrist; but their desire for unity to compete with the Far West and Far East suggests the cohesion that could form such a European alliance.

When this opportunistic leader appears on the international scene, the time will be ripe for his coming. Following his initial conquests, many adjoining nations will willingly submit to him. Having endured a brief period of mob rule, they will probably endorse with enthusiasm his program of peace and unification to achieve a measure of stability. How they and the world will fare in that program is another matter which we will discuss later. It is important to note that he does not come as one who is immoral or antireligious, any more than Judas came on as a greedy devil at the beginning. He may, in fact, be a jolly good fellow and a promoter of culture and religion.

Israel's Pact with Hell

The first predicted event following the church's Rapture is a covenant between Israel and this vaunted leader. Signing that pact will also begin the seven-year end-time period for Israel (Daniel 9:27). God's time clock of dealing with the nation will again be plugged in, a timepiece stopped when Messiah was cut off. God's purposes with the church having been completed, the seventieth week of Daniel's prophecy will begin. This pact will then start the countdown for Christ's coming to set up His earthly kingdom seven years later.

The fact that this bellicose "prince" will make a covenant with Israel implies, of course, that Israel will be in a place of prominence and power. This sounded like a pipe dream prior to 1948, while the Jews were without hope of national recognition. Her position as a political force in the Middle East today, however, is certainly doubted by no one. The signing of this agreement with Israel then suggests that she will have something this leader wants and that he will be able to supply something she wants. This shrewd bargainer would hardly make a national pact with little Israel without ulterior motives, and the Jews would certainly not grant this impostor something for nothing.

THE DESIGN OF ANTICHRIST

The initial purpose of this crafty leader is not hard to discern. Beginning in relative anonymity and competing with many tough customers in world politics, he will obviously need all the help he can get. He will thus use every avenue of diplomacy, making friends and gaining influence wherever to expand his power base. Like Hitler's appeasement at Munich, he will make tongue-in-cheek leagues with many, bargaining for more and more political leverage.

It should also be remembered that the northern power bloc (a reunited Gog and Magog affiliation) will also be in the running for European dominance. That group will, in fact, be a major factor in alluring the nations of Europe and the Middle East to align with this new leader who promises unity and survival through military union.

This posturing then will polarize the two power blocs of north and south. To acquire a foothold in the Middle East, Antichrist will welcome this link with Israel, probably for her strategic land position at the geographical center of three continents. As cul-de-sac of the Mediterranean, the Levant has long been an enviable prize for expansionist regimes. For these political advantages then, Antichrist will sign a seven-year pact with Israel to stabilize the area and fortify his southeastern flank.

The Strategy of Israel

The shrewdness of Israel will no doubt match that of Antichrist. She would obviously not ally with this revenuer without some overpowering ulterior motives. Needing all the friends she can get, Israel may simply seek to break the stalemate with her Arab challengers and reduce her massive defense outlays. Cozying up to this rising potentate of Europe will appear to be her best hope to stabilize her position and fulfill some of her messianic dreams.

With Jerusalem as Israel's chief concern, this pact with Antichrist will probably center on the issue of its rule and worship at the temple. The fact that sacrifices are later halted and the temple desecrated suggests their restitution will be a part of this bargain (Daniel 9:27). This would be an opportune time for Israel to mollify the ultraorthodox by the resumption of these sacrifices at the temple. To enable that, a temple of sorts on the ancient Mount would have to be constructed, for sacrifices could not be offered at any other place. Acquiring this prize will perhaps be the frosting on the cake for world Jewry in their latter-day renaissance.

Such an agreement, admittedly, will incur worldwide Islamic wrath. Their sacred shrine of the Dome of the Rock stands on the temple site (though off-center), and is generally respected by most of the world as nonnegotiable—period. Muslims claim sonship to Abraham (by his eldest son, Ishmael), and consider their right to that real estate to be as ancient as that of the Jews. That Dome is a pillar of Islam, defiantly challenging both Judaism and Christianity by its location, grandeur, and inscriptions. Any pact that allows Israel to resume her sacrifices at this spot will inevitably ignite Arab ire throughout the world. Yet this designing monarch will apparently deem it a risk worth taking in his game of political chess in Europe and the Middle East.

Israel's Growth and Relative Security

This pact with Antichrist will also benefit Israel by providing several years of peace and growth. Ezekiel, in the sixth century B.C., foretold this restoration and the terror-filled days that follow. In describing Israel's situation prior to the northern invasion, he pictured her as at rest, dwelling safely without walls (Ezekiel 38:11). This suggests a period of relative peace for some three years, enabling a large influx of world Jewry to swell her ranks, as well as her banks (Ezekiel 38:12).

Initially, Antichrist's relationship to Israel will be almost messianic, raising unbelievable hope for the nation. That relation, however, will later turn sour and the treaty will become a death warrant. Isaiah described it as "your covenant with death" and "agreement with hell" (Isaiah 28:15). As we will presently see, this cozy co-op will prove to be a paramour relationship in the devil's whorehouse, and one of the great national tragedies of Israel's history. It is matched only by her first great tragedy of rejecting her true Messiah (Zechariah 11). The nation's infatuation with this pseudo-messiah will shortly explode in their faces, as he "makes mutton" of the sheep and a slaughterhouse of the nation (Zechariah 11:16–17).

THE RELIGIOUS SETTING OF ANTICHRIST'S WORLD

Though the period of Antichrist's reign will be ungodly, it will not be without religion. Both true and false religion will, in fact, flourish. Pandering to religion will be part and parcel of everything from politics to economics. Though the true church will have departed, other so-called "churches" will be very much in business.

The World "Church" of Tomorrow

A handy tool of Antichrist to promote culture and unity will be his world church system. It will be a religion of simplicity and centrality—rigidly so. It may be a compromise of all beliefs to their least common denominator, such as a recognition of values and general sincerity. No doubt a tacit subscription to the idea of God's reality will be included, but only as that is useful for human progress.

Of this post-Rapture "church" the Bible has a good bit to say. The apostle John devoted two chapters to describing it as a false woman (Revelation 17–18), before portraying the marriage of Christ to His true bride (19). He called it a "harlot" system. In her developed form this heady harlot is seen as wealthy and wicked. She is characterized as a mother of pimps, living in illicit relations with the world's political leaders. They use each other for their mutual passions and pleasure. Especially is she intimate with this ascending dictator, for John pictures her as riding the beast (Revelation 17:3). Through these leaders she will seduce and destroy many people in her quest for prestige and carnal gratification.

To describe her wretched character, John named her "Babylon the Great" (Revelation 17:5; 18:2, 21). He associates her with demonic worship and false religion (Revelation 14:8). In using this name he evidently makes reference to Zechariah 5:11, where the prophet speaks of religion being joined to commercialism at Shinar (that is, Babylon). The implication is that this harlot represents a counterfeit system of religion, not unlike the great rebellion against God at Babel (Genesis 11).

John's describes it as a religion of convenience. It will afford its adherents a form of godliness without restraints on the lower passions. Such was the prostitute form of religion at Corinth and Ephesus, where fornication spiced up their worship. The system will be a litany of rituals, divorced from morals and spirituality, designed to placate the need for religion, while destroying the soul through dissipation.

As fornication leads to murder, so this religious system will be "drunk with the blood of saints, and with the blood of the witnesses of Jesus" (Revelation 17:6). The false system of Jesus' time demanded His blood, and this final counterfeit will take the lives of many of His servants. Though tolerant of all else, it will be adamant in its rejection of biblical truth. Aligned with Antichrist, it will serve his purposes, acting as his axeman against all who do not pander to the party line.

What "church" denomination is this? Can we identify it today? John describes it as sitting upon seven mountains (Revelation 17:9), and as the "great city which reigns over the kings of the earth" (Revelation 17:18). Though the mountains represent kings or kingdoms, they also allude to a city. The city of ancient Babylon could hardly be meant, for it has no hills, has long been destroyed, and was cursed with eternal destruction (Isaiah 13:19–20; Jeremiah 50:29, 39). The designation "mystery Babylon," also sets it off as other than literal Babylon. The obvious identification seems to be the city of Rome, known from ancient times as the city on seven hills or mountains. John could hardly have named it, but Rome had long been recognized as a city of secular and religious power.

That he refers to the Roman Catholic Church even in its decadent form, however, is doubtful. To assume such is to miss the point. The "mystery" of which he speaks is that of an amalgamation of religious systems united in worldwide ecumenism. It is better seen as all the counterfeit systems welded together into one with a purely humanistic motive, designed to promote the one-world philosophy of Antichrist. Religious in form, it will be devoid of scruples in pursuing the devil's goals of unifying the world under this satanic agent.

Nor is this end-time church related to the Laodicean church of Revelation 3. Though it shares some of its features of wealth and indifference, it is far more blatant in its indulgences. It is not just "lukewarm" spiritually, but ice cold. Chronologically, the Laodicean church portrayed characteristics of the church age, whereas this one concerns the period of "after these things," that is, after church things (Revelation 1:19; 4:1b). This end-time system will work hand in glove with Antichrist and his puppets. In her role as mistress of this beast, this religious system will influence the kings of the earth, and through them, world commerce.

This brand of pseudo-religion is not new, of course, for Satan has always had his counterfeits. Counterfeiting God's work has been his hobby ever since he went into business for himself, saying, "I will be like the Most High" (Isaiah 14:14). And this end-time amalgam of religion will be his masterpiece. He will not only neutralize religion, but will make it his handmaid. As he took over the professional "church" of Israel before Christ's first coming, so he will take over and dominate this religious caricature before His Second Coming. What he will have taken over, of course, will be the religious shell, not the spiritual kernel.

The Underground Saints of Tomorrow

Though the era of Antichrist will be godless and virulent against Christianity, it will not be devoid of true religion. It will, in fact, be a time of gospel preaching like the world has never known. Not that it will be popular or respectable, for it will be under the ban of church and state.

In this crucible of fire, however, the true gospel will be preached through underground means in a daring program of salvaging "brands from the burning." The one salutary result of this world judgment will be its sifting and separating of wheat from the chaff. Uncommitted fence-sitting and pleasurable Christianity it will not be, but a forthright concern to evoke genuine decisions for Christ. Costly and clear-cut discipleship will be restored to their rightful place in Christian resolve.

Its Redemptive Program

To effect this program of salvation in the midst of judgment, the Lord will use a variety of innovative means and people. This is described in the book of Revelation, which is one of the most redemptive books of the Bible (as is John's Gospel). While unraveling this series of judgments, John intersperses several chapters on salvation to emphasize that God has not left Himself without a witness. These are chapters 7, 11, and 14, each following a portrayal of fierce judgment.

The 144,000 Israeli Servants (Revelation 7, 14)

Following the opening of the sixth seal of world judgment (Revelation 6:12–17), John introduces a strange scene of servants of God from all the tribes of Israel. They are being sealed or preserved for service. The question naturally arises as to how these end-time saints are saved, inasmuch as the true Church has been raptured. Who are they? what do they do? and how do they come to salvation? John's portrayal in chapter 7 harks back to his description in chapter 6 of tribulation saints martyred under the fifth seal. He here answers the problem of how they were saved, first by identifying the evangelists and then showing the result of their ministry to all nations.

Who are the 144,000? The church has long debated the identity of this group. The religion of "Jehovah's Witnesses" tries to shoehorn itself into this prophecy, all evidence in the context to the contrary. Traditionally, the church has often assumed that they represent all believers of this age who witness in persecution, being immortal till their work is done. This is admittedly a pious analogy.

In the context, however, the group is specifically called the "One hundred and forty-four thousand sealed from every tribe of the sons of Israel" (Revelation 7:4). John makes their identity as clear and specific as possible. As if anticipating our inclination to baptize them into the church, he drones out the twelve Israeli tribes from each of which come 12,000. If he really meant the Israelis, as is commonly understood, it is difficult to fault him for not being specific enough. Also, the period of time he describes is "after these things" when God again begins to deal with Israel as a nation. The church epistles deny any spiritual distinction between Jews and Gentiles in the church age. Rather, they insist that all are integrated together as common sinners to freely accept God's offer of grace (Romans 3:22).

Some have denied that the 144,000 are true believers, inasmuch as they are not called saints. Others have also questioned whether they are "witnesses," since that is not stated. These Israelis are specifically identified as "servants of our God" (Revelation 7:3). That term is a common identification of true believers in both Testaments, and is used to describe the believing martyrs of the previous chapter (6:11). Israel, Moses, and David were often called the Lord's servant, as was Messiah Himself. The sealing of the 144,000 is an allusion to a similar marking in Ezekiel 9:4, in which the faithful were marked for preservation through the Lord's judgment on Jerusalem. These are sealed for an unspecified period of time.

The 144,000 then are a group of Hebrew believers who are saved as the "firstfruits" of this new harvest of Israel (Revelation 14:4). Were they of the church, they would be a group of "last fruits," rather than first fruits. The result of their ministry brings also a bountiful harvest of "a great multitude, which no one could count, from every nation and all tribes and peoples and tongues" (Revelation 7:9, 14). These are specifically identified as the martyred fruit of "the great tribulation."

The Two Tribulation Witnesses

We naturally wonder how the 144,000 Israelis come to salvation after the church has been retired. "How shall they hear without a preacher?"

(Romans 10:14). This question is left unanswered in Revelation 7, but is strongly suggested in chapter 11. There John describes two time periods of three and a half years each, one a time of witness in Jerusalem and the other a time of desecration. (Though the two periods are of equal length, they are distinguished by their different designations.) During the first period of 1260 days, "two witnesses" appear and are anointed by the Lord for a special ministry. Since they have power to "shut heaven so that no rain falls" and "power over water to turn them to blood" (the first miracles of Moses and Elijah), they appear to be a resuscitation of these two unique witnesses. We recall that they were pressed into service also at the time of Jesus' earthly ministry on the mountain, following which Jesus prophesied a future return of Elijah (Matthew 17:11).

These two witnesses then bear testimony for God to Jerusalem and are slain after three and a half years, as the "beast...comes up out of the abyss" (Revelation 11:7). Their ministry evidently begins at the start of the seven-year period and is abruptly cut off at midpoint. The message they bring appears to parallel that of John the Baptist who called the nation to its knees in preparation for Messiah (Malachi 4:5–6). This suggests that their first converts may be the 144,000 of Israel as the "firstfruits" of their ministry.

The Gospel of the Kingdom

The message they preach is called by Jesus the gospel of the kingdom (Matthew 24:14). What gospel is this? A better question would be, what other gospel is there? It is doubtless the same as that spoken of by Jesus and the apostles, with the added emphasis of the soon appearing of God's kingdom on earth. It will be a message of salvation by faith in Jesus Christ, stressing the fact that the evil rule of Antichrist will shortly be destroyed by Christ as He comes to set up His kingdom. There is obviously no other saving gospel (Galatians 1:8–9).

This gospel will be preached throughout the whole world of that time (cf. Matthew 24:14). It will be God's final salvage operation before Christ's coming and no demon or device will effectively thwart its delivery. To guarantee this, God will empower His two witnesses with miraculous powers till their work is done. And following their ascent into heaven and the martyrdom of the 144,000, God will again press angels into evangelistic service to insure the gospel is proclaimed worldwide (Revelation 14:6). This is not so strange when we recall that He also used angels to proclaim Christ's first coming (Luke 1:26; 2:9–14).

PREPARATION FOR WORLD JUDGMENT

Israel's brief spell of delusion and safety under Antichrist will be in stark contrast to the rest of the world. All nations will be in a state of trauma and terror. The mysterious departure of the church may trigger some of this, unleashing pent-up passions and vengeance against all things moral and spiritual. The need to restore social order after massive gang and mob violence may be the ideal soil for Antichrist to offer strong leadership and begin building his empire.

Nor will it be a bed of roses for true believers in Israel. Jesus described this first-half period as the "beginning of sorrows" for many. Throughout the world there will be wars and rumors of wars, with famines, pestilence, and earthquakes in many places (Matthew 24:6–8). The Lord gave this description of the world in answer to a question about His return and the signs that would immediately precede it. It was not a description of the church age, as the context shows, but of that time when God begins again to deal with Israel as a nation and the new believers among them. The first half of that period will sample those coming sorrows.

The Four Apocalyptic Horsemen

John, in Revelation 6, under the symbolism of four horsemen describes the worldwide aspect of this judgment. After picturing Christ in chapter 5 as the only one worthy to judge the world (having been slain to redeem them), John dramatizes the commencement of those judgments by the unsealing of seven chapters of an awesome book. The content of each seal describes successive aspects of that judgment.

The first four are the "apocalyptic horsemen," which portray a series of judgments by human and natural causes during the first half. Though they come from natural causes, it is Christ the "Lamb" who initiates them by opening the seals. The symbol of "Lamb" signifies His redemptive purpose, as opposed to a mere punitive purpose.

The First Horseman Rides a White Horse (Revelation 6:2)

The first seal portrays a conqueror with a bow and a crown. This horseman evidently symbolizes Antichrist who comes as a pseudo-messiah, conquering first three, then ten kingdoms, and later the whole world (Daniel 7:24). The image suggests a counterfeit of Christ who later comes on a white horse at the end of the judgments (Revelation 19:11).

The Second Horseman Rides a Red Horse (Revelation 6:3–4)

The next three show a progression of devastation begun by the first horseman. Number two on a red horse has a "great sword," symbolizing full-scale war and fierce homicide. This pictures the explosion of pent-up racial anger and gang warfare that literally "takes peace from the earth."

The Third Horseman Rides a Black Horse (Revelation 6:5–6)

Black symbolizes famine, an inevitable consequence of war. It is probable that drought may also be a contributing factor in this judgment (Revelation 11:6). As in most human disasters, the poor man's staples of wheat and barley are made scarce, while the luxury items of "oil and wine" go begging.

The Fourth Horseman Rides a Pale Horse Named "Death" (Revelation 6:8)

The opening of this fourth seal summarizes the results of the first three judgments. They bring death by "sword and with famine and with pestilence and by the wild beasts of the earth." This portrays a vast devastation of mankind, taking an unheard of toll of one-fourth of the earth's population. The idea of wild beasts being involved is not so farfetched when we recall that a lengthy drought often brings animals out of the hills and forests to forage for food and water. By all this human and natural savagery, the bloodshed is described as unprecedented. The fact that "hades" is said to follow "death" emphasizes the fact that this is a judgment on the wicked and rebellious. Hades is always associated with the death of unbelievers in the New Testament. Revelation 20:13–14 describes "death and hades" being cast into the lake of fire. This vast destruction of the wicked concludes the judgments of the "apocalyptic horsemen," portraying earth's decimation under Antichrist.

The Fifth Seal Describing Martyrdom

This portrayal of martyrs following the four "apocalyptic horsemen" is a brief supplement concerning the righteous. It describes the slaying of many martyrs by an altar scene and a word of council from the Lord (Revelation 6:9–11). The scene unveils "souls under the altar," believers who have been slain for their Christian testimony during that period. The point is that the fury of that time will not bypass believers, but will test them sorely, many unto death.

The cry of the martyrs "under the altar" expresses the fact that their slayers are not just the axemen of Antichrist, but "those who dwell on the earth" (a designation in Revelation for all the ungodly). The whole world of ungodly will get into the act. For this injustice these "souls" cry to the Lord (Avenger) for justice. The Lord replies that many other "fellow servants" will also be martyred before the slaughter ends. This John further explains in the following chapter (7:9ff.).

The Sixth Seal Introducing the Great Day of the Lord

The judgments of this sixth seal are different in several ways. Their first distinction is their supernatural character, as opposed to natural causes. A massive earthquake moves every mountain and island, the heavens are blackened, and the sky is "split apart." In the process, the heavens are opened to give all mankind a glimpse of God on His throne as the "wrath of the Lamb" is about to fall. That evil society, drugged with humanistic pragmatism, is left with no doubt as to who is orchestrating these judgments.

The second difference is that this seal introduces another period of judgment, that known as the "great day of their wrath" (Revelation 6:17). The first and last prophets of Israel especially emphasized this period. Joel (c. 835 B.C.) first spoke of it as "the great and awesome day of the Lord," with signs almost identical to those shown in this seal (Joel 2:30–31). Malachi's last word in the Old Testament also spoke of this "great and terrible day of the LORD" (Malachi 4:5). In the Gospels Jesus referred to it as the "great tribulation," a time of carnage unparalleled in human history (Matthew 24:21).

But Malachi also noted that before the coming of this awesome day, the prophet Elijah will return to minister to Israel for three and a half years (Malachi 4:5; Revelation 11:3). This indicates the chronology of this sixth seal. Since Elijah is to minister during the first three and a half years, the supernatural judgments of this seal occur at the midpoint and serve to introduce the great tribulation.

SUMMARY

This story of the rise of Antichrist is one of immense intrigue and opportunism in world affairs. Occurring in the wake of the Church's departure, it will galvanize a shocked and frenetic world to regroup and seek a measure of stabilization. In that regrouping process, two polarizations will take place. The first will be that of the nations of Europe and the Middle East, aligning with either the northeastern European bloc of "Gog and Magog" or that of the southern alliance of Antichrist. In the midst of all this maneuvering will be the island of Israel in a sea of international jockeying for world dominance. Motivated by new threats of annihilation by her Arab neighbors, Israel will form an alliance of trust with the rising Antichrist. Under the presumed safety of this political pact, Israel will enjoy a brief period of "peace" in the midst of a raging world of international wars and turmoil.

A second polarization will be that of religion. During that period of three and a half years, much religious activity will transpire of both a true and false nature. Motivated by the ministry of God's two resurrected witnesses, an underground nucleus of newly saved believers will give courageous proclamation of the gospel. The fierce religious struggle that will ensue will be accentuated by a vast martyrdom of saints who come under the ban of Antichrist's church and state.

These martyrs remind us of God's continuing redemptive program during the end times. John sees it necessary to emphasize this in chapter 7, before elucidating the further supernatural judgments of the last half. Only with this redemptive perspective can the purpose of the following supernatural judgments be properly understood.

The opening of the sixth seal then brings the drama of history to its most climactic hour. The trumpeting of God's wrath is about to sound and be executed on an increasingly rebellious world. How that wrath begins and who is involved is a solemn and somber story, to be sure. It is an essential reminder, however, of what God thinks of sin as He cleanses and prepares the world for its coming day of glory.

CHAPTER TEN

ISRAEL'S FINAL HOLOCAUST

Few races of people have suffered as much as the Jews. Before the coming of Christ they were constantly between the hammer and anvil of Gentile powers. Their location made them the brunt of international intrigue. That bitter role of scapegoat tended to intensify if anything, driving many to ghettos for sheer survival. The sordid "final solution" pursued by Hitler only epitomized the plaintive plight of the wandering Jews.

A new day dawned in 1948 and they now have a homeland of their own. Though jubilant and euphoric at times, they have had little time to savor victory or gloat. Rather they have united to wielded trowel and sword in an effort to carve out what they see as their messianic future. Hard work and sheer doggedness have paid off. Their massive feat of rebuilding Palestine from a barren, malaria-ridden land into a thriving garden and industrial beehive is almost without parallel. In half a century they have planted an oasis of democracy in the Middle East, hoping to fulfill their age-old dreams in a modern world.

SHADOWS OF A GATHERING STORM

Before their day of predicted glory actually comes, however, things are going to get worse—much worse—before getting better. Though they have known trouble throughout history as a constant companion, an unprecedented storm lies ahead. Under a deceptive antichrist, they will experience a brief period of peace and growth, but it will be short-lived. It will only presage a time of greater holocaust. The reason? Their age-long rejection of truth in refusing the Messiah God sent.

Though prophesied, we naturally ask why this coming generation of Israel should be subjected to that time of predicted tribulation. Since God does not punish children for the sins of their fathers (Ezekiel 18:20), why this calamity on such a committed, industrious people? The obvious answer is that a moral crisis is also coming. That coming generation under Antichrist will have developed an apostate and degenerate condition deserving that prophesied judgment (Ezekiel 39:23–26). Their impious relations with Antichrist and his apostate cronies will implicate them in executing Christians and an unprecedented besmudging of the name of Jesus. For this cause God said through Ezekiel, "I shall make you pass under the rod…and I shall purge from you the rebels, and those who transgress against Me (Ezekiel 20:37–38).

This time of great tribulation, of course, will not be restricted to Israel. It will be worldwide. Many factors will contribute to its buildup, and numerous events will make up the mosaic that brings it to a head. Its plot involves not only a massive world war, but an unparalleled war in heaven. Key figures will include angels and devils, Antichrist and his allies, the Russian north and her allies, Egypt and her allies, with Israel caught in the middle. Much Scripture is given to describing this as a cataclysmic point in world history. All the major prophets wrote of it as did many of the minor prophets. How does it all begin? How do the various parts fit, and what will be the outcome?

THE BUILDUP FOR WORLD WAR III

Prior to this time the world will have tooled up for its most crucial armed confrontation. Following more than three years of international tension, bluff, and buildup by Antichrist's coalition and the northern bloc, world tension will be at a fever pitch. Europe will again become a vast military bastion as the nations polarize around these two military giants. Egypt and the Arab nations will be somewhat divided, but mainly with the northern bloc. In the final months of that buildup, plowshares will be hurriedly turned into swords, war being more important than agriculture (Joel 3:10). Although numerous wars will precede this decisive one, they will be minor by comparison. This confrontation will be the real World War III between the superpowers, for the battle of Armageddon will be later and of a much different character.

The Crucial Issues Involved

The little nation of Israel will be in the midst of this. Her land will be the major battlefield and she will be the vortex around which the great struggle swirls. The question is why the superpowers would commit all their resources to fight over the small state of Israel and her limited resources.

Ezekiel 38:12 describes some of their reasons: "to capture spoil and seize plunder" from a people gathered from the nations who have come with great wealth and "live at the center of the world." Two tantalizing plums seem to attract the nations: her wealth and her strategic location. The in-gathering of Jews from around the world will have swelled this booty, and her wealth of minerals locked in the Dead Sea is said to be without calculation. All this will be a coveted prize for the marauding powers, especially after being pauperized by three years of drought and world plagues. Having lived and pursued her own messianic vision under the temporary favor of Antichrist, Israel will have flourished in many ways. But this will make her a sitting duck for the hungry nations.

These developing issues and sinister preparations suggest that the midpoint of the seven-year period will find the world a powder keg that needs only a spark to ignite. We naturally wonder who will be fool enough to strike that match?

The War of Two Archangels in Heaven

We get a clue by noting that a similar cataclysmic event will take place in heaven just prior to this midpoint battle on earth. This period has been called the Day of the Lord, and He is the one who orchestrates its agenda.

Though the nations will rage in cosmic battle with each other, it is the sovereign Lord who will call the shots from heaven. This reminder is given in the explanatory passage of Revelation 12, which introduces several important figures not yet mentioned. To this point in Revelation, Satan's part in this drama has not been mentioned, nor has his agent Antichrist been officially introduced. In this chapter John begins those introductions by showing how Satan will be involved and the reasons he unleashes his savagery at this time.

SATAN'S EVICTION FROM HEAVEN

At God's command, Michael and his angels will make war with the "dragon" and his minions, casting them out of heaven (Revelation 12:4–9). The identity of this "dragon" is not left in doubt, but is specified as Satan, the serpent of Genesis 3:15. John says little of the massiveness of this battle in heaven, but suggests it by its outcome. One-third of the angels of heaven are evicted, giving us some idea of the vastness of Satan's kingdom and rule. His being bounced from heaven also terminates his pernicious work of accusing the saints before the throne of God (Revelation 12:10; cf. Job 1:6ff.; Zechariah 3:1).

This unceremonious ejection of Satan from the heavenly realm will be the spark that ignites the fiery conflagration on earth. Indignant at this insult by a lesser dignitary, he will vent his wrath on the earth. Though his removal from heaven brings rejoicing there, it brings woe on earth as the devil devises his final strategy (Revelation 12:12). He will know his time is short, not because of any gift of prophecy, but because he knows God's Word—and believes it (James 2:19).

SATAN'S WRATH ON EARTH

The pent-up fury of the devil at this time will be turned in two directions. He will first persecute the "woman," identified as Israel, and will pursue those who are true believers in Jesus (Revelation 12:17). Israel will feel his wrath because she is the nation that produced the "man child" Jesus, and true believers will experience his fury because they hold the testimony of Jesus. Having usurped the kingdoms of this world, the devil will be infuriated as the "seed of the woman" seeks to divest him of that rule in the earthly sphere (Luke 4:6; 1 John 5:19).

The date of this event is precisely given by John, as he twice declares that the woman is driven into the wilderness for three and a half years (Revelation 12:6, 14). This obviously relates to Daniel's description of Israel's time of unprecedented trouble that occurs at the last half of the end-time period (Daniel 12:2, 7).

Satan's wrath is here described as first a frontal attack on Israel and then a flood of water that drives her into the eastern wilderness of Edom. As Daniel often traced Israel's problems to the spiritual realm, John also reveals Satan as the perpetrator (Daniel 10:13, 20–21; 12:1). To counter this, Israel is helped by both Michael and the earth, enabling her to find refuge in the eastern mountains, perhaps the high plateau of Petra. This "spewing of water after the woman" is John's way of reminding the reader of the Old Testament prophecies of these end-time events, inasmuch as several prophets had long ago detailed these battles (Ezekiel 38–39; Daniel 11–12; Zechariah 13). They portray two great world empires invading and colliding on the hills of Palestine at some time after Israel's return when they are peacefully settled in the land. That which Revelation 12 pictures as instigated and carried out by the devil, the prophets detailed from the perspective of the earthly battles that will be waged.

RUSSIA'S FINAL FIASCO ON THE HILLS OF PALESTINE

At Satan's prompting, Russia and her confederates will make a dramatic plunge into Palestine. This attack will ignite the fuse of world conflict by bringing four major world power blocs into head-on collision. It will force a showdown, not only on the Palestine question, but on the broader issue of who will dominate the world.

The Major Adversaries

The identity of "Gog of the land of Magog" (Ezekiel 38:2 ff.) is quite generally accepted as the final ruler of Russia (ancient Scythia) by most lexicographers. He is said to be the ruler of "Rosh, Meshech, and Tubal"

(v. 3), which are identified as the lands of Russia and Tobolsk (eastern Russia) with the capital city of Moscow. Affiliated with them will be Persia, Ethiopia, Libya, Gomer, and Togarmah (Ezekiel 38:5–6). The Ethiopia and Libya spoken of here are not the north African countries, but ancient Japhethites contiguous with Persia. Gomer (Gimarrai) refers to the Cimmerians who moved from the Crimea to northern Turkey, and Togarmah is located in northeastern Turkey and Armenia (ancient Assyria). These are lands north of Israel from eastern Persia or Iran to ancient Scythia or modern Ukraine.

The text of Ezekiel 38–39 identifies this invader as a great northern confederacy descending on Israel. There are some who see this adversary as a coalition of the Islamic powers stretching from Iran to western Russia. That is certainly a possibility. Islam today claims nearly one billion adherents and is the world's fastest growing religion. Its strong militaristic base in the Koran makes it a growing religious competitor, aggressively seeking a unified political power base. The special challenge of Islam is against Christianity and Judaism.

It is not our business, however, to identify this northern power or to peg its religion. As Sir Robert Anderson once wrote, "Prophecy is not given to enable us to prophesy," but "by patient contemplation we may clearly discern the main outlines of the landscape of the future" (*The Coming Prince,* 271). We simply leave it as the text describes it—the land of Magog to the north and far north of Israel with their leader, Gog, who see the land of Israel a prize to pillage. Recent and continuing changes in that area show how quickly political and religious changes can take place, but that does not change the biblical location.

Ezekiel's Portrayal of the Destruction of Gog and Magog

The story of this invasion is detailed by Ezekiel (38–39). To appreciate his prophecy, we should recall how he develops his theme in his book. Having prophesied the destruction of Jerusalem in chapters 4 to 32, he then predicts her final restoration in chapters 33 to 48 (33 being a recommissioning). After warning of false shepherds in chapter 34 and God's ancient judgment on Edom in 35, he describes Israel's regathering from all nations and her renewal as the flock of God in 36. Chapter 37 then shows, in the parable of "dry bones," how this regathering will take place in the "latter days."

In that end-time period her "very dry bones" will reassemble, but without spiritual life ("very dry" signifying having been dead a long time). The nation will regather while yet in unbelief. At a later point the "house of Israel" will be given spiritual life, but only after a cataclysmic purging takes place. Therefore, before describing the coming blessings of the messianic age in chapters 40–48, Ezekiel elucidates that judgment that will precede it and cleanse the land. In the process he describes how God will destroy the godless northern empire that He uses for Israel's purging. This story is the subject of Ezekiel 38 and 39.

Russia's Calculated Gamble

At a propitious time the northern confederacy will elect to go for broke in an international gamble. They will make a lightning strike into the central heartland of Palestine. This will not be a minor skirmish, but an all-out committal of their army, fleet, and air force. Ezekiel describes it this way: "And you will go up, you will come like a storm; you will be like a cloud covering the land, you and all your troops and many peoples with you" (Ezekiel 38:9). In this they will be joined by various Arab states from the south.

Their objective will be no paltry prize. It will be both economic and political. They will come "to capture spoil and to seize plunder," but also to secure a foothold at "the center of the world." With Antichrist in covenant relations with Israel, this move by the confederate North will obviously be at great risk, but calculated to check the growing world influence of Antichrist and seize the balance of power.

God's Personal Response from Heaven

In answer to this impudence God says, "I shall call for a sword against him on all My mountains" (Ezekiel 38:21). That "sword" will bring both cosmic judgment from heaven and military blitzkrieg from the West. Ezekiel elaborates on the former:

> And in My zeal and in My blazing wrath I declare that on that day there will surely be a great earthquake in the land of Israel. And the fish of the sea, the birds of the heavens, the beasts of the field,...all the men who are on the face of the earth will shake at My presence; the mountains also will be thrown down, the steep pathways will collapse, and every wall will fall to the ground. (Ezekiel 38:19–20)
>
> And with pestilence and with blood I shall enter into judgment with him; and I shall rain on him, and on his troops, and on the many peoples who are with him, a torrential rain, with hailstones, fire and brimstone. (Ezekiel 38:22)

This description is similar to that given by Joel (2:30–31) and John in Revelation (6:12–17), as they each introduce the coming of the "great and terrible day of the Lord." Ezekiel's point here is to highlight God's wrath as He levels it against the impious nations of the North who from ancient times have despised God's people Israel.

The Challenge from the West

Besides supernatural judgment, the Lord will also employ the sword of nations to destroy Gog and Magog. That will include both treacherous civil war among them and a massive onslaught by a western alliance. This is suggested in the challenge by "Sheba and Dedan, and the merchants of Tarshish, with all its villages [Hebrew young lions]" (Ezekiel 38:13). The lands of Sheba and Dedan, grandsons of Abraham by Keturah, were trading points in the Persian Gulf with whom the ships of Tarshish did business (Genesis 25:3; Ezekiel 27:12–24). Those ships also carried on a brisk trade throughout the Mediterranean to Tarshish (Spain) their home port in the far west. This mention of the fleet of Tarshish with its young lions is a probable reference to the western alliance of Antichrist. It is also a rare reference to the future empires of the West—Great Britain, the U.S.A. and their allies—the only suggestion of the modern West in Scripture. To this invasion by the North, Antichrist will quickly respond. It is a challenge to his treaty with Israel.

Daniel's Portrayal of Antichrist's Conquest

Daniel, who views it from another angle, also gives a blow by blow account of this battle. His prophecy emphasizes the involvement of Antichrist, progressively bringing his activities in the end times into the open. In Daniel 11:36ff. this mysterious "king" is seen in his rise to power, becoming increasingly anti-God. The prophet specifically dates this prophecy as coming at the time of the end, just prior to the great tribulation (Daniel 11:35; 12:1; cf. Matthew 24:15, 21).

Four Major Powers Collide

Daniel's prophecy identifies four blocs of nations: the first is this blasphemous king, Antichrist and his allies; second, the king of the South, Egypt and her confederates; third, the king of the North, Russia and company; and fourth, an Eastern bloc of kings. Daniel gives a description of their massive engagement:

> And at the end time the king of the South will collide with him, and the king of the North will storm against him with chariots, with horsemen, and with many ships; and he will enter countries, overflow them, and pass through. He will also enter the Beautiful Land, and many countries will fall; but these will be rescued out of his hand: Edom, Moab and the foremost of the sons of Ammon.
>
> Then he will stretch out his hand against other countries, and the land of Egypt will not escape. But he will gain control over the hidden treasures of gold and silver, and over all the precious things of Egypt; and Libyans and Ethiopians will follow at his heels.
>
> But rumors from the East and from the North will disturb him, and he will go forth with great wrath to destroy and annihilate many. And he will pitch the tents of his royal pavilion between the seas and the beautiful Holy Mountain; yet he will come to his end, and no one will help him. (Daniel 11:40–45)

The campaign can be traced as follows: The kings of the North and the South (Russia and Egypt) conspire to invade Palestine. Antichrist, in league with Israel, will have plans to retain the land as his own. Egypt will make the initial attack from the south as a detracting action. As Antichrist responds to this southern ploy, the northern alliance will descend on him and his forces with their massive armament and swarm over the whole northeastern Mediterranean area. This appears to be the same invasion described in Ezekiel 38–39, which is here shown to be challenged by the western alliance of Antichrist.

Divine Wrath on the North

Then an unbelievable thing happens. God intervenes to bring judgment on the Russian invasion of Palestine with cosmic upheavals. A great earthquake and heavenly disturbances destroy the northern army as the forces of Antichrist also join in the battle. At this turn of events, Antichrist's most vicious foe will be obliterated, allowing him to extend his power over the surrounding countries. Egypt will also be consolidated under his rule, with only the areas of ancient Edom, Moab, and Ammon being denied him. The reason for this is not given, but perhaps they are too small to bother with as he feverishly undertakes the massive task of consolidating his enlarged empire.

The Eastern Challenge

As he mops up Egypt, however, he will suddenly become greatly disturbed by a report that an alliance in the North and East has formed to challenge and corner him (Daniel 11:44). To this he quickly responds, increasing his brutality and destruction as he confronts this dying axis and others who dare to oppose him. How far he pursues these challengers is not described, but he apparently emerges from the campaign as world dictator. He appears in Revelation 13 as the undisputed dictator.

At this midpoint, Antichrist will establish himself in Jerusalem, building "his royal pavilion between the seas and the beautiful Holy Mountain" (Daniel 11:45). This place on Mount Zion may be only his summer headquarters, but it will figure quite prominently in his program.

Daniel's final statement in chapter 11 that "he will come to his end, and no one will help him," has suggested to some that this battle takes place at the time of Armageddon, just before Christ's return. That is hardly the case, for Daniel dates it in the following verse as occurring at the beginning of the great tribulation (12:1). During the last half, the Antichrist is in undisputed command, forcing all the world to do his bidding. This brief statement of his ignominious end is simply a word of encouragement to Israel about his final defeat after this gloomy prophecy of his rise as the great archenemy of Israel in the end times.

ISRAEL'S FALSE SHEPHERD TURNS WOLF

During this victorious campaign of Antichrist over the northern invader, some convulsive changes will take place in Antichrist himself. Not only will he adopt a vicious attitude toward Israel, he will have a complete change of character. As he comes on the scene in Revelation 13, he appears as a "beast" with the character of Satan.

The reason for this radical change may simply be the result of his sudden ascent to political dominance; his lust for power may be so insatiable as to drive him to revoke former friendships to achieve his world ambitions. That may be possible, but several other factors appear to be involved in this abrupt change in the man's psyche.

Antichrist Returns from the Abyss

John introduces him as coming on the scene at the midpoint, as the "beast out of the sea" (Revelation 13:1). He appears to have been called up by the dragon as one who had a death stroke ("slain unto death") and was healed (v. 3). This might conceivably mean that he was on his deathbed and experienced a miraculous healing. The language, however, hardly allows that, since both his death and resurrection are described as point actions in the past, and are referred to six times (Revelation 11:7; 13:3, 12, 14; 17:8, 11). So unusual is the event that it causes the whole earth to bow in worship.

He is also described as having come out of the abyss. This is the place where the wicked dead are kept, awaiting judgment (Revelation 9:11;

17:8; 20:1–3). God seems to have allowed him a brief reprieve. At the time of the harlot's destruction (midpoint), it is said that he "was, and is not, and shall come." Though he "was" and "shall come," John says at the midpoint, he "is not."

This "beast" is also portrayed as representing the last of a group of eight kingdoms, five of which were history at that time (Revelation 17:8–11). Assuming that the sixth was present at the time of John, the seventh was future, and Antichrist, who represented the eighth, would also be "of the seventh." Thus the seventh and eighth would be different, but also the same (as the first-half kingdom will be the same as the last half). Antichrist, being raised out of the abyss, would actually be the same.

These passages strongly suggest that Antichrist will die briefly at midpoint and be resurrected for a new role. Such a resurrection admittedly presents a problem, since God alone has the power to give life. It might be recalled, however, that Satan, the "fallen star" of Revelation 9:1–11, is there given the key of the abyss to allow certain escapage. God might allow him the same power to restore Antichrist. If so, Satan will have produced his greatest counterfeit, simulating Christ's resurrection, thus providing the false prophet a great deceptive tool. This he will use to the limit to deceive the world and make the beast an object of worship (Revelation 13:14).

Antichrist Empowered by Satan

A second factor contributing to the radical change in Antichrist at the midpoint is his empowerment by Satan (Revelation 13:2). The infuriated dragon will give this resuscitated leader "his power, and his throne and great authority." Having been warned of his great wrath (12:12), the earth will immediately experience it through this puppet of the dragon. He is seen as blasphemous and vile, seeking to destroy all the saints (13:5–8). As such, he will rule for forty-two months (13:5).

In summary, we note that Antichrist comes on the scene at the beginning of the seven-year period as a man of brilliance in politics and a patron of religion. At the midpoint, however, a unique crisis takes place in his career. During his violent struggle with the northern invaders, he is evidently killed. The accompanying earthquakes and heavenly disturbances could account for his death, though his being "slain to death" suggests conflict (Revelation 13:3). However, he is soon raised to life and assumes the role of dictator in a far more vicious and depraved manner. He then operates during the last half completely in the power of Satan. Having desired world rulership more than anything else, he will sell his soul to the devil to receive the "glory" Satan long ago boasted he could give: "I will give it to whomever I wish" (Luke 4:6).

ISRAEL BETRAYED AND EMASCULATED

Like Judas Iscariot, this "son of perdition" will also be a betrayer. After ascending to the role of world dictator, he will discard all his paper pacts and serve only his own interests. His covenant with Israel will probably be but one among many such treaties made to be broken. Having gained his objective, he will be obliged to no man, and will violate anything that restricts his absolute world dominion.

That covenant will doubtless bring benefits to Israel for three and a half years, allowing her to grow and flourish. A vast immigration of Jews will flock to the land from all parts of the world, stimulating prosperity under the umbrella of Antichrist. With her sacrificial system reinstituted, the people will believe her messianic age is about to dawn. Though his rule will bring great turmoil outside the land, Antichrist will appear as Messiah to many in Israel.

At the midpoint, however, they will be rudely disabused of that delusion. Following the massive destruction of the northern invaders and the restoration of order, Israel will discover that a new kind of antichrist is in charge. He will suddenly become a wolf that slaughters the sheep, rather than a shepherd that feeds them (Zechariah 11:6). He will be the devil incarnate, or at least his clone. They will find their highly touted covenant to be an "agreement with hell" (Isaiah 28:18).

Israel's Religious Reversal

This turnaround will begin the period Jeremiah called "the time of Jacob's trouble" and Jesus called the "great tribulation." Many of the prophets wrote of it. Several excruciating events will make it the time of Israel's supreme calamity, the first of which will be religious. Their newly established system of ritual sacrifices will again be terminated (Daniel 9:27). This will be followed by the institution of dragon worship in the temple where an image of Antichrist will be set up. This is the final "abomination of desolation" spoken of by Daniel and others (Daniel 12:11; Matthew 24:15; 2 Thessalonians 2:4).

Israel's National Distress

A second calamity will be the devastation of the people of Israel themselves. They will endure a "time of distress such as never occurred since there was a nation until that time" (Daniel 12:1). Not even the destruction in A.D. 70 or the modern holocaust will compare. As they once basked in the favor of Antichrist, they will suddenly become the brunt of his fury. Under this new reign of terror, "many will be purged, purified, and refined" (Daniel 12:10). The maligned witness of the 144,000 will receive a belated response by many as their message begins to come true.

Though many Israelis will be forced by circumstances to remain in Jerusalem, a vast crowd will flee in panic to the mountains. Jesus solemnly warned of this day of distress. He admonished those in Jerusalem to flee to the mountains as they see this act of abomination in the temple (Matthew 24:16). So urgent will their escape be, Jesus said they should let nothing hinder them. Those delayed by restrictions of the Sabbath, anticipation of childbirth, or other circumstance will be in great danger. Were this massacre and desolation to continue, Jesus said, it would consume the whole of humanity (Matthew 24:22).

For those who do flee, however, supernatural help from Michael the archangel will be given. He will accord them special protection in their flight to the hills, hovering over them in a mountain sanctuary for three and a half years (Revelation 12:6, 14). The high mountain fortress and plateau of Petra has often been speculated as a possible hideaway, as it often served the ancient Edomites and Nabataeans. In his own peculiar way, Michael will give this remnant of Israel "two wings of the great eagle...that she might fly into the wilderness to her place, where she was nourished for a time and times and half a time, from the presence of the serpent" (Revelation 12:14). It is evident, however, that many of Israel will not avail themselves of this escape, for thousands will be slain in the succeeding months in Jerusalem (Zechariah 13:8; Revelation 11:13).

In discussing this supernatural side of the story, John portrays Michael as playing a twofold role in the drama. He commences the fireworks by first bouncing Satan from heaven and then protecting the faithful of Israel from his fury on earth. Having lost their erstwhile benefactor, Antichrist, they will receive the protection of Michael. As the ravens once fed Elijah in the wilderness for three and a half years, Michael will feed and hover over this remnant for a similar period. His power to evict Satan from heaven certainly demonstrates his ability to care for this remnant at God's command.

THE NEW WORLD RELIGION OF DEVIL WORSHIP

The resurrected Antichrist will be full of surprises. A significant reversal he will effect will be his colossal change in world religion. During the first three and a half years, he will patronize the world ecumenical church and be one of its leading members. He and the prelates will work hand in glove in efforts of unification. This sinister union of church and state will produce a popular religion that pretends to worship God, but is, in reality, the epitome of religious hypocrisy. As a tool of Satan, it will be corrupt to the core.

The World Ecumenical Church Destroyed

The devil, however, will not be satisfied with a system that merely counterfeits worship of God. Vilifying God's work is only half his agenda; his final goal is to take the place of God, to be worshiped as God Himself. That travesty he will force on the world during the last half, using two prominent stooges as his agents. One is the Antichrist and the other will be the false prophet who will officiate as the ecumenical pope of the system.

That change appears to take place as follows. Returning from his conquest of the North, Antichrist will unleash his wrath on his former religious accomplice, the false church. Through the ten puppet kings associated with him, he will institute a thorough purge of all religions, especially the harlot church system. That touted, fence-sitting religious system will have a great fall.

> And the ten horns which you saw, and the beast, these will hate the harlot and will make her desolate and naked, and will eat her flesh and will burn her up with fire...For her sins have piled up as high as heaven, and God has remembered her iniquities. Pay her back even as she paid, and give back to her double according to her deeds. In the cup which she has mixed, mix twice as much for her. To the degree that she glorified herself and lived sensuously, to the same degree give her torment and mourning; for she says in her heart, "I SIT AS A QUEEN AND AM NOT A WIDOW, and will never see mourning." For this reason in one day her plagues will come, pestilence and mourning and famine, and she will be burned up with fire; for the Lord God who judges her is strong. (Revelation 17:16; 18:5–8)

Having used this religious counterfeit as a pawn to promote his own political ends, Antichrist will discard her at his moment of triumph. Their former intimacy will only make her more vile in his eyes. Both true and false Christianity will then be banned from the earth and hunted down. The pillaging of this false system with its dazzling riches will be quickly accomplished in one day (Revelation 18:8). In destroying it, however, Antichrist will not only fulfill his own selfish designs, but also the intentions of God concerning this harlot. All heaven will rejoice and feel avenged at the judgment of this deceptive, seductive system that has fawned itself under Antichrist as the church of God (Revelation 18:20).

In its place he will set up an even more vile system, worship of the dragon. This will be a blatant worship of Satan through his agent the Antichrist. John describes this travesty in Revelation 13:3–6:

> And I saw one of his heads as if it had been slain and his fatal wound was healed. And the whole earth was amazed and followed after the beast; and they worshiped the beast, because he gave his authority to the beast; and they worshiped the beast, saying, "Who is like the beast, and who is able to wage war with him?"...And he opened his mouth in blasphemies against God, to blaspheme His Name and His tabernacle, that is, those who dwell in heaven.

The Temple Converted to Devil Worship

To accomplish this conversion of the world to devil idolatry, Antichrist will use several basic means. The first will be the conversion of Jerusalem's temple into a satanic holy of holies. Having called a halt to the revived religious system, he will exterminate any form of Jehovah worship and set up dragon worship in its place. Paul declared that this man of sin would exalt himself "above every so-called god or object of worship, so that he takes his seat in the temple of God, displaying himself as being God" (2 Thessalonians 2:4). In his absence he will place an image of himself on the sacred altar (Revelation 13:14–15). Nor will he make any bones about the fact that he works in Satan's power to promote devil worship. If "every dog has its day," this will be the devil's day of fulfilling his age-long dream to receive worldwide worship.

The False Prophet As High Priest

A second means Antichrist will use to extend dragon worship throughout the world will be through a dedicated lieutenant known as "the false prophet," or "beast out of the earth" (Revelation 13:11; 19:20). His name distinguishes him from the beast out of the sea, perhaps in the fact that he arises out of the land of Israel, rather than the Gentile area of the Mediterranean. It also suggests he may be an apostate Jew, a Judas who also sells his soul as a henchman of Antichrist.

Whatever his origin, his purpose will be to bring the world to its knees in worshiping Satan. How could sane people possibly submit to such a delirium? This false prophet will use several unique tools to bring it off. One will no doubt be the death and "resurrection" of Antichrist as a counterpart to Christ's resurrection. He will delude the world into believing in a dualism of God and Satan, convincing them that Satan is now winning and taking over the world. That will not be difficult with wickedness in seeming triumph. To demonstrate this, he will perform great miracles similar to Elijah's making "fire come down out of heaven" (Revelation 13:14). He will even give a semblance of life to the image of Antichrist in the temple. All who refuse acquiesce to Satan worship will be slain. This he will justify by reference to Elijah's slaying the 450 prophets of Baal who defied Jehovah worship (1 Kings 18:38–40).

The Economic Power Play: 666

To force this satanic worship throughout the world, the false prophet will make it a bread and butter issue. All buying and selling will require each one to display a "mark of the beast," either his name or his number, 666 (Revelation 13:16–18). This will signify their subjection and allegiance to Antichrist and Satan. Those who refuse will either die of famine or be rounded up for the guillotine (Revelation 20:4). Many of the faithful will be forced into martyrdom or underground activities, but exemptions or compromise with the system will not be tolerated.

What should we make of the number 666? It has been ingeniously interpreted through history by many theological sleuths scenting the trail of mystery in Antichrist. Its mathematics has intrigued many. Over the centuries numerical games have been played with such names as Judas, Nero Caesar, Caligula, and various popes in attempts to uncover the culprit. The name "Hitler" (using the numeric of the English language, A = 100, B = 101, etc.) comes out 666, for instance.

All this is futile speculation and outside the purpose of this prophecy. The biblical command to "calculate the number" has to do with end-time believers in the context of this worldwide coercion of satanic worship. For those believers under the heel of Antichrist, this prophecy of "666" will serve as a light in the darkness. It will kindle hope in their hearts that God's prophecies are being fulfilled and deliverance is on the way. Biblical prophecy is not given to entertain the curious with tricky puzzles, but to stimulate the saints to active patience in the outworking of God's program. This mysterious number, 666, will be God's reminder to them that He has not forgotten them in their hour of great trial.

SUMMARY

A glimpse at these crucial events at the midpoint of Daniel's seventieth week portrays the desperation of those bleak days of which Jesus gave warning. It will be a time when sin and evil will appear to have gained world dominance as righteousness is driven underground. It will be the day of testing Satan's "lie" (2 Thessalonians 2:11), that human nature is in an evolutionary spiral upward, revealing rather its inevitable spiral downward without the restraining influence of God's Spirit. It will show the personification of sin in human nature and its ultimate rejection of God's redeeming grace.

With respect to Israel, it will bring to a climactic end the results of rejecting God's Messiah for two millennia. The false messiah they embrace will tickle their fleshly aspirations for a brief honeymoon, to be sure. But, having used them as gullible pawns to further his own devious ambitions, he will, like the thieves on the Jericho road, leave her half-dead and naked in her own native soil.

All these midtribulation events will be traumatic in the extreme for the fledging nation, but necessary to bring about her spiritual revival. It will prepare both Israel and the world for their eventual reception of God's Messiah as the long-sought Prince of Peace.

In the following months, however, a final, more awesome confrontation will take place in the massive engagement of God and man at Armageddon. The events that lead to that assize are entirely unique to man's history and require a special chapter to unfold. The buildup for Armageddon lies ahead.

The Seven-Year End-Time Period

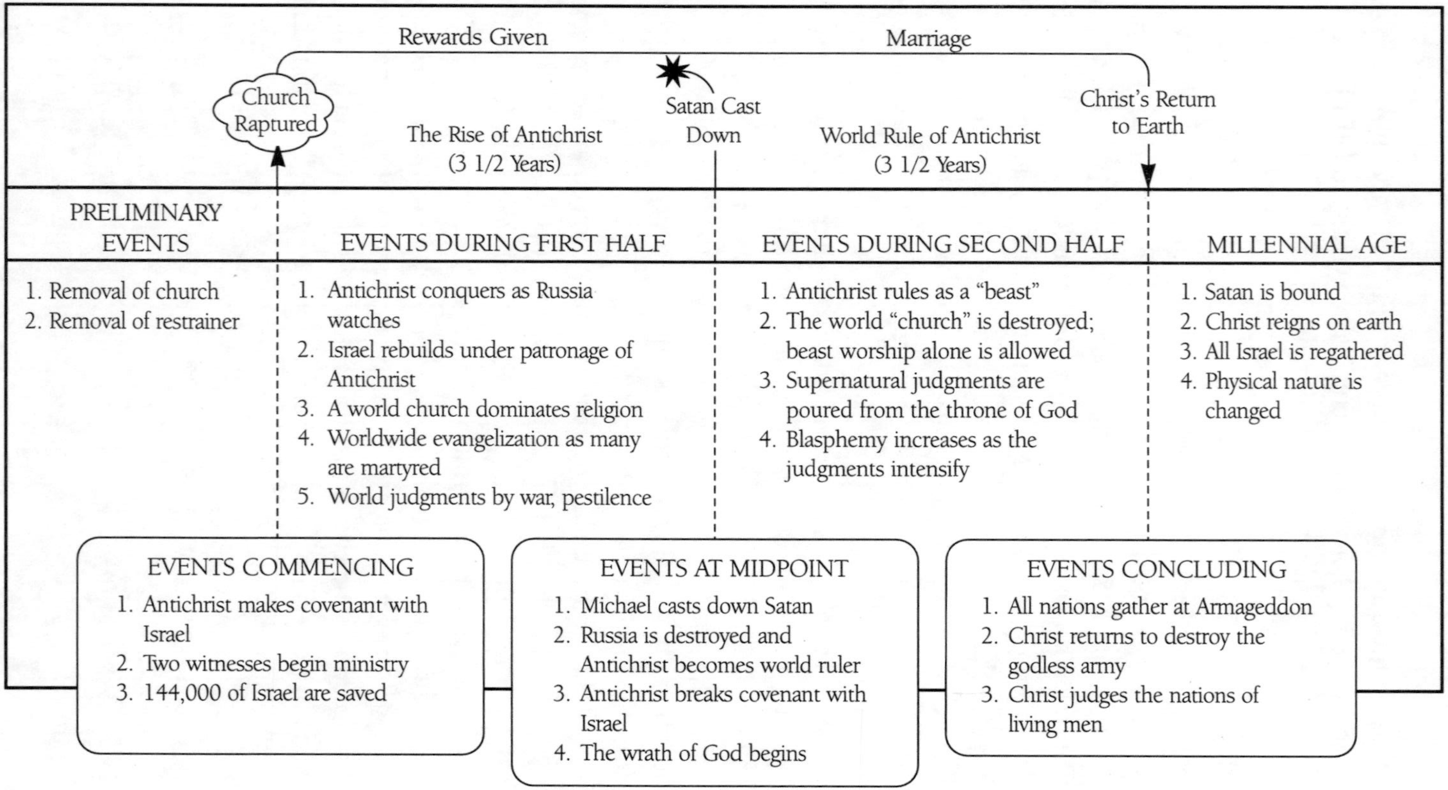

Rewards Given
Marriage
Church Raptured
Satan Cast Down
Christ's Return to Earth
The Rise of Antichrist (3 1/2 Years)
World Rule of Antichrist (3 1/2 Years)
PRELIMINARY EVENTS
1. Removal of church
2. Removal of restrainer
EVENTS DURING FIRST HALF
1. Antichrist conquers as Russia watches
2. Israel rebuilds under patronage of Antichrist
3. A world church dominates religion
4. Worldwide evangelization as many are martyred
5. World judgments by war, pestilence
EVENTS DURING SECOND HALF
1. Antichrist rules as a "beast"
2. The world "church" is destroyed; beast worship alone is allowed
3. Supernatural judgments are poured from the throne of God
4. Blasphemy increases as the judgments intensify
MILLENNIAL AGE
1. Satan is bound
2. Christ reigns on earth
3. All Israel is regathered
4. Physical nature is changed
EVENTS COMMENCING
1. Antichrist makes covenant with Israel
2. Two witnesses begin ministry
3. 144,000 of Israel are saved
EVENTS AT MIDPOINT
1. Michael casts down Satan
2. Russia is destroyed and Antichrist becomes world ruler
3. Antichrist breaks covenant with Israel
4. The wrath of God begins
EVENTS CONCLUDING
1. All nations gather at Armageddon
2. Christ returns to destroy the godless army
3. Christ judges the nations of living men

CHAPTER ELEVEN

MOVING TOWARD ARMAGEDDON

At this point in the unfolding drama, we note that a period of silence is observed in heaven. The angelic cast is given a half-hour break (Revelation 8:1). During this intermission let's briefly reflect on where we are and what these studies mean for us today. The plot may be getting a bit unnerving. Why should we be bothered with these eerie descriptions?

PREPARING FOR THE FINAL DRAMA

Weird though they may seem, these apocalyptic pictures are neither fanciful nor irrelevant. Nor are they just to inspire the emotions, for that is not the purpose of any Bible book. Rather, they are given to reveal a dimension of reality about to confront us that is not a mere recycling of the past. To view prophecy with uniformatarian lenses is to miss its revelational character. Prophecy, in other words, is a revelation of the unknown future which God has elected to make known.

The Purpose of Prophecy

It should also be recognized that the design of prophecy is not merely to reveal future events. More basic is its purpose to reveal the overall philosophy of God's program. It not only dramatizes God's activities in the world, but also shows why He allows those events to take place. It ties all the pieces together in a meaningful whole.

More important is its purpose to unveil the character of God. Prophecy sets in balance His qualities of love and holiness as displayed in His acts of grace and judgment. While accentuating each, it waters down neither. His gracious activities do not mean that He overlooks sin, for He sternly judges the wicked. In it all, His redemptive purposes complement His kingdom program. Prophecy is preeminently a revelation of God.

This reminds us that the study of prophecy is essential for all who would gain a true perspective of life. It adds the third dimension of the future to our limited vision of the past and present. If we fail to find the study practical, we have probably bogged down in its mechanics and lost sight of its challenging motif. The nitty-gritty of life is its native soil, giving meaning and focus to practical Christian living.

The Context of Revelation 8–9

Returning to Revelation 8, we note that the stage is set for some ominous events. Its initial period of silence is a lull before an awesome storm (Zephaniah 1:7; Zechariah 2:13). The purpose is to impress all with the solemnity of the coming drama. A milestone has been reached, and a new level of terror is about to break. Prominent in this series are seven angelic trumpeters who alert the earth (Revelation 8–9). During the first three and a half years, much of the earth will have been devastated. Wars, famines, and pestilence will have taken their inevitable toll. Following the midpoint battle of "Gog and Magog," Antichrist will flaunt himself as victor, but will be left with a war ravaged and grief-stricken world. Just burying the dead will be monumental (Ezekiel 39ff.).

In the wake of this midpoint war then, there will be little to go home to. Besides the ravages of man's destruction, there will be the effects of over three years drought which the two witnesses will bring upon the earth (Revelation 11:6). How extensive this will be is not disclosed, but drought will be a distressing factor in the period. Drought was often used by God to chastise His people in the Old Testament (Leviticus 26:19–20; 1 Kings 17:1), and it is probable that He will use it again in the end times. Drought and famine will be a major curse of the time.

The Supernatural Character of Coming Judgment

Although God could allow sin to judge and destroy itself, He will not remain passive in this judgment. The period has been introduced as the time of the wrath of God and of the Lamb (Revelation 6:16–17). The previous judgments of the "seals" came as the results of war, famine, and pestilence, with little said of the supernatural. In the forthcoming judgments the source is specifically traced to God, with little said of man's conniving. In fact, the more intense the plagues become, the more careful John is to declare their divine origin (Revelation 8:5; 15:7–8).

This supernatural emphasis during the last half of the tribulation is important to recognize. The Bible has much to say of man's activities at the midpoint, after which Antichrist emerges as a world potentate. It also has much to say of man's deviltry at the end of the tribulation which is climaxed by Armageddon. But the actions of men in between are mainly described in Revelation 13, where Antichrist and his false prophet are in supreme control of the world. No wars are described in this period, for who could defy the arch dictator with satanic authority and his miracle-working accomplice? They are busy forcing the world to worship Satan and "blood-hounding" the earth to drag to the guillotine any who dare to resist their edicts. Even the 144,000 appear to be martyred during this time (Revelation 14).

The last half of the tribulation then is described as the time when God opens heaven to pour out His wrath on a sinful world. That is what especially characterizes the "trumpet" and "bowl" judgments. God's angels at His command mete them out. Men are seen as the recipients, but not the perpetrators of these plagues. Furthermore, these judgments are portrayed as coming from God's holy altar, rather than just from His throne. John is careful to emphasize this to show the absolute holiness of these judgments against those who have violated God's Law.

SEVEN TRUMPETS INTRODUCE DIVINE JUDGMENTS

Each of the three series of divine judgments (seals, trumpets, bowls) is introduced by a striking storm warning: "Thunders, voices, lightnings, and an earthquake" (Revelation 4:5; 8:5; 11:19; 16:18). These are reminiscent of God's descent on Mount Sinai to give Moses the book of laws and judgments. There He also came with thunders, lightnings, the voice of a loud trumpet, and the quaking of the mountain (Exodus 19:16ff.). In Revelation 8, this thunderous prelude breaks the silence of heaven, alerting all that the divine fireworks are about to begin.

This use of trumpets also suggests the redemptive purpose of the coming judgments. Joel the earliest writing prophet first used this as a call to repentance before the Lord's judgment (Joel 2:1, 15; cf. Hosea 8:1). The trumpet or "shofar" was Israel's alerting siren to summon the people to solemn assembly. This salvaging theme is also noted in that the trumpet judgments are fifteen times said to destroy "one third," rather than a complete destruction. They appear to be "samples" of the final judgments, urging all who will to repent.

The time of these trumpet judgments probably extends over a period of two years or more, as suggested by the fifth which involves five months (Revelation 9:5). The seven are divided into three groups. The first four are cast down from heaven, the next two arise from demonic or earthly sources, and the last is from heaven, announcing the coming of the Judge Himself.

Trumpet 1—Consumes Vegetation (Revelation 8:7)

The first trumpet is a judgment by fire on earth's grass and trees. Massive blazes are ignited all over the world by the "hail and fire, mingled with blood." Consumed by these is a third of earth's depleted vegetation. The plague is evidently a curse on men for their thanklessness for what God has provided in a productive earth. Coming after several years of drought, such a rash of brush and forest fires would certainly not be unusual, especially accompanied by lightning.

In evaluating these judgments, the question often arises as how literal we should understand them. A common approach is to allegorize the weird scenes as personal, social, or political blights that seem offensive to the occasion. That method was long used by the medieval church, making interpretation as pliable as one's imagination. Applied to the book of Revelation, that approach is a slippery slope that easily ends in a virtual denial of the truths being taught. Its practical effect is to reduce the book to a museum piece or an insoluble puzzle.

It is therefore essential to stay with the grammatical-historical method, if consistency and the authority of the book are to be preserved. Interpretation must derive from the context. Since the book of Revelation is strongly imbedded in the Old Testament, we are obligated to observe those evident relationships. The plagues of Egypt, for instance, have an obvious similarity to these trumpet judgments (Exodus 7–10). The first judgment of hail, fire, and blood is almost identical to the seventh plague of Egypt, which nearly everyone accepts as literal (Exodus 9:23–24; 1 Samuel 4:8). If those historic judgments were literal, we are on precarious ground in making these otherwise. John's prophecies often relate to Moses' histories.

Trumpet 2—Pollutes the Sea (Revelation 8:8–9)

The second judgment is on marine life and shipping through a "great burning mountain" which is cast into the sea. This could be a huge burning meteor that pierces earth's atmosphere and fragments into the sea. Its effect is to pollute the sea, causing one-third of marine life to die and one-third of shipping to be destroyed. It no doubt produces tidal waves that extend across the oceans and gives off gaseous pollution that turns the sea to crimson.

In this cataclysm, God's judgment will extend to an area not touched by the drought of the first half. That drought will have made seafood a common and welcome delicacy for those near the sea. Here that supply will also be affected, bringing judgment to the uttermost part of the sea.

Trumpet 3—Pollutes Drinking Water (Revelation 8:10–11)

The third trumpet brings down a "great star" called "Wormwood" that is cast on the rivers and their mountain sources of water. This extends the pollution to one-third of the drinking supply. In this way, judgment strikes men and women with thirst as well as hunger. It is similar to the first plague of Egypt, taking a large toll of earth's population through the polluted and embittered water (Exodus 7:20).

Trumpet 4—Brings Darkness (Revelation 8:12)

The fourth judgment is a plague of darkness over much of the earth. Again, it is not total, but partial, restricting the light from one-third of the sun, moon, and stars. While this plague portrays actual darkness, it also reflects the deep spiritual darkness settling over the world. Darkness in Scripture often accompanied the judgments of God (Exodus 10:21; Matthew 27:45). It was, in fact, prophesied as one of the signs of the great day of the Lord, and is again used here to spur repentance (Joel 2:31).

Trumpet 5—Brings Locust Plague (Revelation 9:1–12)

The last three trumpets are called "woes" and are prefaced by a special warning. An "eagle" from midheaven is dispatched to alert the earth of their greater intensity and more awesome character (Revelation 8:13). The first two originate from demonic sources.

This fifth trumpet (or first "woe") unleashes a plague of smoke and locusts from the abyss, that is, from deep within the earth. This abyss is opened by a "star" fallen from heaven, who is identified in two languages as the "destroyer" and as the "king" over the marauding troops from the pit. As if the intense pollution of smoke was not enough, scorpionlike locusts are here loosed to torment men for five months. Whether these are normal or specially prepared locusts may be questioned, but their counterparts in Joel 2 were described as normal. These descriptions, in fact, are quite similar. Contrary to their nature, however, these are instructed not to eat grass or vegetation (if such is available), but to afflict men. Only the 144,000 sealed by God are exempt, suggesting they have not yet been martyred.

This affliction is the most hideous yet encountered. So intense is the torment that people will prefer death to life with the locusts. Worse still, death will not be an option. John says, "In those days men will seek death and will not find it; and they will long to die, and death flees from them" (Revelation 9:6). Jumping off bridges or resorting to poison will not be an escape route in those days. During this five-month judgment, God calls a moratorium on death.

Trumpet 6—Death by Demonic Horsemen (Revelation 9:12–17)

The judgment of the sixth trumpet (the second "woe") is executed by four death angels who command an army of 200 million horsemen. They are released from the Euphrates River to destroy one-third of all mankind. The area of the Euphrates was often associated with judgment in the Old Testament, being the locale of Assyria and Babylon whose armies destroyed Israel and Judah. These angels are described as having been long prepared for this mission of mass destruction. If death was cheated of its prey during the previous five-month moratorium, it will more than recoup its loss in this judgment.

Adding this to the one-fourth of mankind who die in the fourth seal, at least one-half of earth's population will have perished by this time.

This mysterious 200-million-man army from the Euphrates is often equated with the sixth bowl judgment, which also comes from the Euphrates (Revelation 16:12). Many see this as that massive army from China and the orient who join in the final Armageddon confrontation. Since the weird horses seem to describe military tanks armored with missiles, and the next trumpet announces Christ's coming, there are similarities. That they are the same, however, is doubtful because of the chronological differences. Revelation 9:20 shows that there is a time lapse after this sixth trumpet in which the depravity of men is again intensified. That is not possible after Armageddon. Also the long series of "bowl" judgments take place after this sixth trumpet, each involving a time period, as God continues to seek those who will repent.

It seems preferable, therefore, to leave them as an unsolved enigma, rather than identify them with Armageddon. Whatever this army is that rides on horses with lions' heads and brimstone spitting mouths, the path of destruction they leave is unsurpassed. It leaves less than half of earth's population alive at its close. As Jesus said, "Unless those days had been cut short, no life would have been saved" (Matthew 24:22).

Before presenting the last trumpet judgment, John again takes an intermission in Revelation 10–11 to catch up on some needed explanations. Chapter 10 reasserts Christ's title deed to the earth as He is about to complete His judgments, and chapter 11 shows how men deserve the judgments given: they had adamantly refused the two resurrected witnesses God sent. This prepares for the blowing of the final trumpet judgment.

Trumpet 7—Christ's Coming (Revelation 11:15–19)

This final trumpet gives a preview of Christ's coming, being announced by a great chorus in heaven. For the world of rebels it will constitute their final "woe." He will come in great power to judge the wicked, reward the saints, and assume supreme rule over the earth (v. 18). For the wicked to experience His personal presence will be the third woe and the supreme shock of their lives.

This last trumpet does not bring the actual coming of Christ, but gives a brief preview of it. It is here announced as a foregleam for the faithful and as a warning for the wavering. Its character is that of a last call to repentance before God "lowers the boom." The last series of seven plagues will be more of a punitive nature on the rebels.

As a prelude to those final judgments, another "storm warning" is sounded in Revelation 11:19 of "lightning, voices, thunder, an earthquake, and great hail." These issue from the "ark of the covenant" in the heavenly temple, again stressing the justice of the final judgments.

THE FINAL BOWLS OF JUDGMENT POURED OUT

With the stage set for the last series of judgment, John again takes an interlude for some essential explanations in chapters 12–15. The many events already described have left many questions as to who is involved. To this point, he has not yet formally introduced the important personages in the drama: Satan as the dragon; Michael as the archangel; Antichrist as the beast and his henchman the false prophet; and Christ as the Son of Man in heaven. Therefore, he now flashes the spotlight on various scenes that introduce these figures. Let's briefly review them to see their significance at this point.

In Revelation 12, John gives the spiritual side of the drama, showing the involvement of Satan and Michael in the coming fury against Israel and the saints. Chapter 13 then brings Satan's two henchmen on earth into full view, relating them to the revived Roman Empire predicted by Daniel. In chapter 14 the spotlight again shifts back to heaven, especially highlighting the Son of Man as He sharpens His sickle to reap the ripened "grapes of wrath" on earth. Chapter 15 then introduces the final bowls of chapter 16 by again emphasizing their righteousness as coming from God's holy altar. Each of these is important as the final curtain comes down on the world's judgment.

Although these final judgments are more intense, their durations are progressively shorter than the previous. The "seals" occupy over three years, the "trumpets" perhaps two years, and the "bowls" about one year. These appear to be triggered off in rather rapid succession. They are said to complete the plagues of the wrath of God (Revelation 15:1).

There is admittedly a strong similarity between the trumpet and bowl judgments. The first of each group is on the earth; the second, on the sea; the third, on rivers, etc. These similarities, however, do not make them identical. The bowls are of much greater intensity. Whereas the trumpets have more the character of samples (e.g. "one third"), with an emphasis on repentance, the bowls are more universal and final. They invoke unalterable punishment. Let's note the prominent features of each.

Bowl 1—Antichrist's Kingdom (Revelation 16:1–2)

John introduces the bowl judgments as the "wrath of God," and the first is specifically targeted at Antichrist's crowd. Those baptized into his ranks by the "mark of the beast" will experience dreadful malignant sores. Believers who refuse to worship his image are exempt from this judgment, which no doubt further infuriates the kingdom of Antichrist.

Bowl 2—On the Sea (Revelation 16:3)

This second bowl extends God's wrath to the sea, polluting it with blood as from a dead man. Its judgment on sea life appears to be universal, destroying all life in the sea. The terminal character of this judgment on sea life suggests the need for Christ to return in a new creative capacity. It corresponds to the first plague in Egypt which turned "all the water that was in the Nile" into blood (Exodus 7:20).

Bowl 3—On Fresh Water Sources (Revelation 16:4–7)

The third bowl has a similar effect on the rivers and fountains of water. Though it is not said to be universal, it sorely depletes man's sources of drinking water. So devastating is this judgment that a double reminder is given the earth concerning its divine justice. The reason assigned is that "they poured out the blood of saints and prophets, and Thou hast given them blood to drink. They deserve it" (v. 6). Since they asked for blood, God assures them they will get their fill.

Bowl 4—The Heat of the Sun (Revelation 16:8–9)

This judgment brings intense heat from the sun that scorches men with fire. Such will inevitably produce massive forest and brush fires throughout the earth. This plague has the reverse affect of the fourth trumpet judgment which brought darkness. The definite article before "men" in the text suggests its special application on those previously identified as worshipers of the beast. Their blasphemy of God is the first blasphemy noted in response to these judgments, suggesting their incorrigibility (Revelation 16:9; cf. Matthew 12:31).

Bowl 5—Darkens the Kingdom of Antichrist (Revelation 16:10–11)

This plague shows the progressive focusing of judgment on the beast and his kingdom, here narrowed to his throne. Having rejected light, his people get a taste of real darkness. Their response is again blasphemy of God, showing they recognize the source of their judgment.

This judgment of darkness is similar to the ninth plague of Egypt, which brought darkness to the Egyptians, but not to the Israelites

(Exodus 10:21–23). So oppressive was that darkness, it could be "felt." As that plague was followed by the final judgment of blood, this one will also be followed by the bloodshed of Armageddon.

Bowl 6—The Euphrates Dries Up (Revelation 16:12–16)

This drying up of the Euphrates speaks of both drought and coming bloodshed. Called the "Great River," the Euphrates is the longest and largest river of western Asia running from the Armenian mountains to the Persian Gulf (1780 miles). With the droughts already described, its drying up is not hard to conceive.

The purpose of this judgment, however, is far more than the drying up of a river. It introduces us to the climactic events of the battle of Armageddon by showing the chief instigators of it. They are the dragon and his two agents, Antichrist and the false prophet. These, aided by demons, invite and entice all nations to send their armies to "the war of the great day of God the Almighty" (vv. 13–14). Their gathering place will be Armageddon ("Hill of Megiddo") in the Plain of Esdraelon. Before noting that final battle in an extended discussion, we will first review the last of the bowl judgments to observe God's response.

Bowl 7—Massive Earthquake (Revelation 16:17–21)

The seventh bowl concludes the series by atmospheric and geophysical eruptions. A great earthquake produces convulsions that dwarf even those of the great flood. This seismic rumble will completely devastate much of the earth's surface, changing its physical contours. With these eruptions, enormous hailstones (114 pounds) fall from heaven, adding to the havoc. These evidently come at the climax of Armageddon and coincide with the return of Christ to the earth. They constitute a brief statement of God's response to the challenge of demon controlled men at Armageddon. John describes them as the "fierceness of God's wrath," the rawest statement of God's anger in the New Testament, but applauded by heaven, as we shall presently note.

GOD'S SALVAGE OPERATION THROUGH THE JUDGMENTS

Having previewed these judgments of God's anger and wrath on a rebellious world, we need to recall their purpose. Why does a loving God invoke such violent wrath on the earth? He has excellent reasons. The three rounds of divine judgments (seals, trumpets, and bowls) have both corrective and punitive purposes. God is not indulging in a temper tantrum, but is indulging the remainder of men with a final "come hither" before He comes personally to judge the nations. The judgments have a redemptive purpose, for God is here wringing out the world, so to speak, to salvage every vestige of repentant individuals. Before finally closing the door on salvation, He puts them in a decision "hot-house," to draw out their responses in one direction or the other.

We have already noted that this divine operation is a significant part of the tribulation period. The gospel of Christ and His coming Kingdom will be preached throughout the whole world during this time (Matthew 24:14). Various messengers will be used. The two witnesses (Moses and Elijah), the 144,000 Israelis, and the great multitude of Gentiles will be active. Many martyrs will die, giving testimony of their faith and devotion to Christ. Total abandonment to Christ will be demonstrated by many as never before. It will be a time of stand-up-and-be-counted for God or join the Antichrist. Neutrality will be impossible. In that soil of rugged polarization many courageous Christians will "be strong and do exploits" for their God.

On the other hand, there is also noted an increasing degeneracy during the period. Wickedness will dramatically increase. This is seen in the development of blasphemy in the Book of Revelation. Blasphemy of God is not seen in the first half of the tribulation (except in the blasphemous names of the harlot), but is introduced by the "beast" in Revelation 13. Toward the end, however, there is a marked increase in blasphemy as seen in the last three bowl judgments (Revelation 16:8, 9, 12). They blaspheme God because of the plagues. This blasphemy is not just a string of oaths involving God's name, but a direct damnation of God for their pains which they attribute to Him. There appear to be no atheists in the crowd, for that delusion will have ceased. Rather they recognize God and curse Him for their plight.

This again puts the lie to the notion that purgatory will fry the wickedness out of sinners. Those who willfully turn from God and allow sin to do its work in their souls place themselves in an irretrievable state of corruption. Sin inevitably personifies itself in individuals, acting as a creeping cancer that is finally beyond arrest (Romans 1:24–32). Satan is the Bible's outstanding example of what sin will do in an individual who rejects God in his life. That process will show up in the increased depravity of rejecters toward the end of the tribulation period. For such, these judgments will be punitive, not ameliorative. Having refused to be a part of God's building, they will be disposed of by the Lord as obsolete "scaffolding" in the building of His house.

THE WORLD BREATHES REVENGE AT ARMAGEDDON

The campaign of Armageddon logically follows the divine judgments before it. It is the world's response to God's call for repentance. Their continuous strain and increasing intensity, however, will furiously enrage them. Antichrist and his henchman will be infuriated, dedicated as they are to the proposition that Satan has taken over the world and deserves worship. In that satanic delusion, they will perhaps see those plagues as the vengeful acts of a defeated and retreating deity who is gradually succumbing to Satan. As previously noted, this dualistic notion of God and Satan vying for dominance is certainly not new, dating at least back to the Essenes who borrowed it from the Persians. Their triumphs in wickedness will suggest to them that Satan has finally come up the winner.

The Purpose of Armageddon

The battle of Armageddon is popularly known as the final, decisive battle of the nations as they destroy themselves. It is often related biblically to the concluding conflict of east and west, as the battle of Gog and Magog is seen as the final battle of north and south. According to this view, the armies of Antichrist will be arrayed against the 200-million-man army of the Orient and the North (Revelation 9:16).

As previously noted, however, that view is fraught with contextual difficulties that make it difficult to accept. This battle of Armageddon is mentioned only once in the Bible and relates specifically to this final battle just prior to Christ's return (Revelation 16:16). It refers to the "hill of Megiddo," the locale of the "battle of the great day of God Almighty." It is not primarily a battle among nations, but between a Satan-inspired world and Christ. It involves the nations gathering for the purpose "to make war with the Lamb" (Revelation 17:14; 19:19). That is not only the way it ends; it is the way it begins. It is incited by Satan, Antichrist, and the false prophet, who gather the armies of the world for a decisive confrontation with Almighty God. They gather for a massive demonstration, to menacingly shake their fists at God.

If we think such insanity too much to believe, we need only recall the strong delusion and depravity under which they will labor. After several years of satanic brainwashing with wickedness dominating the earth and a miracle-working false prophet showing supernatural signs, the mass of mankind will think the power of Antichrist and the dragon invincible (Revelation 13:4–6). Using their best in advanced missile and nuclear gadgetry, they will believe they can blow God out of His heaven. Having once put the nails to the incarnate Christ, the world will not hesitate to turn modern weaponry against an ancient deity they feel is defeated.

SUMMARY

This then is the significance of Armageddon. It will be the response of unrepentant men to divine judgment, siding with Satan in cosmic battle. Joel the earliest writing prophet, described the place of this battle as the "valley of decision" (Joel 3:14). There the decision will be made in a climactic way as to who is "King of the earth." David also spoke of this final confrontation in Psalm 2:1–6:

Why do the heathen rage,
and the people imagine a vain thing?
The kings of the earth set themselves,
and the rulers take counsel together,

Against the Lord,
and against his anointed, saying,
Let us break their bands asunder,
and cast away their cords from us.
He who sitteth in the heavens shall laugh;
the Lord shall have them in derision.
Then shall He speak unto them in his wrath,
and vex them in his great displeasure.
Yet have I set my king
upon my holy hill of Zion.

Christ's return to the earth, of course, will be God's crisp response to man's satanic outburst at Armageddon. That heralded coming is the most prophesied event in the Bible, being God's ultimate remedy for a sick and deranged world. It is the climactic point of prophecy. We shall attempt to portray its highlights in the following chapter.

CHAPTER TWELVE

THE KING'S RETURN IN GLORY

The King is coming! If you wonder what's wrong with the world, why injustice, poverty, and violence seem to reign, just remember—the King is absent. Israel's Messiah came as the Prince of Peace for all people, but failed to "pass muster" in both Jewish and Gentile courts (Isaiah 9:6). Though once rejected as an impostor, He is coming again as an Imperial. He will then rule the world as the King of kings, establishing His kingdom of righteousness and peace throughout the earth.

Christ's return to the earth will be the silver lining behind the storm clouds of judgment. Coming as the "Sun of righteousness...with healing in its wings" (Malachi 4:2), He will cleanse the earth and bring joy to all creation (Romans 8:23). His day of coronation will also be a day of liberation and personal fulfillment for all the children of God.

Because this Second Coming is portrayed in so many passages of the Old and New Testament, it is necessary to group the major events by categories to get the overall picture. They involve His coming to judge and to save, to destroy the wicked, and to deliver the righteous. They also describe His restoration of Israel, new relations to the nations, and various accompanying changes in the earth itself. Let's review them under the categories of His judging and saving work.

CHRIST'S COMING TO JUDGE

When Christ returns to the earth, His judgment work will not yet be finished. He will come to a world arrayed against Him, determined to blast Him out of His heaven. At His first coming, He was met by a threat of slaughter at Bethlehem, and at His return a similar welcoming committee will meet Him. Only this time all the armies of the world will be massed against Him. In contrast to that first arrival, He will not again flee to Egypt, but will personally confront and destroy those intent on His destruction. Before He can minister healing to the nations, He must first perform radical "surgery" to close up the wounds of a broken and bleeding world.

His Coming with Power and Great Glory

At the height of the Armageddon struggle, lightning of unprecedented brilliance will strike. As the cause of righteousness appears all but lost in the earth, the brightness of God's glory will shatter the darkness and reveal in the heavens the most stupendous scene ever conceived. On a "white horse" Christ will descend through the clouds, leading a vast heavenly troop also on white horses (Revelation 19:11ff.). Concerning this descent the Lord Himself gave the classic description:

> For just as the lightning comes from the east, and flashes even to the west, so shall the coming of the Son of Man be.
>
> Wherever the corpse is, there the vultures will gather.
>
> But immediately after the tribulation of those days, THE SUN WILL BE DARKENED, AND THE MOON WILL NOT GIVE ITS LIGHT, AND THE STARS WILL FALL from the sky, and the powers of the heavens will be shaken; and then the sign of the Son of Man will appear in the sky, and then all the tribes of the earth will mourn, and they will see the SON OF MAN COMING ON THE CLOUDS OF THE SKY with power and great glory.
>
> And He will send forth His angels with A GREAT TRUMPET AND THEY WILL GATHER TOGETHER His elect from the four winds, from one end of the sky to the other. (Matthew 24:27–31)

Although His coming will be of transcendent glory for the righteous, it will be tumultuous for the wicked (Isaiah 28:21). Brilliant signs of lightning and thunder will pierce the sky and banish the darkness, calling the entire world to attention. Some will be sleeping, some working, and some warring (Matthew 24:40–41). All however, will be instantly awakened to the fact that God is breaking into human history in a new and personal way. His descent from heaven may include a trip around the globe with His train of saints and angels, for John declares that "every eye will see Him" (Revelation 1:7). That grand scene will hardly be just a television spectacular for most of the world, captured by alert cameramen in Jerusalem. The evidence is that that descent will involve a brief span of time in which He will be observed by all the earth, as well as by the armies gathered against Him. His train of saints will then have a grand flight around the globe to glimpse the promised land.

Perhaps His actual place of "landing" will be the Mount of Olives, just east of Jerusalem (Zechariah 14:4; Acts 1:11). There He will come as a man of war to meet the challenge of Satan, Antichrist, and all the evil forces assembled. As they will have gathered for battle against Him, He will not disappoint them. The "gentle Jesus" will meet His enemies as a man of war (cf. Exodus 15:3).

His Rescue of the Jerusalem Remnant

Jerusalem at that time will be under a massive siege by the nations, as they prepare for Armageddon. That final gathering of the world's armies, as we have noted, will be like a satanic hysteria, challenging the Almighty. "And I saw the beast and the kings of earth and their armies, assembled to make war against Him who sat upon the horse, and against His army" (Revelation 19:19). The area to which they gather is the great plain of Esdraelon near the Hill ("Har") of Megiddo south of the hills of Nazareth. This vast plain is a natural field of battle and was once described by Napoleon as the ideal battleground for all the armies of the world. The "little general" inadvertently spoke prophetically. To this bivouac area the armies of the world will gather and spill over into the hill country of central Palestine, pillaging as they go. They will move south to the Valley of

Jehoshaphat near Jerusalem and extend their troops to the southern hill country of Judea (Joel 3:12).

Jerusalem Pillaged

Though their main mission will be to defy the Lord, they will also come to assault Jerusalem (Zechariah 12:2–3). This is obviously not their primary mission, for they would hardly need all the armies of the earth to attack Israel or its capital. In their malicious contempt for God, however, they will vent their fury on the ancient people of God, and Jerusalem will catch the brunt. While waiting for a divine confrontation, they will practice on the traditional holy city, vilifying everything sacred.

That is the picture Zechariah paints of this assault on Jerusalem as the Lord descends to defend His people (Zechariah 12). The prophet describes first their physical deliverance and then their spiritual conversion. In his depiction of the nations' attack, Zechariah describes the city as a "goblet of wine that causes intoxication" (12:2). The prophet also portrayed the city as a heavy stone that will rupture the nations as they try to lift it. Jerusalem, in other words, will be the focus of the nations' fury as they in delirium vent their wrath against the Lord.

Jerusalem Purged

The result of this wrath of the nations will be a final purge of Jerusalem. Before Christ comes to deliver His faithful remnant, that city will endure another great anguish. The lewd crowd with Antichrist will plunder the city, ravish the women, and take half the people captive (Zechariah 14:2). Throughout the whole land, Zechariah declares, two-thirds of Israel's population will be destroyed (13:8).

Jerusalem, however, will not capitulate without a valiant struggle. Though trodden down by Antichrist for over three years, they will find this final brazen assault to be the catalyst to jolt them into action. It will bring the faithful together to take on this Antichrist, a reincarnation of all the Hamans, Herods, and Hitlers in a life and death struggle.

This final revolt of Israel against the godless horde will be like a replay of the Maccabeans' struggle against Antiochus Epiphanes in 167

B.C., who also sought to stamp out Jehovah worship. As then, many of the Jews will rise up in holy horror against this blasphemous foe, in spite of the overwhelming odds against them. Their courage and godly disgust will have finally jelled into a spunk that defies even the devil. Zechariah portrays their defense as a counter movement inspired by sheer trust in God. Both leaders and people will fight as with superhuman strength, the weakest being "like David" (Zechariah 12:8). Many will be slain in the uneven battle but, like the Maccabeans, they that "know their God shall be strong and do exploits."

How long this herculean struggle will continue before the Lord arrives is not indicated, but it appears to be of short duration. The Lord will suddenly descend on their enemies and rescue these courageous defenders in their hour of great need.

Edom's Vengeance Revisited

Isaiah describes the Lord's coming as a final judgment on Edom (Isaiah 63). The prophet sees Him beginning His judgment with this ancient enemy of Israel, as He sloshes through a wine press of blood that runs throughout the land (Isaiah 63). In so doing He stains His garments with the blood of His enemies. He treads this wine press alone, asserting that this is His "day of vengeance" (63:3–6). His weapon is a "sharp sword" from His mouth, a symbol of His Word (Isaiah 49:2; Hebrews 4:12; Revelation 19:15). The same powerful Word by which He created the universe is the weapon He uses in this final rescue of His people and destruction of His enemies.

The fact that He commences judgment at Edom is striking for two reasons. The first is the ancient animosity of Edom toward Israel, cursing her when she was up, and trampling her when she was down. For this insatiable bloodthirstiness, Edom was promised total obliteration (Isaiah 34:5; Jeremiah 49:7ff.; Obadiah 1:8; Malachi 1:4). Though ancient Edom has long been destroyed and her progeny lost, the mountain plateau of her glory will yet be the place of God's judgment: "For My sword is satiated in heaven, behold it shall descend for judgement upon Edom, and upon the people whom I have devoted to destruction" (Isaiah 34:5).

Many end-time prophecies speak of Edom's judgment, and Isaiah portrays the Lord beginning His cleansing operation there.

A second significance of Christ's judgment beginning in the land of Edom relates to the faithful remnant who flee to the mountains (Daniel 12:1; Matthew 24:16ff.; Revelation 12:6, 14). Though the archangel Michael will have protected them for over three years, the Lord also will come to their rescue. The probability is that a large concentration of Antichrist's troops will have surrounded them in this secluded mountain area, ready to devour them. Therefore, as Christ comes to deliver His people, He will begin by rescuing this remnant who have heeded His warning to flee the terrors of Jerusalem to this wilderness sanctuary.

The Encounter at Armageddon

From Edom the Lord will move swiftly to the valley of Jehoshaphat near Jerusalem and proceed to the bivouac area of Antichrist's army at Armageddon. The length of this valley of slaughter is given by John as 1600 furlongs or 200 miles (Revelation 14:20). That approximates the length of Israel's former territory from southern Judah or Edom to the Lebanon mountains in the north. John even gives the depth of the slaughter as up to the horses' bridles, suggesting the massiveness of this destruction. As the angel of the Lord slew the Assyrian army of 185,000 gathered against Jerusalem in the time of Hezekiah (2 Kings 19:35), so Christ will bring wholesale destruction in this final gathering against Him and His people. So thoroughly planned is this operation that even the clean-up committee has been appointed. They are the birds of the air who are invited to "the great supper of God" (Revelation 19:17, 21).

His Harvest of the Grapes of Wrath (Revelation 14:14–20)

In reviewing this massive slaughter at Christ's return, we should not miss the divine perspective of the sordid scene. The apostle John portrays this in Revelation 14, where Christ is seen swinging His sickle as the "Son of Man" (14:14; cf. John 5:27). As such, He reaps the "grape harvest" of the earth, which is seen to be thoroughly ripe. What kind of a harvest is this, and why is it called the "grapes" of God's wrath?

Ripeness of the Harvest

The symbol "grapes of wrath" is taken from Joel 3:13 where the prophet envisions Jerusalem being assaulted in the end times by the heathen from the Valley of Jehoshaphat. As the Lord roars out of Zion to rescue His people (like a lioness rescuing her whelps), the wickedness of the nations is portrayed in the metaphor of grapes ready for reaping. Their ripeness is seen to need immediate harvest. At the close of the tribulation, that ripeness will be evident by the fruit of their blasphemy and utter contempt for God. As in the time of Noah, the condition of men will be "only evil continually" and the earth "filled with violence."

This symbol of "grapes," however, also implies rejoicing in heaven. From the divine standpoint, that harvest will be refreshing in its judgment of wickedness. As sin is a blight on God's universe, its eradication at its greatest time of triumph will call for great rejoicing. Having extended His grace to all who will receive it, God will take pleasure in vindicating His holiness by His wrath on sin.

Sweetness of the Harvest

This concept of God's wrath on sin is not popular, but is essential to rightly perceive the nature of God. His love cannot be fully appreciated apart from His holiness. The fact that He extends mercy without compromising His holiness makes the marvel of His love so much greater. God's holiness means the stability and purity of His nature, the unshakable standard on which the universe runs. The nature of sin and the nature of God are such that they cannot eternally coexist. In this light, the cry for vengeance in the imprecatory psalms is a righteous prayer, echoing the concern of the godly of all ages (e.g., Psalm 69:22–28). Their prayer that God destroy the wicked is a call for the vindication of God's holiness and the extension of His nature into all aspects of life. The nature of sin is to lock God out or deny an essential part of His being. He does not impart His love without His holiness, for His nature cannot be divided.

These divine judgments then serve to rescue God's righteousness from a long misunderstanding by many people. His long-suffering and forbearance with sinners must not be misconstrued as acceptance of sin; they only allow postponement of judgment to make His mercy more available. The cry of those who know God (as the martyrs of Revelation 6:10) is that God's vengeance be quickly executed on sin. When this is finally accomplished in Revelation 19:1ff., the grand response of heaven will be the *Hallelujah Chorus* (the first in the New Testament). His judgments may sound harsh and even barbarous to those unacquainted with God, but it is applauded by heaven and the deep desire of all who long for His kingdom to come.

From heaven's view then, this judgment of intractable sinners is seen as a harvest of "grapes," refreshing in its affirmation of the whole nature of God. It is that work of God which Isaiah called "His strange work" (Isaiah 28:21, NIV). It will be strange for the wicked in that He no longer tolerates wickedness; but it will be an act of mercy for the earth and God's universe, as Christ assumes His rightful role as King of kings and Lord of lords (Revelation 19:15–16).

His Judgment of the Living Nations

Following the battle of Armageddon, the Lord will enter into judgment with all those yet living. The conclusion of that battle will be swift and decisive as the Lord destroys the armies gathered against Him like they were nonexistent. John's description is to the point:

> And I saw the beast and the kings of the earth and their armies, assembled to make war against Him who sat upon the horse, and against His army.
>
> And the beast was seized, and with him the false prophet who performed the signs in his presence, by which he deceived those who had received the mark of the beast and those who worshiped his image; these two were thrown alive into the lake of fire which burns with brimstone.
>
> And the rest were killed with the sword which came from the mouth of Him who sat upon the horse, and all the birds were filled with their flesh. (Revelation 19:19–21)

Consignment of the "Infernal Trinity" (Revelation 20:1–3)

Besides destroying the malicious armies gathered against Him at Armageddon, Christ will personally dispose of its prominent leaders. Antichrist and his false prophet are scheduled for special handling; they will be cast alive into the lake of fire. The first to taste of this eternal flame, they will arrive a thousand years before the devil and the rest of the wicked. They are cast alive into this inferno without even the privilege of death. Such are the solemn words of Jesus as John completes the story of Armageddon.

The ringleader, Satan, however, will be temporarily consigned to the abyss, for the Lord has yet another service for him. An angel on special assignment from heaven will bind him with a "great chain," and lock him in the abyss where he will remain for a thousand years (Revelation 20:1–3). He will then be loosed for the final service of rounding up the rebels before he is disposed of. His entire career is a picture of a plummeting star, beginning in the highest heaven and descending to the deepest hell, portraying the tragic trajectory of one who willfully strays from the will of God.

Judgment of Living Israelis (Ezekiel 20:35–38)

Besides those destroyed in the battle of Armageddon, everyone still living at that time will also be judged in a personal meeting with the Lord. The purpose of this judgment will be to cull out the wicked from among the righteous who will enter the millennial kingdom. Millions of people throughout the world will have survived the great plagues, both saved and unsaved. Each of these will stand before Christ to be judged as to his or her true relation to God. This judgment will involve both Israel and the Gentile nations.

Christ's judgment of the surviving Israelis is portrayed in Jesus' parable of the "ten virgins" (Matthew 25:1–13). The Lord had just described His future coming to Israel as with power and great glory in fulfillment of Daniel's prophecy (Daniel 7:13). This is to occur after the tribulation when He comes as the "Son of man" to receive His glorious kingdom (Matthew 24:15, 30). Besides several other precautions, the Lord warned them of the ever-present danger of mere profession in claiming to be His followers. Kosher ritual and good intentions will not suffice to gain one entrance into His kingdom. The reason five virgins gained entrance, while five were denied, was because they had made proper preparation. Procrastination is always an enemy of the soul.

Those described here as virgins are evidently those Israelis who had received a knowledge of the gospel during the tribulation. They are obviously not the same as those of Zechariah 12 who represent the remnant in the wilderness and are not as yet fully aware of Messiah's identity. The ten virgins of Matthew 25 are those who have received that knowledge, many of whom failed to act on it. These He will cull out as superficial. Only those of Israel who have made a clear-cut decision for Christ will enter His kingdom.

Judgment of the Gentile Nations (Matthew 25:31–46)

The Lord will also hold a great tribunal to evaluate the millions of Gentiles yet alive at His coming. "All the nations will be gathered before Him; and He will separate them from one another, as the shepherd separates the sheep from the goats" (Matthew 25:32). This separation of sheep and goats is obviously not that which takes place at the Rapture, which is an instantaneous event. It is a later judgment of those yet alive after the tribulation, judging how each responds to an issue following the Rapture. That issue will be how they respond to God's people during the tribulation.

CHRIST'S COMING TO DELIVER HIS PEOPLE

The purpose of this special scrutiny of the Gentiles will be to determine or reveal who enters the millennial kingdom. Its result will be to separate the superficial from genuine believers, exposing their inward hearts by their outward actions. That litmus test will be their treatment of Christ's "brethren," His tribulation witnesses. Those witnesses will have suffered scorn, hunger, nakedness, and imprisonment by the world of Antichrist and the false church. Some will be Jews and some Gentiles who have stood for Christ. Receiving any such into one's house or treating them with mercy will be an act of great personal jeopardy, but will show whose side one is on. Jesus declared that to receive one of these will be like receiving Christ Himself (Matthew 25:40).

This passage is often used as an exhortation to show mercy to the Jewish people ("brethren") or to those who are down and out or in prison. That is certainly an excellent application, but it is not the point or interpretation of this passage. The "brethren" Jesus mentions are those who do "the will of My Father in heaven," whom He also calls His disciples (Matthew 12:50; 28:10). The context is a tribulation scenario of great animosity toward Christ, a time when showing mercy to these brethren will be a crucial test of true discipleship. It will distinguish those with living and active faith from those with mere passive pretensions, but without genuine commitment. The Lord will in this way cull out the counterfeits before He inaugurates His millennial kingdom.

The Changes in Earth's Topography

Christ's coming will not only affect humanity, but nature as well. The topography of the planet is scheduled for a cataclysmic change. As the earth erupted and convulsed at the judgment of the great flood, so will it sustain an even greater upheaval when Christ returns in judgment. Isaiah the prophet described it as a time when the Lord will "arise to shake terribly the earth" (Isaiah 2:19, 21).

Both Old and New Testaments speak of this topographical rearrangement many times in relation to Christ's coming. Jesus described the whole seven-year end-time period as a time of repeated earthquakes (Luke 21:11). At the midpoint, however, a mighty earthquake will occur as an introduction to the awesome time known as the "wrath of God" (Revelation 6:12). John said of that quake, "Every mountain and island were moved out of their places." This, however, does not compare with the final eruption, but is only a foretaste of the last crust-settling event.

That final earthquake will occur in connection with the last bowl judgment, changing earth's surface (Revelation 16:18). John describes it as the greatest earthquake since the creation of man, dwarfing even the seismic convulsions of the Noahic flood. So great will this jolt be, it will destroy many cities of the world (16:19). Rome is especially singled out for destruction, though her false Babylonian system will have been destroyed three and a half years earlier. Concerning this cosmic shake John says: "And every island fled away, and the mountains were not found" (16:20). It is definitely not a common, run-of-the-mill earthquake. How extensive it will be in reconstituting continents and ocean floors is not specified, but it appears to change mountain contours and ocean floors.

A specific area of this change will be Palestine, the central focus of Christ's return. As He descends on Mount Olivet, the great hill will split north and south, creating a great valley east and west from Jerusalem to the Dead Sea (Zechariah 14:4). The result will be that Jerusalem will be lifted up and the surrounding hills leveled into a descending plain from Jerusalem (Zechariah 14:10). This relandscaping of central Palestine will make Mount Zion "Beautiful in elevation" (Psalm 48:2). From the city will flow "living waters," lively streams as from a subterranean fount, flowing to both the Dead Sea and the Mediterranean (Ezekiel 47:1–10). The result will be a healing of the Dead Sea so that it is filled with large quantities of fish. These topographical changes will emphasize the great preeminence of Jerusalem and the temple in the millennial age.

Though the bases of these changes are not scientific, they are not without some seismological evidences. It is well known that geological faults honeycomb much of the earth's surface, making seismology a very practical science in our day. Many shakes, in fact, are said to be overdue. Such a fault has been discovered near Jerusalem, running east and west under the Mount of Olives. Such corroboration does not prove the Scriptures, but they do contribute to the realism of prophecy.

These changes in nature also suggest that the stage is being set for the final drama of Christ's return. When He comes the earth will convulse for its final shakedown to welcome its Creator, preparing for a millennium of peace on earth. Till then, "the whole creation groans and suffers the pains of childbirth together until now" (Romans 8:22).

Christ's Coming to Save

Though Christ will come as the world's Judge and nature's Creator, He will also come in His saving role as the deliverer of His people. Besides His "strange work" of judgment, He will complete His "saving work" of redemption. All aspects of creation anxiously await the liberation He will bring to the world and His people. Like His judgment work, His work of salvation will also be multifaceted. The following are some of the major areas or groups that will be affected.

His Coming with the Church

As Christ returns from heaven on a white horse, He will be accompanied by a heavenly army also on white horses (Revelation 19:14). These accompanying riders are identified by their fine linen as the "bride" of the Lamb (19:7). Paul also spoke of Christ's relationship to the Church as that of husband and wife or bride (2 Corinthians 11:2; Ephesians 5:23–32). As the Lord returns to the earth, the church will accompany Him to serve with Him in judging and reigning over the earth (Matthew 19:28; 1 Corinthians 6:2; Revelation 3:21; 4:4; 20:4). This makes quite obvious the fact that two other major events will have already taken place before He comes.

THE LAMB'S MARRIAGE

As Christ returns, the event of His marriage is portrayed as a past event (Revelation 19:7). It is evident then that the marriage ceremony takes place in heaven some time after the Rapture of the Church. As Jesus told His disciples, He will first take His bride to the "Father's house" (John 14:2–3). What an ideal place for the joyful occasion of this marriage ceremony—the Father no doubt officiating! This heavenly marriage is seen by Paul to be the ideal toward which all marriages point (Ephesians 5:31–32). It will, in fact, be one of the greatest events in the history of God Himself, judging from the significance of a son's marriage in the Old Testament (Genesis 24).

This marriage ceremony (19:7) is not to be confused with the "marriage supper" (19:9). John speaks of both these events, but, in keeping with Jewish marriage customs, distinguishes them. The marriage ceremony takes place in heaven at the Father's throne; the marriage supper will be celebrated on earth. The latter is what Jesus referred to in Matthew 25 in the parable of the "Virgins Awaiting the Bridegroom." That passage portrays Him as returning to the virgins of Israel who are guests invited to the marriage supper. "Virgins" is a frequent Old Testament designation for Israel (2 Kings 19:21; Isaiah 37:22; Jeremiah 14:17; Amos 5:2). That supper will occur on earth, with Israel and the nations invited as guests, a "honeymoon celebration," perhaps, that may take the entire millennial age.

The Church's Rewards Already Given

A second event already past when Christ returns is the judgment of believers. (Romans 14:10; 2 Corinthians 5:10). This judgment is not to determine one's salvation, for only true believers will be at this tribunal. Rather, it will be a time for each believer to stand before the Lord to be examined concerning his or her life as a believer. Every word, thought, or action will be reviewed on God's screen, assessing its worth or motivation. Was it done for Christ or for self? The Lord will then present each believer with His special awards, earned by his or her faithful service.

The fact that this awards ceremony occurs before Christ returns is evident in Revelation 19:8 where the bride is described as already clothed in "fine linen [which] is the righteous acts of the saints." She will have already received her rewards. The "fine linen" of which He speaks is not her "righteousness" for salvation (which is really Christ's righteousness given at salvation), but her "righteousnesses" (pl.), that is, her "good deeds" in service for Christ. These rewards were often discussed by Jesus and the apostles as one of the motivations for service (e.g., Matthew 19:27–20:16; 2 Peter 1:4–11). They often made the point that God's rewards will not be given merely on the basis of production or length of service, but on the basis of faithfulness in serving God with the gifts He has given.

John's portrayal of the church dressed in wedding garments of her own making is most appropriate. It follows the ancient custom of each bride tailoring her own wedding dress and impresses the need for all believers to be persistent in "taking stitches." God allows each believer to be involved in the process of determining his or her eternal rewards. Every "glass of water" given in Christ's name will have immense value in terms of building greater capacity to glorify God and enjoy Him forever.

It is evident these two heavenly events will have taken place before Christ returns to the earth. The church will then be associated with Him as He returns to restore society and all nature in preparation for His millennial reign.

His Coming to Israel

One of the long-standing purposes of Christ's return will be the deliverance of His people Israel. This glorious event was predicted in many Old Testament passages. Though Israel rejected its Messiah the first time, the covenant Lord did not on that account annul His promises made to the fathers. Even in the darkest days of Israel in the Old Testament, the Lord said through Jeremiah: "I have loved you with an everlasting love; therefore I have drawn you with lovingkindness. Again I will build you, and you shall be rebuilt, O virgin of Israel!" (Jeremiah 31:3, 4). Paul also affirmed this in the New Testament:

> And thus all Israel will be saved; just as it is written, "THE DELIVERER WILL COME FROM ZION, HE WILL REMOVE UNGODLINESS FROM JACOB. AND THIS IS MY COVENANT WITH THEM, WHEN I TAKE AWAY THEIR SINS." From the standpoint of the gospel they are enemies for your sake, but from the standpoint of God's choice they are beloved for the sake of the fathers; for the gifts and the calling of God are irrevocable. (Romans 11:26–29)

These promises to the patriarchs and prophets concerned what was most dear to them, the continuance of their physical seed and their place in God's program. To Abraham, David, and Jeremiah the Lord swore that His Word and promises concerning Israel could not be altered (Psalm 89:35–36; 105:8ff.; Jeremiah 31:36–37). Jesus also declared that He would not forsake them in their hour of great need, but would come to them (Mark 13:26).

When He does come, Israel will have undergone a spiritual upheaval, along with its political and social devastation in the last half of the tribulation. Any fleeting delusions of bringing in the messianic age by courting Antichrist will have vanished. They will be jolted into a radical reconsideration of their spiritual foundations. Perhaps the ministry of the two witnesses and the 144,000 during the first three and a half years will be recalled, inspiring an underground current of revival. A large contingent will have fled to the wilderness under the protection of Michael. Many others, of course, will be stuck in the Jerusalem area under the heel of Antichrist and his henchman. All these will no doubt experience an unprecedented revolution in their thinking, making them ripe for a spiritual turnaround.

Some Jews will already have received Jesus as their Messiah and Savior through this terror, but most will not have come that far. The larger remnant of Israel will not have acknowledged Him, though a spirit of receptivity and penitence will have developed. It is to this group Christ will come with a special anointing of grace (Zechariah 12:10). They will first embrace Him as their long-sought Messiah, but will not as yet recognize Him as the Nazarene. However, as they meet this one who has rescued them from the ravages of Armageddon, they will suddenly be aghast at what they see in His hands:

> And one will say to him, "What are these wounds between your arms?" Then he will say, "Those with which I was wounded in the house of my friends." (Zechariah 13:6; cf. 12:10)

This remnant will then experience the most convulsive spiritual revolution in all of history. As with doubting Thomas, they will cry, "My Lord and My God!" A spiritual fountain will then be opened to them for sin and uncleanness (Zechariah 13:1). Zechariah pictures this cleansing stream as a subterranean fount, long available but untapped, now opened for all the house of Israel. Spontaneously, the people will avail themselves of this antidote for sin and uncleanness, Christ's blood shed on the cross. In deep mourning and yet great joy, they will recognize Him as the one who once came to Bethlehem in fulfillment of prophecy, but was dubbed a blasphemer and given to the Romans for crucifixion.

Concerning this national sin of rejecting their Messiah, all Israel will join in national mourning (Zechariah 12:10–14). "They will mourn for Him, as one mourns for an only son." In their bitter remorse, they will doubtless recall the words of Isaiah: "But He was pierced through for our transgressions, He was crushed for our iniquities; the chastening for our well-being fell upon Him, and by His scourging we are healed" (Isaiah 53:5). That penitence, however, will be more than national; it will be individual, each in personal heart-searching and deep contrition (Zechariah 12:14). Great travail and lamentation will be expressed for this most astounding tragedy of their nation's history. They will frankly acknowledge before all that Jesus of Nazareth is the Jehovah of their fathers and the Savior-Messiah long anticipated by the prophets.

The Nation Reborn

Paul spoke of this future revival as the beginning of a new era for Israel. He saw it as a rejuvenation of the nation, a regrafting of the people back into the "olive tree" of God's favor (Romans 11:23). This united act of receiving Jesus as Messiah will be like a new birth to the nation, restoring them to their long-abandoned place of God's favor. It will inaugurate their time of millennial blessings, the details of which we shall discuss in the following chapter.

His Resurrection of the Righteous Dead

The final phase of the "first resurrection" will take place shortly after Christ returns. John describes it in Revelation 20:4:

> And I saw thrones, and they sat on them, and judgment was given to them. And I saw the souls of those who had been beheaded because of the testimony of Jesus and because of the word of God, and those who had not worshiped the beast or his

image, and had not received the mark upon their forehead and upon their hand; and they came to life and reigned with Christ for a thousand years.

The Tribulation Martyrs

The resurrection here described is that of tribulation saints who died by martyrdom or by resisting the threats of Antichrist. John's evident purpose in this account is to show the outcome of the tribulation conflict and God's disposal of those involved. Having shown the fate of the wicked, he then portrayed also the destiny of the righteous: "they came to life and reigned with Christ for a thousand years" (Revelation 20:4). This he called the "first resurrection."

Jesus had previously identified the "first resurrection" as that of the righteous dead, the second being that of the wicked dead following the millennium (John 5:29; Revelation 20:4–5). It is really the "first" of two kinds of resurrection described in Daniel 12:2. In the Book of Revelation, however, John mentions only the resurrection of tribulation martyrs. He assumes his readers know Daniel 12, 1 Corinthians 15, and 1 and 2 Thessalonians, which describe those other phases of the "first resurrection." Let's recall them for review.

The Church Saints

Though John does not speak of the church's resurrection in Revelation 20:4, he does refer to the church as already raised prior to this time. Of them he said: "And I saw thrones, and they sat upon them, and judgment was given to them." He portrays them as "throne sitters," the twenty-four elders associated with Christ in judgment (Revelation 4:4). Jesus' last words to the church in Revelation 3:21 spoke of this: "He who overcomes, I will grant to him to sit down with Me on My throne, as I also overcame and sat down with My Father on His throne." He said the same thing to the disciples in Matthew 19:28: "Truly I say to you, that you who have followed Me, in the regeneration when the Son of Man will sit on His glorious throne, you also shall sit upon twelve thrones, judging the twelve tribes of Israel." Revelation 20:4 describes the church on these thrones, associated with Christ in His judgment work.

In this passage then, John does not describe the resurrection of church saints, but only alludes to them as having been raised to fulfill their judgment work with Christ. As Paul noted in 1 Corinthians 6:2, the church will participate with Christ in governing the world. They will evidently be raised prior to the tribulation to fulfill this role. As He prepares for His kingdom reign in Revelation 20, He also raises the tribulation martyrs to complete the resurrection of the just in preparation for that thousand-year reign on the earth.

The Old Testament Saints

The question then arises as to when Old Testament believers will be resurrected. Since John does not mention their resurrection in Revelation 20, he evidently assumes our knowledge of Daniel 12 where it is described. There the prophet was informed about the two resurrections before receiving some specific information about the great tribulation. He is then told that he himself will rise again and be rewarded at the conclusion of those days of Israel's tribulation: "But as for you, go your way to the end [of your life]; then you will enter into rest and rise again for your allotted portion at the end of the age [literal, days]" (Daniel 12:13).

This fits also with Isaiah's classic passage on resurrection in 26:19–20. He there notes that the faithful of Israel will arise after the Lord's final indignation and judgment of the wicked, just before the joy of the messianic age. In Matthew 24:31, Jesus also described this in conjunction with His second coming: "And He will send forth His angels with A GREAT TRUMPET AND THEY WILL GATHER TOGETHER His elect from the four winds, from one end of the sky to the other." This indicates that all Old Testament saints, whether of Israel or not, will be raised at this time, presumably with the tribulation martyrs.

All these resurrections of the righteous then constitute the "first resurrection." They are set in contrast to the resurrection of the wicked that occurs after the millennial period (Revelation 20:5). The "first resurrection" does not mean a single event, but the first of two kinds of resurrections spoken of by both Daniel and Jesus (of the righteous and the wicked). Resurrection of the tribulation martyrs and Old Testament saints will complete this first resurrection.

SUMMARY

Christ's return to earth is the crowning event toward which all creation looks. He is the "Desire of Nations" and of nature. At His coming He will first attend to much unfinished business with respect to sin and judgment. Having then destroyed His enemies who despise His rule, He will then liberate His people, rejuvenate the earth, and gather His elect from all nations, and establish His glorious reign on earth. No longer a God afar off, He will be the constant companion of His people and the ever present king of the nations.

That new world order will doubtless be full of surprises. The Scriptures, however, are not without some intriguing clues for believers to ponder as we anticipate it. Concerning that much-prophesied age of wonder our next chapter will deal. In many ways that new world order under the Prince of Peace constitutes the capstone of Bible prophecy.

CHAPTER THIRTEEN

GOD'S SHANGRI-LA

Who among us has not dreamed of utopia? Everyone has their own image of that "beautiful isle of somewhere." To some its a fishing pole by a lazy river; for others, retirement in the Bahamas, or suddenly falling heir to a million bucks—"How else can you be happy?"

Utopia, however, is more than a fantasy from Sir Thomas More. The Bible presents it as the "promised land" toward which God is leading His people. That coming utopia portrayed by the prophets will far exceed the wildest expectations of our dreamy fantasies. Those juicy dreams are meager foretastes of God's envisioned paradise, mere candles in the night awaiting the morning sun.

Such optimism admittedly sounds like ecstasy gone berserk, especially in our day of prophecy bashing. Yet it rests on the surest foundation. It rests on the biblical predictions of Christ's return to rejuvenate the earth and inaugurate His new world order. That certainty is illustrated by the 300 literal fulfillments of His first coming. So broad will be the changes of that world of tomorrow that nearly every aspect of life will be affected. Many of its glamorous details have not been revealed to prevent their alluring charms from becoming mere fleshly appeal. The Lord as one of His future surprises reserves its full revelation. On the other hand, much has been revealed to suggest the character and broad pattern of that life to come. Let's put this "dream" together as the various passages of the Bible describe it.

THE PERSONAL PRESENCE OF CHRIST

The greatest distinction of that coming world will be Christ's personal presence among His people. His dwelling with them in everyday life will make it the messianic age. Though He is omnipresent in this age, localized in heaven at the Father's right hand (Ephesians 1:20; Hebrews 1:3), He will then be personally present on earth with His people.

The Millennial Age Identified

That time of Christ's future dwelling on earth is called the "millennium" by John in Revelation. Since the term is never mentioned elsewhere in the Bible, much controversy has arisen as to its meaning. How should we best understand it? It is simply another term for the "messianic age" portrayed by the prophets. John describes it here as commencing immediately after the tribulation period. Since the prophets so thoroughly discussed that age, John in Revelation assumes that his readers know those prophecies and simply supplements them with further elaboration from the Lord.

A THOUSAND YEARS OF MESSIAH'S GLORY

Among other things, John reveals the duration of that age and the key events that enclose it. It will last a thousand years (Revelation 20:4–6). It will begin when Christ returns, at which time Satan will be consigned to the abyss. It will end a thousand years later, at which time Satan will be released for a brief time. He also notes that it will begin with the resurrection of the just and conclude with the resurrection of the unjust. That is almost the sum and substance of John's revelation on the millennium.

This brevity of comment on the millennial reign appears surprising, especially since John alone deals with it in the New Testament. Some have therefore questioned its importance. That brevity, however, is not so surprising when we recall that his major emphasis concerns the judgments of the end time, already described by the Old Testament prophets. John assumes our knowledge of those prophecies and gives additional data on the messianic age not previously noted.

The question is often debated as to what John meant by the "thousand year" reign of Christ. Many have taken it as a figurative description of the church age or of eternity. Their reasoning is that Christ's reign is heavenly and will last forever, not merely a thousand years (2 Samuel 7:13; Daniel 2:44; Luke 1:33; Revelation 11:15). They further assert that the many symbols of Revelation caution against taking the "thousand years" as literal. Their fear is that it will make heaven "too earthy, too materialistic." Giving it an allegorical meaning supposedly preserves its "mystery" and majesty.

With due respect to the piety of those intentions, such manipulations inevitably play havoc with sane interpretation. They leave interpretation to the subjective whims of each interpreter. Allegorism, applied to Revelation, has shown itself to be a subtle way of aborting the declared purpose of the book which is to reveal new truths about Christ's coming. The Lord Himself solemnly cautioned against any such adding or subtracting to the text in His final warning of the book. Though this book does utilize symbols, most are drawn from the Old Testament where they portray literal truths of history or prophecy. The "beast out of the sea" in Revelation 13:1, for instance, is a direct reference to Daniel's identification of the Roman prince (Daniel 7:8). The plague judgments of Revelation 8 and 9 are similar to those in Egypt, which nearly everyone recognizes as literal. It is essential to interpret Revelation in the wider context of the Old Testament. Besides these many Old Testament figures, others are added, most of which are explained in the text itself in quite literal terms.

It is therefore brash to conclude that the book is an allegorical puzzle and therefore the "thousand years" is a symbol for something else. Of the twenty-one cardinal numbers used in the book, each makes good sense when taken in the literal sense. John, in fact, used the term "thousand years" six times in Revelation 20:2–7 to leave no doubt as to the duration of this period of Christ's reign. If he meant something else, he leaves no clue as to what it might be.

This does not mean that Christ's reign as King of kings and Lord of lords will end after the thousand years. He designates this period as just the time of His earthly rule in which "He must reign until He has put all His enemies under His feet" (1 Corinthians 15:25). It is described as the era that consummates human history with God's king in place. During that time He will fulfill His covenant promises to Israel and demonstrate to all the world how He meant the world to run, before closing the drama of humanity's sojourn on earth.

The Binding and Loosing of Satan

As Christ will dominate all aspects of that millennial age, the devil will be conspicuous by his absence. His removal will, in fact, be one of the unprecedented blessings of that era (Revelation 20:3). Though not destroyed until after the thousand-year period, he will be bound and out of business until the end of that time. Not only bound and inactive, he will be entirely absent from the earthly scene, sealed in the abyss. The Lord's purpose in this removal is that Satan should not deceive the nations during that age. Whereas "the devil walks about as a roaring lion" today, "seeking whom he may devour," he will then be out of sight, out of mind, removed from any influence on men (1 Peter 5:8).

THE PURPOSE OF SATAN'S REMOVAL

This solitary confinement of the devil for a thousand years is not designed mainly for his punishment; nor is it just to eliminate violence and make the earth more pleasant during the reign of Christ. Its deeper purpose is to demonstrate the real cause of sin. Though Satan will be absent, sin will continue, showing it is not just a product of the devil. People sin without his help even under the gracious governance of the Prince of Peace. The handy excuse that "the devil made me do it" will be forever silenced. It will dramatize the fact that sin is a depravity that finds its cause, not in the devil, but in the rebellious heart. Satan's temptation was not really the cause of man's sin in Eden—only the occasion. Thus his isolation during the millennial age will not eliminate sin, but only force it underground, stifling its overt expression.

This demonstration will be crucial in God's final judgment at the great white throne. It will effectively answer the argument that sin is just an influence from which men could be saved by a proper environment, which God failed to provide. It will thus lay the ground for His final judgment by eliminating handy excuses. The essence of sin is a condition of the heart for which each one is responsible, and passing the buck will be forever invalidated, even before that final judgment occurs.

Satan's Short Reprieve

As his binding will serve a divine purpose, so his reprieve for a brief season will also do divine service. Following the thousand-year period, the devil will be loosed to deceive the nations of the earth for a brief season (Revelation 20:3, 7–9). He will quickly incite Gog and Magog, that is, rebels from all nations of the world, to gather in a final rebellion against God. These are not the "Gog and Magog" of Ezekiel 38–39, who come on the scene a thousand years earlier, but are similar to them as enemies of God's people from all the world. Although the assembling of these rebels may take some time, their destruction will be swift. Like Elijah's enemies of old, they will be quickly destroyed by fire from heaven (2 Kings 1:10–12).

Satan's Service for God

This final act of Satan will serve at least two purposes in the divine program. First, it will bring to the surface all those living at that time who are unbelievers at heart and enemies of God. At Satan's inducement, they will come out of the woodwork from everywhere, "as the sands of the sea," showing their real allegiance. Though the millennial age will begin with all redeemed, the children born during that time will need to be saved, many of whom will reject the salvation Christ offers. That rejection will take place in spite of the continual presence of the King. As Jesus once said about those who reject truth, "neither will they be persuaded if someone rises from the dead" (Luke 16:31). "Faith comes by hearing" and acting on the Word, not merely by spectacular experiences. They will have rejected the intense light of Messiah's personal presence.

Second, this gathering of the wicked by Satan will dramatize the unique service the devil inadvertently performs for God. In this final tour of freedom, he will polarize the wicked and draw them from among the righteous. Acting like a giant magnet, he will draw off the dross from God's kingdom in preparation for the eternal state. This exemplifies his age-long service to God, suggesting the reason God has tolerated his rebellion so long and delayed his final execution.

The binding of Satan during the Millennium and his later release will be immensely important. It will dramatize the wisdom of God concerning an inexplicable mystery of life—His daring use of the devil. Satan's most diabolic schemes ironically fulfill God's purposes, as the devil himself becomes mere scaffolding God uses in the building of His house. Thus the Lord will demonstrate His ability to make the wrath of men to praise Him and all His enemies to serve Him (Psalm 76:10).

Christ's Reign As King of Kings

That millennial age will especially exhibit the personal presence of Christ. As Son of God and Son of Man He will serve as both supreme King and humble "Servant" of His people. Having highly exalted servanthood at His first coming, Christ will then "gird himself to serve and have them recline at the table, and will come and wait on them" (Luke 12:37). Like David of old, He will combine rulership and service in His grand office of King. As He daily walks among them, He will display His true character as Son of God and Son of Man.

His Residence on Earth

It may seem strange that the Son of God should set up residency and headquarters on this small planet in His mighty universe. Doesn't He have other important business, perhaps some "foreign affairs," to attend to? Why take up residency on tiny planet earth for all that time?

Such questions obviously make unwarranted assumptions. The fact that the earth is just a speck in a faraway corner of the Milky Way, and by no means the orbital center of a vast universe, does not suggest the deistic notion that humanity is subsidiary to God's concerns. The truth is that humanity is so central to God's program that the Almighty gave His only begotten Son to save and become a part of the human species. This Son has, in fact, taken the church as His bride and has become the new Head of the race (Ephesians 1:22; 5:31–32). Though not the orbital center of His universe, men and women are the orbital center of God's program, as far as the Scriptures reveal.

From this divine perspective then, Christ's coming to reign as King of the earth is supremely important to God, as well as to humanity. Jesus looked with grand anticipation to that future time when He will enjoy intimate fellowship with His people. He created them and redeemed them for intimate relationships, and the millennial age will enable that fulfillment on earth.

His Role As King of Kings

As King of the earth, He will enact a program of righteousness, equity, and compassion. Though He will rule the world with a "rod of iron," He will gently lead His people (Psalm 2:9; Isaiah 11:4; 40:11). Jerusalem will be His capital and Mt. Zion the locale of His palace (Psalm 2:6; Jeremiah 3:17; Zechariah 14:16). From there He will execute judgment and proclaim His law to all people. The whole earth will benefit from His discerning counsel. Peace will reign among all nations, and plowshares will not again be turned into swords. "The earth will be filled with the knowledge of the glory of the LORD, as the waters cover the sea" (Habakkuk 2:14). The knowledge of His glory will be the captivating theme of the nations and the central core of education.

His Ruling Associates

As sovereign Ruler, Christ will have many serving with Him in His vast administration. His will be a monarchy with various subordinate kings and agents. Some will be in their resurrection bodies of glory (similar to Christ's), and others still in their earthly bodies. David, for instance, will be resurrected as one of His preeminent deputies, exercising rule over the nation Israel (Ezekiel 34:24; 37:24–25). Though Christ will sit on the "throne of his father David," David will evidently serve as a prince before the Lord (Jeremiah 30:9; Hosea 3:5). Jesus promised the twelve apostles they would also sit on thrones of leadership judging Israel (Matthew 19:28). All saints, in fact, will serve as judges over the world in various capacities (1 Corinthians 6:2).

Besides these resurrected leaders, there will also be those from among the earthly people who will rule (Jeremiah 30:19–21). Such an arrangement will promote rapport between the earthly and resurrected classes of people. Their areas of responsibility will be in all aspects of life, civic, social, religious, business, and education. Over all these the Lord will rule and give counsel as the "Wonderful Counselor." Not isolated in a gilded castle, He will walk with His people in the marketplace, as well as at the temple.

THE DAY OF ISRAEL'S GLORY

The millennial (messianic) age will also be the great day of national glory for Israel. For this the children of Abraham have long waited, looking for the fourfold blessings of the Abrahamic covenant. The vast area of land Abraham was promised when told to look north, south, east, and west, is still in escrow; her national blessing of being the preeminent "head" of the nations is yet unfulfilled. Only after her time of national repentance at Christ's return will these elusive blessings be given. Out of the tribulation crucible a remnant will be plucked as a "brand from the burning" to reap the fulfillment of these promises (Zechariah 3:2).

With joy they will then "draw water from the springs of salvation," and beseech God to mold them as clay in the Potter's hand (Isaiah 12:3; 64:8). Out of this humble remnant the Lord will make up His "jewels" (Malachi 3:17). They will demonstrate His model theocracy. Though there have been many children of Abraham in history of whom Abraham would be ashamed, these reborn children will be the delight of his heart—and of God's.

Israel's Expansion As Promised to Abraham

That age of glory will begin with the regathering of Israel to Palestine from all parts of the globe (Deuteronomy 30:3ff.; Isaiah 11:12). They will return, never again to be evicted from their land (Amos 9:15). In numbers they will far exceed that of their forbears (Deuteronomy 30:5). As Abraham was promised children "as the stars of the heavens, and as the sand which is on the seashore," that new Israel will be almost without number. Though greatly reduced during the coming great tribulation, the millennial remnant will multiply to an innumerable company.

To accommodate this increase, the nation Israel will occupy a large land mass extending from the Euphrates to Egypt (Genesis 15:18; Deuteronomy 11:24). This was God's promise to Abraham in response to his faith. Notice the interesting exchange that took place in the giving of that covenant. When Abraham offered his "only son" to God in Genesis 22, the Lord promised him children as the stars of heaven. When he gave up his choice real estate on the Jordan in the interest of peaceful relations with Lot, God promised him all the land he could see in every direction from that mountain height. Though neither the patriarch nor his children ever fully possessed that land, it was saved for them for when they returned in penitence to the Lord (2 Chronicles 7:14).

So firm was that promise that even after Israel was ejected from the land for their idolatry, the Lord renewed His promise through Jeremiah (30–31). Far from annulling that covenant, He further elaborated it. More than that, He also gave the prophet Ezekiel a geographical sketch of the land, describing in detail the temple and city with the twelve tribes around them (Ezekiel 40–48). These chapters describe the new nation of Israel following the chaos of the tribulation which is portrayed in chapters 37–39. The tribes of Israel will then occupy parallel strips of land running east and west (48:1–8). At the center will be the prince's portion, including Jerusalem; the temple area; and the suburbs for the priests.

North of the prince's portion will be seven tribes each occupying a parallel strip. Their order from the prince's portion north will be: Judah, Reuben, Ephraim, Manasseh, Naphtali, Asher, and Dan in the far north. South of the city will be five tribes: Benjamin, Simeon, Issachar, Zebulun, and Gad. This arrangement puts the four tribes from the handmaids, Bilhah and Zilpah, farthest from the center: Dan, Asher, and Naphtali at the far north, and Gad at the far south. Each, however, will have its special gate of access to the city. This detailed description by Ezekiel portrays a greatly enlarged temple and city. The city alone is one hundred square miles and is only a small part of the prince's portion. It will be much larger than anything in Jerusalem's history.

Ezekiel's account is unique in its boldness and preciseness of details, suggesting that the prophet believed in their literal fulfillment. Such precision makes little sense otherwise. The Lord evidently gave this careful blueprint to them to impress all future generations with the certainty and precision of what God intends to do for Israel when they will respond to Him.

Israel's New Temple and Ritual System

Ezekiel's prophecy has many other surprises. Being a priest as well as a prophet, he gave special emphasis to the temple and its services. With numerous measurements, he described its floor plan and structure, all of which fit exactly when plotted on a drawing (as one of my former students, John Schmit, has demonstrated in his miniature replica of Ezekiel's temple). The prophet even includes the many extra chambers for the priests and Levites with their appointments.

The Temple Furniture

A most unique feature of this temple, however, is what is left out. As previously noted, Ezekiel makes no mention of the ark of the covenant, the mercy seat, cherubim, lamp stand, showbread, incense, or inner veil. Nor does he speak of the high priest. Were this simply a symbolic portrayal of the New Testament church, these omissions would be inexplicable, for they constituted the heart of the system. For a priest to omit them would be unpardonable.

Accepting them in their normal sense, however, these omissions make a significant point about that millennial temple. All the pieces left out of this new temple typify Messiah, who will then be physically present. He will be the "law" of the ark of the covenant, the "light" of the lamp stand, the "bread" of the table of showbread, etc. More specifically, they typify Messiah in His work in the inner chambers of the holy place

(Hebrews 9:2–5). He will be the physical fulfillment of all those hidden, missing parts. Not only will He be King of kings on the throne, He will be the ever present great High Priest as well (Zechariah 6:13).

Renewal of the Sacrificial Offerings

It comes as a bit of a shock to note that Ezekiel sees a reinstitution of animal sacrifices in that new temple (Ezekiel 40:39; 43:18–27). Though he does not mention the Passover lamb, he describes the five Levitical offerings, all of which pointed forward to Christ's work on the cross. We naturally question why such a bloody ritual should be reinstituted in the millennial age, inasmuch as Christ completed His redemptive work on the cross. Doesn't the writer of Hebrews militate against such a resumption of offerings as he emphasizes the total adequacy of Christ's one offering (Hebrews 9:11ff.; 10:18, etc.)?

The very idea of resuming the offerings admittedly leaves us aghast, almost driving one to seek some kind of allegorical interpretation. That solution, however, is purely subjective. It gives short shrift to the text or its context and has nothing substantive to offer as to the true meaning of the passage. We do well to remember that the prophecies of Ezekiel that were fulfilled historically were all fulfilled in a most literal way. Consider, for instance, the prophecy of Jerusalem's destruction (Ezekiel 4:7), or the detailed prediction of Tyre's being destroyed and swept clean (Ezekiel 26:4). Those prophecies were fulfilled to the letter, almost with a vengeance. In all honesty, we are obligated to interpret unfulfilled prophecies with the same degree of literalness as those fulfilled, whether we understand them or not.

How then can we square this reinstitution of animal sacrifices with the fact that Christ's offering was "once for all" (Hebrews 9:28)? We get the first clue by recalling the main argument of the writer of Hebrews. His basic point is not that animal sacrifices were done away forever, but that animal sacrifices never did take away sin. They were like IOUs. But because some believers at that time were tempted to return to their colorful mystique (Acts 21:26), the Hebrew writer emphasized their obsolescence and the total sufficiency of Christ's one offering. Nothing can be added to His one sacrifice for the remission of sin.

That finality, however, did not invalidate any subsequent ritual to commemorate Jesus' death. The Lord's Supper, for instance, was instituted as a remembrance of Him "until He comes" (1 Corinthians 11:26). The "cup" spoke of His death, in place of the blood of animal sacrifices under the old economy. Neither one takes away sin. The purpose of the Lord's Supper is to call the Church to reflect on the significance of that "once-for-all" offering for sin—lest we forget.

That is precisely the purpose of these renewed offerings in the millennial temple. As the church has a memorial of Christ's death, "till He comes," so that new society will also have a similar reminder of their salvation. A myriad of children will be born during that age, all in need of the salvation Christ offers. With Jesus reigning as King, however, it will be difficult for those children to think of Him as a sacrificial offering for sin. That is where these memorial offerings will come in. They will continually provide a graphic portrayal of the redemptive work of Christ on the cross. As children inquire about the meaning of these animal sacrifices, their parents will explain how Messiah once came as a babe to Bethlehem, was rejected by His people and was crucified to bear our sins. The continual observance of these Levitical offerings will give many opportunities to portray the full meaning of His "once-for-all" offering for sin. They will provide many object lessons of those redemptive truths throughout the year, lest they be forgotten in that age of glory and prosperity.

Israel's New Covenant

The nation Israel is a covenant people with whom the Lord has related Himself by special agreements (Romans 9:4). As previously noted (Romans 3), most of those covenants were unconditional (dependent on God alone) in their ultimate fulfillments. Though individual blessings were conditioned on obedience, the covenants themselves were irrevocable and guaranteed forever (Romans 11:29).

The question then arises as to why Paul speaks of the Mosaic covenant as being "old" or obsolete (2 Corinthians 3:14; cf. Hebrews 8:13). How was this an exception? His explanation was that this covenant was added to fulfill a temporary purpose till the coming of

Christ (Galatians 3:19–24). As a covenant system it was a working relationship between the Lord and His covenant people, designed to evoke individual responses to the divine leadership. Whereas the other covenants were more national, guaranteeing specific ultimate blessings to the nation, the Mosaic was personal, involving each one individually with his covenant Lord. It elaborated on the first part of the Abrahamic covenant, conditioning their individual participation in the covenant benefits (John 8:39).

Because the nation so continually broke this covenant code (Jeremiah 11:4–5), she was evicted from the covenant land in 586 B.C. It was at this time that Jeremiah the prophet announced a new covenant that the Lord would make with united Israel (Jeremiah 31:31–34).

> "Behold, days are coming," declares the LORD, "when I will make a new covenant with the house of Israel and with the house of Judah, not like the covenant which I made with their fathers in the day I took them by the hand to bring them out of the land of Egypt, My covenant which they broke, although I was a husband to them," declares the LORD.
>
> "But this is the covenant which I will make with the house of Israel after those days," declares the LORD, "I will put My law within them, and on their heart I will write it; and I will be their God, and they shall be My people.
>
> "And they shall not teach again, each man his neighbor and each man his brother, saying 'Know the LORD,' for they shall all know Me, from the least of them to the greatest of them," declares the LORD, "for I will forgive their iniquity, and their sin I will remember no more."

The Time Zones of the New Covenant

This exchange of covenants presents two problems: when did the old terminate, and when does the new begin. Though the Mosaic Law was broken many times in the Old Testament period, it came to an end when Christ died on the cross (Galatians 3:19; Colossians 2:14). It was then that the Levitical priesthood ended, terminating also the legal system to which it was joined. "For when the priesthood is changed, of necessity there takes place a change of the law also" (Hebrews 7:12). It did not just gradually peter out, but came to an abrupt end when the veil of the temple was torn asunder, ending both the priesthood and the legal system. As noted in chapter 3, the Law's eternal principles continue, but the covenant system terminated at the cross.

The time the New Covenant begins is quite precisely stated as "after those days" (Jeremiah 31:33). That time is given as following the scattering and regathering of Israel (31:27–28), or after "the time of Jacob's distress," when "he shall be saved from it" (30:3–7).

As discussed in chapter 3, this covenant is not a covenant with the church, but with the returned "house of Israel and the house of Judah" (31:31). The reference to this covenant in Hebrews 8:8ff. is simply for the purpose of showing that the Mosaic covenant had ended; the "old" was not designed to be permanent, as some Jews thought, only temporary. The church today is not under covenant relations, as such, except as partakers of the "blood of the eternal covenant," a reference to the protoevangel of Genesis 3:15 (Hebrews 13:20). The New Testament gospel does not replace the Mosaic covenant for redemption, but only as a guidance system. We do not follow a legal letter, but the living Lord (Romans 14:9). Paul declared that we are ministers of the Spirit of "a new covenant," which Spirit he identified as the Lord (2 Corinthians 3:6, 17). His blood ratified our redemption and became a covenant itself (Luke 22:11; 1 Corinthians 11:25).

The Substance of the New Covenant

Though the substance of each of the previous covenants is precisely stated, Jeremiah does not give the details of this one. He simply announced that the Lord would establish a new covenant relation with both houses of Israel after He has renewed them to fellowship by forgiving their sins. Not written on tablets or kept in the ark, it will be engraved on their hearts (Jeremiah 31:33–34). In other words, it will be spiritual in nature, rather than a manuscript or legal document for scribes to manipulate or distort. Each will relate personally to the Lord without instruction from others (31:34).

In this sense, the New Covenant with Israel will strongly resemble the present relationship of Christ and the church. It will certainly not be a retrogression back to law, but a reinauguration of God's grace with the nation Israel. Having been grafted back into the place of God's favor, they will have a new spiritual relation with the Lord as a channel of His blessing. This new gracious relationship will be the basis on which God will bless His people throughout the millennial age.

THE NEW WORLD ORDER

Besides great changes in Israel, the millennial age will introduce radical changes in every area of life. We often think of the believer's hereafter as being heaven, but that is not the whole story. All resurrected saints from both Old and New Testament times will be very much involved in the millennial age on earth. After Christ's return to set up His kingdom, we will be very much down to earth as we pursue with Christ the development and immense possibilities of that kingdom. We will return to a new environment and in resurrection bodies.

The Various Classes of People

God has many kinds of children, and in that millennial age they will all be together as a happy family. As the age begins, all will have been born into God's family by the new birth (John 3:5), both those resurrected and those redeemed and yet in earthly bodies. By new birth each will have received spiritual life, which the natural man does not have. To properly contemplate that unique society, let's recall the various classes of people that will be involved.

EARTHLY PEOPLE IN MORTAL BODIES

Life on the mortal plane will continue as today. All people who survive the tribulation to enter the millennial kingdom will be redeemed as the "sheep" approved by Christ (Matthew 25:32–34). These will be saved, but not translated, entering the new age in their mortal bodies. They will carry on life as usual, bearing children and repopulating the earth. It appears that these earthly people who enter the millennial age will continue to live throughout the thousand-year period. Of them Isaiah wrote: "They shall not build, and another inhabit, they shall not plant, and another eat; for as the lifetime of a tree, so shall be the days of My people" (Isaiah 65:22). Old age and death will not overtake people in the messianic age, depriving them of the fruit of their labors. The righteous will continue to live throughout the period, exceeding the great ages of the antediluvians, all of whom fell short of 1,000 years.

The children of these redeemed people, however, will not necessarily live throughout the period, but could die young. The Lord will judge overt sin, and He will not withhold capital punishment where that is required. Isaiah declared that sinners in that day will die a youthful death under 100 years of age (Isaiah 65:20). Only the wicked will die, however, for only the fate of the wicked is mentioned at the final resurrection and judgment at the great white throne (Revelation 20:11–15). Funerals will perhaps have strange eulogies, for only the wicked will be cut down. That means no accidental deaths of the righteous, whether by falling off tall buildings or violence. Righteousness and justice will prevail and extend to every aspect of life.

The Resurrected Saints

Mingling with these earthbound saints will be the resurrected saints of all ages. This will include those from the Old Testament, New Testament, and tribulation periods. Each group will have a different status and function in that millennial society. Old Testament saints will constitute the "old friends" of God, including many with whom He began His program (Hebrews 11). Of such will be Enoch, Noah, Melchizedec, and Abraham. Also the resurrected saints of Israel will have a special place as those with whom He enacted His covenants and conveyed His Word. Moses, Joshua, Samuel, and David will occupy special places of honor. Many unnamed and unheralded will be among them.

To the New Testament church, however, God has assigned the unique position of the bride of Christ (Revelation 19:7–8). Paul often referred to this union as the intimacy of husband and wife (Ephesians 5:31–32). This is the bride He is winning out of the world during the present age while rejected by His Israeli brethren. It is a marriage relation distinct from that of Israel, called the "wife" of Jehovah, the triune God, which is an earthly relation of Israel in the land (Hosea 2). The exalted position granted the church is uniquely the "unspeakable gift" of God's grace (2 Corinthians 9:15), one that continues into the eternal state.

A third group of resurrected saints will be the martyrs of the tribulation period. They are slated also to reign with Christ during the millennial age (Revelation 20:4). This group from both Israel and Gentile nations will evidently serve in a special priestly capacity (Revelation 20:6). Like the Levites who stood by Moses in a time of spiritual defection (Exodus 32:26; Numbers 1:47–53), these will fill varied roles of heavenly Levites. Recall that the 144,000 Israelis who are martyred, appear to have the specialized function of "Levitical singers," providing music for the Lamb wherever He goes (Revelation 14:3–4).

Adapted for Heaven and Earth

All these resurrected saints will enjoy fellowship with both heavenly and earthly beings, evidently not restricted to the earth. Although the heavenly city of New Jerusalem will not yet have descended to earth, it will already be built and accessible for resurrected saints (John 14:2; Revelation 21:10). More will be seen of that city in our discussion of the eternal state. For this twofold interaction our bodies will be specially equipped, adapted for fellowship with both human and spirit beings, even with angels (1 Corinthians 6:3; 15:44).

The question is often asked whether we will really see the Father. Obviously, no one will see Him in bodily form, for "God is a Spirit"; He has no body as such. That does not deny, however, that we will see Him in a meaningful way, for the "pure in heart...shall see God" (Matthew 5:8; Revelation 22:4). Having "spirit bodies" (rather than mere soul bodies), we will interact with angels and evidently have face to face fellowship with the Father (1 Corinthians 15:44). As Christ and the angels regularly behold the Father's face, resurrected saints will likewise behold the face of their heavenly Father (Matthew 18:10).

This idea of interacting with spirits admittedly appears somewhat spooky to us today—bordering on the ghoulish. If it does, we need only recall Christ's sojourn on earth for forty days after His resurrection. In His glorified state He exhibited in living color our future life of resurrection. On several occasions He ate food, though He didn't need to (Luke 24:43; John 21:12–13). At the garden tomb He was recognized by His voice as He spoke to Mary Magdalene. His resurrection body was so like that of other men that He was mistaken for just another stranger on the road to Emmaus. He evidently didn't even wear a halo. Yet He entered rooms and disappeared without opening doors. On His resurrection day He evidently went to the Father's throne in the third heaven and returned the same day (John 20:17–19). When He later ascended into heaven, however, He rose up through the clouds in a slow and deliberate way.

In all these experiences, the Lord's relations with His disciples were not phantomlike, but intimate and real. One of His purposes in this forty-day stay over was to demonstrate some of the features of our future resurrection life. As John says, "We shall be like Him, because we shall see Him just as He is" (1 John 3:2). We will enjoy a dual fellowship with both heavenly and earthly beings in a natural and normal way.

Changes in Physical Nature

That millennial age will also see great changes in nature itself. Immense energy resources will be opened up for that era of progress. An increasing concern of our world today is that the earth is quickly being depleted of its energy reserves. That concern is certainly a healthy one for our greedy and exploitive age. The fact is, however, that the surface has hardly been scratched in the vast energy resources with which God has invested man's terrestrial home. The greatest of them have probably not yet been tapped. They have been wisely restricted from our present self-serving age. In that age to come, however, with violence subdued and selfish exploitation checked, vast new energy sources will no doubt be opened up.

To reduce its obvious appeal to human greed, of course, the Bible does not reveal the specifics of these power resources. It does, however, have much to say of the unparalleled prosperity and vitality of that messianic age. More than a mere nuclear age, it will be a time of great scientific and social progress. Its horizons will be vastly greater. Under Messiah's rule, that age will doubtless showcase unparalleled physical and scientific growth.

An Explosion in Knowledge

Knowledge is essential to progress, but it is sorely limited without right relations to God. "The fear of the Lord is the beginning of knowledge" (Proverbs 1:7). In that future earth this gift will be maximized not only to resurrected saints, but also to those in mortal bodies. "The earth will be full of the knowledge of the LORD as the waters cover the sea" (Isaiah 11:9). Several factors will enable this increase in human comprehension. With the Great Physician at hand, human frailties will be at a minimum (Isaiah 35). Men's eyes will not be dim, nor will their tongues stammer in speech (Isaiah 32:2–4). Second, the Lord will be present as the "Wonderful Counselor" to teach and supervise universal education. If Einsteins arise among us today, using only a small percentage of their brain potential, what great scientists and artists will be produced in that time of unlimited knowledge! Exploring the universe may be mere field trips in the schools of science.

All Nature in Harmony

To enhance peace and tranquillity on earth, the whole of nature will be reconciled (Romans 8:21). The wolf and the lion will lounge with the lamb and the calf (Isaiah 11:6–7). Carnivores will no longer be carnivorous; they will munch on vegetation like the cow (Isaiah 11:7; 65:25). The point is that violence will be eliminated in much of the animal kingdom. To illustrate this point, the prophet declared that a little child will lead the lion as a romping pet. Ferocity will be extracted from animal nature.

This facile environment will also extend to inanimate nature. It will be a day of liberation for both the believer's body and creation itself (Romans 8:21–23). The curse imposed on the ground at the advent of sin will be removed. No more will thorns and weeds infest the ground, nor storms of heat and cold devastate the earth (Isaiah 49:8–10). Physical nature will work with rather than conspire against the work of men's hands. Under the supervision of the Creator Himself, all nature will become a handmaid to complement the work of men for the glory of God.

As previously noted, great topographical upheavals will have changed the contours of the earth. The final earthquake after Armageddon will rearrange mountains and coastlines (Revelation 16:18). At Christ's return, the Mount of Olives will be leveled and much of the landscape reformed into a plane, gradually rising to a high point at Jerusalem (Zechariah 14:4, 10). The probability is that this renovation of the earth's crust will be worldwide. A rich, new environment in Edenic form and productivity will be restored for the glorious reign of the Man from heaven.

These many changes will bring about the utopian abundance portrayed by the prophets. Amos described it in terms of terraced gardens drooping with overloaded vines of grapes (Amos 9:13). Ezekiel saw it as a restoration of the Garden of Eden (Ezekiel 36:35). To Jeremiah it was seen as a time of replacing mourning with dancing, the young and the old rejoicing together (Jeremiah 31:13).

The apostle Paul also described that new age as a time of society's resurrection from the dead (Romans 11:12, 15). So vibrant and exciting will its agenda be, the highest joys of our present age of contrived theatrics will seem dead by comparison. His explanation is that a new channel of blessing will energize that age. Israel will be grafted back into the "olive tree" of God's blessing (Genesis 12:3). This is the way it was intended to be. His argument is that, if God is able to bless the world with redemption through Israel's disobedience, what untold riches will He bring through her obedience in that future day (Romans 11:12)! The nightmare of violence, crime, poverty, and fear will end as the world itself experiences a resurrection to life as it was meant to be.

These glimpses of tomorrow's world are admittedly sparse and meager, but they give a measure of substance to our hope. That meagerness reminds us again that the real attraction of faith is not the glitter of tinsel, but the beauties of the Savior Himself. The glory of His Person will be the real focus and satisfaction of His people, all else being mere fringe benefits (Romans 8:32).

Those peripheral benefits, however, will constitute the background and environment of that coming messianic age. In His presence there will be fullness of joy, and these accouterments will contribute to the ecstasy of that time when Christ will dwell with His people in God's "Shangri-La."

CHAPTER FOURTEEN

THE DAWN OF GOD'S ETERNAL DAY

Eternity! What an awesome thought! Nothing boggles the mind like the thought of eternity. We reel in tailspins, as if it is off-limits to human thinking. However, the Bible often refers to it as basic to ultimate meaning. In the apostle Peter's final vision, he saw it as the "day of God," an endless period following the final judgments of the "Day of the Lord" (2 Peter 3:12). That day will terminate the present order, as the Lord creates "new heavens and a new earth" (v. 13). It is a day toward which God has programmed all things, a morning of joy for believers beyond earth's long night of sin and sorrow. How can we properly appreciate such an incomprehensible thought? We need to recall its purpose.

God created men and women for fellowship. To enhance that divine-human relationship, He made them in His own image. His purpose was to extend His divine nature into human personalities, enabling their ultimate fulfillment in joy and pleasure (2 Peter 1:4). Since God does nothing accidentally, it follows that He Himself had a desire and hunger for their fellowship as well. Though the entrance of sin seemed to destroy that plan, it did not abort or nullify it; it only postponed it. While first attending to the sin question, the Lord simply delayed its final fulfillment till after the millennial age. In the eternal ages, that fellowship will be perfected in a new and redeemed environment.

The Bible's description of that eternal day is admittedly rather brief; but it is quite explicit. Many passages point to it. The classic chapters on the subject are 2 Peter 3 and Revelation 21–22. Its description by John constitutes the capstone of God's revelation to man, portraying the final bliss of those who put their trust in God. The apostle introduces the eternal ages by first describing the final judgment of the great white throne, after which he gives a breathtaking view of the new heavens and earth.

THE FINAL JUDGMENT OF THE GREAT WHITE THRONE

We have previously noted that the millennial age will end with another massive rebellion of men against God. In their madness that generation of revolt will have forgotten the costly lesson of Armageddon. Satan will again instigate this final rebellion, as he is released from the abyss; but it will also serve God's purpose of rounding up all rebels for judgment. Similar to Armageddon, this crowd will be quickly destroyed as they surround the holy city. The upshot of this revolt will be the immediate destruction of all those still living who have rejected God's mercy during the millennial reign of Christ. It will also be the first step in God's judgment of the wicked as He purges unbelief from the universe in preparation for the eternal ages.

Resurrection of All the Wicked

This purging will evidently climax with a monumental blast that will dissolve the present heaven and earth in a massive ball of fire—a future and final "big bang" (2 Peter 3:12; Revelation 21:1). As that happens, the unbelieving dead of all ages will be retrieved and resurrected for judgment. They will appear at some spacious location before the "great white throne" of God (Revelation 20:11–13). No unbeliever in history will miss this muster, with two exceptions. John noted that Antichrist and the false prophet will go directly to the lake of fire, not having even of the luxury of death and a waiting period before judgment (Revelation 19:20; 20:10). They will, in fact, still be there at the end of the thousand years (20:13).

Otherwise, all unbelievers from the time of Cain will stand before God to give account in this judgment. Judas will be there, as will Pharaoh, Haman, Antiochus Epiphanes, Herod, Pilate, Caiaphas, Nero, Hitler, and all the celebrated unbelievers of all time. Sinners, both good and bad, rich and poor, big and little, religious and irreligious, will appear for this final meeting. John noted that "death and hades" will spew forth their occupants and even the sea will obediently round up its victims (Revelation 20:13). The dissolution of cremation will instantly reverse to reassemble all its ashes and souls for judgment. This resurrection is called the "second resurrection," or the "resurrection of judgment" (John 5:29).

The Purpose of Final Judgment

This Great White Throne Judgment is different in many ways from all previous judgments. It contrasts with the judgment of the nations in Matthew 25, in that it occurs after the millennial age and does not divide "sheep and goats." It is a judgment of unbelievers only. Also, it is not a so-called universal or general judgment of all men, deciding the fate or destiny of each. It makes no mention of the just or saved, dealing only with those raised for damnation. These are distinguished from the "blessed and holy," who are raised in the "first resurrection" (Revelation 20:6).

The question then arises as to why this resurrection of the wicked or unsaved takes place. Why not simply consign them to their fate? The obvious reason is that justice requires that a final reckoning or appraisal be given before the condemned are delivered to their final destiny. God does not consign sinners to judgment with a mere wave of the hand. Each recipient of judgment will stand before God to have his or her case individually reviewed.

The purpose of this careful accounting will be to demonstrate the perfect fairness and absolute necessity of the judgment meted out. God will not allow His place of eternal retribution to become a madhouse of cursing Him or staging demonstrations. All concocted notions of charging God for being unfair or too severe will be removed. Though that judgment will certainly be harsh, it will not be fickle or capricious; it will be in strict keeping with eternal justice and the essential nature of cause and effect. In other words, God will clear the air of all dissent as the destinies of the lost are pronounced.

The Justice of Final Judgment

On what basis then will these solemn decisions be made? John is quite explicit in noting the judicial basis of this judgment to be two sets of books kept by the divine recorder (Revelation 20:11–15). One is the "book of life" and the other is the "book of works." These scrolls record the decisions of the sovereign God and the free-will actions of men.

The book of life contains the names of all the redeemed, drawn up by God before the foundation of the world (Ephesians 1:4; Revelation 13:8; 17:8). It represents God's election in the redemptive process, revealing also that many are excluded (20:15). Since this appears unfair and arbitrary from the human view, God will then open another set of books, the record of each one's works. In this review all pertinent facts and evidences will be subpoenaed to make the case crystal clear, including the thoughts and intentions of the heart (Ecclesiastes 12:14; Romans 2:16; Hebrews 4:12). In will also be a time of righting all wrongs, those remembered and those forgotten. In this judgment God will demonstrate to all the lost that their works and God's election confirm each other, neither being watered down by the other (Romans 8:28–29). As Abraham once said, anticipating God's judgment on Sodom: "Shall not the Judge of all the earth deal justly?" (Genesis 18:25). He will, indeed, and that justice will be transparent to all.

The Finality of Judgment

The Lord clearly revealed the final fate and state of the lost in two basic descriptions—the "lake of fire" and the "second death" (Revelation 19:20; 20:10, 14–15; 21:8). The first describes a place and the second, a state.

THE LAKE OF FIRE

We would like to think of the lake of fire as simply a state of mind (sufficiently horrible as that would be), but the text describes it as a physical reality. Certainly the resurrection of the unjust is a physical one, not just spiritual. Never having seen a lake of fire, we can only shudder and surmise the horror of such a place. The Lord's portrayal is one of indescribable torment.

The words themselves are overwhelming. They constitute the most solemn revelation of Scripture concerning the awesome destiny of the lost. Nothing remotely approaches it in all of human literature. So devastating are the words, we are prone to wince and move on to happier thoughts, as if from a case of delirium tremens. To do so, however, would be to hush God's siren and contribute to the damning of the lost for whom these words were spoken. The fact is that Christ Himself is the author of this revelation on the fires of hell—and who would be so brash as to downplay His words and authority (Mark 9:43ff.). We can but relay His warning on the subject.

The Second Death

The other description of the destiny of the lost is the second death (Revelation 20:14). Though related to the previous, this alludes more to the state of the lost. Many have assumed this final death means the annihilation of the wicked. Humane and generous though that may seem, it is never suggested by the biblical text. The Lord portrayed the destiny of the lost as a state where existence never ceases and the fire is never quenched (Mark 9:48; Luke 12:5). The life God gives is part of His divine image and cannot be obliterated; it is eternally existent. He describes the torment as continuing "forever and ever," the same expression that describes the eternal bliss of the redeemed (Revelation 20:10; 22:5) and the eternality of God (Revelation 4:9; 10:6; 15:7). It is therefore the part of prudence to recognize the horror of it and leave the exoneration of God's justice to the time when He will make all things clear. He is not in the habit of using exaggeration to "deceive" sinners into repentance. The Judge Himself is the one who has spoken on the subject.

This term, "second death," speaks of a condition that first began when Adam died. Death is basically separation, physical death being separation of body and spirit, and spiritual death, separation of the individual from God. The second death will be the final severance of the individual from the life of God and the inevitable consequence of that state of existence in a "living death." In that inexorable state, a person's sin has crowded out every vestige of God-capacity and any desire for His presence. The nature of sin being diametrically opposed to the nature of God, those personified by sin will only be repulsed and enflamed by His presence. The only alternative for such is their dismissal and eternal exclusion from His presence. This is the second death.

The Impossibility of Reversal

One of the final notes the Bible makes with respect to the fate of the lost is the eternal fixity of their lost condition. The apostle John put it this way:

"Let...the one who does wrong, still do wrong; and let the one who is filthy, still be filthy; and let the one who is righteous, still practice righteousness; and let the one who is holy, still keep himself holy" (Revelation 22:11). Following physical death, in other words, it is impossible to change one's direction or eternal destiny. Each one makes a choice in this life as to whether he or she will be eternally holy and righteous or eternally filthy and wicked. That decision is sealed at death. If the goodness and severity of God have not brought repentance and turning to God in this life, the fires of hell will not do it in the afterlife. The notion that one can repent and turn to God after death is never taught in the Bible (though some have misinterpreted Luke 16:23–31 to suggest it).

The reason for this finality is not God's vengeance or caprice, but the incorrigibility of those personified by sin and crystallized in their lost condition. Could the infinite God of love, might, and miracle alter that fact, the decisive pronouncements of the great white throne would be mere rhetoric. The pity is that many suppose quite piously that they will change and become holy after death. The Lord's solemn warning to all in these final words is that death forecloses all hope of changing one's direction. There is no "crossing over" after death (Luke 16:26).

THE GLORY OF GOD'S RESTORED KINGDOM

As we turn to the glory side, it is like awakening on heaven's shore. We begin with the most climactic event of all history, Christ's formal presentation of the usurped kingdom back to the Father. Without enlarging on the details, the apostle Paul gives the time of its occurrence and some brief facts about the ceremony. After describing Christ's final conquest of His enemies, Paul declared about that celebration:

> Then comes the end when He delivers up the kingdom to the God and Father, when He has abolished all rule and authority and power. For He must reign until He has put all His enemies under His feet. And when all things are subjected to Him, then the Son Himself also will be subjected to the One who subjected all things to Him, that God may be all in all. (1 Corinthians 15:24–25; 28)

Nothing remotely approaches the grandeur of this occasion. It is really the consummation of God's whole program with respect to the issue of sin. As noted in chapter 2, God's kingdom program is that process by which He is reclaiming His usurped kingdom and demonstrating His sovereignty in all realms. That program required His forthright confrontation with the problem of sin and the final restoration of the kingdom to God. Corollary to it is His redemptive program, and the two constitute the Bible's story in a nutshell.

Those programs began at the onset of sin in the Garden of Eden. It was then that Christ, the seed of the woman, was commissioned by the Father to fulfill both programs (Genesis 3:15). Man in sin was in need of redemption, and God's usurped kingdom authority was in need of reclaiming. Having accomplished both of these missions, Christ at this time will make a grand presentation of that restored kingdom back to the Father. This celebration will bring to an end forever the long saga of sin and Satan.

Christ's presentation of the kingdom to the Father, however, does not mean that His reign as king then comes to an end. His reign is "forever and ever" (Revelation 11:15). On the contrary, this ceremony will celebrate the fulfillment of His commission to restore God's authority in all spheres. So important is this accomplishment that a special pageant will celebrate its completion. In unprecedented pomp and glory, Christ will march through heaven with the torch of victory to symbolically present to the Father the usurped reins of His kingdom authority. It will not be a restoration of "lost sovereignty," but a reassertion of His sovereign authority and an end of His tolerance with rebels. It will emblazon the eternal truth that God is indeed "all and in all." At the same time it will demonstrate the unity of the Godhead and the joyful submission of all intelligences to His sovereign leadership.

Nor does this subjection of the Son to the Father suggest inequality of the Son with the Father. They are forever equally God (John 5:18). It simply stresses the continuing unity of the members of the Godhead with respect to kingdom authority. In other words, Christ's conquest of the world's kingdom will not be merely a separate satellite kingdom, carved out of chaos for Himself, but of a piece with God's eternal kingdom. As John described that coming kingdom, "the throne of God and of the Lamb shall be in it…and they shall reign forever and ever" (Revelation 22:3–5). The final reestablishing of that kingdom order under the Lord will be a time of consummate joy for both God and His people.

The New Heaven and Earth Described

Though that victory celebration will be a grand consummation, it will be an even grander commencement. The glory of that triumph will not be lead to a humdrum, business-as-usual aftermath, as many earthly triumphs do. Rather, it will be followed immediately by the creation of a new heaven and earth (Isaiah 65:17; 2 Peter 3:13; Revelation 21:1). This new creation will form the framework and "real estate" of man's eternal fellowship and dwelling with God.

As a "new creation," that world will be both old and new. It will be old in that the present earth will be the raw materials of the new. As King Solomon once said, "the earth abides forever" (Ecclesiastes 1:4; Psalm 104:5). But it will also be new, for the old will be completely renovated. The apostle Peter dramatized this renewal:

> Looking for and hastening the coming of the day of God, on account of which the heavens will be destroyed by burning, and the elements will melt with intense heat! But according to His

> promise we are looking for new heavens and a new earth, in which righteousness dwells. (2 Peter 3:12–13)

This awesome prophecy has admittedly challenged the credulity of many, but it no longer needs much defense in our age of nuclear fission. The wonder is that such a disaster will be delayed that long, with our present nuclear proliferation. In God's time and by whatever means, He will melt and recycle the present earth to fulfill His divine purposes. Every vestige of sin and corruption will be obliterated. No telltale fossils of death will be left for an archeologist's spade to dig up and bring to our remembrance. The biblical evidence is that the present era of sin and violence will not even return as a haunting memory to the redeemed: "the former things shall not be remembered or come to mind" (Isaiah 65:17). That renewed planet will be an untainted earth, refashioned for the boundless exploits of righteousness.

The New Jerusalem

An example of the new earth being refurbished is John's description of the "New Jerusalem," its central city. That city will come fresh from the hands of God, not as the product of man's engineering genius (Revelation 21:2).

Its Building

Interpreters have long debated the makeup of this city and the time of its descent to the earth. Some have related it to the Jerusalem of the messianic age where Christ will rule for a thousand years. This new city, however, as described in Revelation 21:10ff., appears to be much different. Its structure and dimensions are especially different and do not fit the millennial temple. The enormous size of this city, for instance, would cover the whole Middle East.

A better view is that, according to the context, this New Jerusalem is entirely unique; it will descend to earth from heaven after the earth's re-creation at the end of the Millennium. Many believe it will hover above and in sight of the earth during the thousand-year period as the central residence of resurrected saints. Orbital cities are even now on the drawing boards of our satellite planners. This hovering arrangement during the millennial age would also fit the description of the nations walking in its light as the resurrected saints dwell there (Isaiah 60:3; Revelation 21:24). Following the earth's re-creation, however, this gigantic city will dramatically descend to the new terra firma as the celestial jewel of God's handiwork.

From at least the time of Abraham, many saints have expressed their anticipation of this city built by God (Hebrews 11:10). It can also be identified as the place Christ alluded to in saying that He was going away to "prepare a place for you" (John 14:3). In keeping with His earthly carpenter's trade, He went away to undertake the construction of this immense celestial metropolis as the permanent residence for His people. If creation was the work of His fingers in a moment of time (Psalm 8:3), what will be the finesse of these mansions which have been under His architectural construction for the past two millennia!

Its Structure and Prominent Features

Though little is said of its structural plan, several clues are given as to its prominent features in Revelation 21–22. Here John speaks of its size, walls and foundations, gates, building materials, and its occupants.

The city is laid out as a square, 1500 miles long and wide. It is also described as 1500 miles high (Revelation 21:16). This great height could suggest either a cubical or pyramidal form. If this means multiplied layers of streets, no one's view would be blocked, for its materials will be "crystal-clear," the true "crystal city" (Revelation 21:11, 21). Whatever its configuration, the dimensions suggest some impressive, innovative engineering, to say the least. Its square contour would stretch over the whole Middle East or half the United States from the Atlantic Ocean to the Rockies and from Canada to Mexico. All great cities of our time put together would be villages by comparison.

Its Twelve Walls and Twelve Gates

The special features of the city emphasized by John are its great walls and munificent gates. The wall is 216 feet high and is built on twelve foundations, each named after one of the twelve apostles. Each foundation in the wall is adorned by a precious stone (from jasper to amethyst, from which we get many of our birthstones). These evidently symbolize the New Testament church which is built on a similar foundation (Ephesians 2:20). So prominent is the church in this metropolis that the city itself is called "the bride, the wife of the lamb" (Revelation 21:9; cf. Ephesians 5:27). The Lord's grand "estate" will be named after His bride.

A second feature John emphasizes concerns the gates around the city. Like the millennial Jerusalem (Ezekiel 48:31–34), this city will have twelve gates, each named after one of the tribes of Israel. These will be distributed around the city, three gates on each side. The significance of naming the gates after Israel suggests the idea of access or entrance. As in Ezekiel's temple, the gates will provide free access for these tribes to the city, but not necessarily residence there. The contrast seems to be that the church or bride, after whom the city is named, is given residence there, whereas Israel has free access by the gates to all the joys of the city. Attending each gate will be an angel, perhaps symbolizing the guarding angels of the Old Testament.

Its Fabulous Materials

In describing the materials that make up the city, the interpreting angel seems almost at a loss for words. Enshrined with the glory of God, the city itself is said to be as brilliant as "crystal-clear jasper" (Revelation 21:11). In appearance it is like a modern diamond of pure carbon in crystalline form, transparent and unflawed in brilliance. The basic structure of the city will be of gold, described as so pure as to be transparent. Its foundations will be constructed of twelve precious stones (vv. 19–20). The first and most prominent of these is jasper, a stone that also symbolizes the Father (Revelation 4:3). Each of the gates will be sculptured out of a single pearl. The significance of these precious stones, however, is not their own value, but their ability to reflect transparently the glory that surrounds them. These structural materials and gems will constantly reflect the glory of God.

Its Missing Features

Several negatives are noted that will also enhance the glory of that eternal city. Two are seen as no longer necessary and two as no longer tolerated (Revelation 21:22–22:3). The first is the absence of a temple. The ancient temple was always a prominent part of Israel's capital, symbolizing the place where God and His people met. In this eternal city, however, there will be no such restricted approaches to the Lord. Rather, "the Lord God Almighty and the Lamb are its temple" (21:22). John declared that "they shall see His face" (22:4). All the temporal symbols of God's presence in a temple will be discarded as mere shadows in the glory of His continual presence.

In the same way there will be no need of the sun or moon (21:23). Though these luminaries will still be part of that eternal sky, they will not serve their present purposes of giving light, governing day and night, etc. The new source of light will be "direct current," direct from the ultimate source of Him who is the Light. These will make both night and darkness unknown to that world. The glory of God and of the Lamb will provide brilliant illumination for all in that land of fadeless day. "Sonlight" will replace sunlight.

Besides the absence of good things no longer necessary, there will also be the absence of debilitating things no longer tolerated. Death with all its terrors will be gone, eliminating man's last enemy. Also nothing unclean will arise to pollute that city (21:4; 27). With these will go all tears, pain, or sorrow that might disturb the joys participated in by all.

No More Sea?

Many would add the sea to this list of things missing in the new earth, as noted in Revelation 21:1. That would dramatically alter the original creation of the earth for man's habitat. It would also pose a question as to the actuality of the river that flows from the throne, for where would the river of abundant waters go in that land of the "water of life"?

Perhaps a better view is that of Joseph Seiss (*The Apocalypse,* 488) that the old sea will pass away to make way for the new. The point of the passage is that the old heaven, earth, and sea will pass away in preparation for "a new heaven and a new earth." As in other passages (Genesis 1:10; Exodus 20:11; Revelation 10:6), the sea is listed separately here as being so vast as to be considered an entity in itself. He who makes all things new will create, in this view, a new crystal sea that will no longer be a thing of danger and dread, but only of beauty, joy, and exhilaration (Revelation 21:5; 4:6).

Its Emphasis on "Life"

John highlights two elements of life as prominent in the New Jerusalem. These are the "river of the water of life" and the "tree of life" (Revelation 22:1–2), located at the central park of the city flowing from the throne of God. Spiritually, they speak of eternal verdure and vitality. The water of life flows as a crystal stream from God's throne and is bordered on both sides by the tree of life. Water and trees are essential to life as we know it today, and they symbolize that future state of abundant provision. The fruit of the trees is said to provide eternal sustenance, and the leaves, eternal health. All that man forfeited at the entrance of sin in Eden will be renewed in that new earth with endless supply. They speak of an abundant life of satisfaction and fulfillment flowing from the throne of God.

The question is often raised as to whether this river and these trees are actual or just symbolic. Many regard the concept of actual water and trees as too carnal and materialistic, and better understood here as mere symbols of spiritual truths.

The probability is that either approach would convey the basic lesson, but that is not all that is at stake. Denigrating the physical as less spiritual is an old ploy used by heretics of history to reject even the bodily resurrection of Christ. On the contrary, there is nothing inherently evil about the physical world, as the Manichaeans taught, for God is also the Creator of the physical world. His redemption was intended to extend to the physical world, as well as to the spiritual (Romans 8:23). With sin extracted from both human nature and physical nature, there will be nothing carnal or indulgent about enjoying the literal "water of life" and "tree of life" in that eternal city.

THE NEW HORIZON

All these portrayals are mere hints of life in God's eternal ages. Their scantiness of details is doubtless for good reason, for the central attraction of that city will be the person of God. Beholding His glory will be man's most captivating and exhilarating experience. Jesus' prayer for His people was "that they may behold My glory" (John 17:24). The apostle Paul declared that "the sufferings of this present time are not worthy to be compared with the glory that is to be revealed to us" (Romans 8:18). When he did catch a brief glimpse of that glory, he had no words to express it (2 Corinthians 12:4). He just called it "inexpressible."

In that coming day, however, the saints will have glorified bodies in which to appreciate the glories of God's new heaven and earth. To enjoy God and heaven one needs a spiritual maturity and a glorified capacity. You don't thrill a three-year-old, for instance, with the thought that he will one day be married. He has no appetite for that and his response would probably be "Ugh!" Likewise, the thrills of God's future would likely devastate and benumb us with our present capacities. For this reason the Lord has graciously withheld most of those details, reserving them as future surprises.

SUMMARY

In concluding this survey of the eternal age, we should again recall the basic cohesion and dynamic by which God relates to His people. It is not by fear and the force of legalism, but by the intense fascination of His person and nature. His central features are love and holiness, both of which describe His character. True love is simply the receiving and communicating of His nature. It is by this dynamic of love that God is winning His ultimate victory, not by the coercion of might. He does not impose His will on anyone by forcing their allegiance. Rather, He imparts His life and love to change their whole motivational makeup. Jesus' last prayer for the disciples was "that the love wherewith Thou didst love Me may be in them, and I in them" (John 17:26). The fabulous love of the Father is what He seeks to implant in all those who put their trust in Him.

By this ingenious strategy of grace, God is preparing His people for eternal fellowship. In that age, love will indeed "make the world go round." That redeemed environment will allow the free, uninhibited flow of God's love and kindness to all. As "it is more blessed to give than to receive," the giving Lord will also receive immense joy and fulfillment in that fellowship. His grand intention for His people is "that in the ages to come He might show the surpassing riches of His grace in kindness toward us in Christ Jesus" (Ephesians 2:7). "Amazing Grace" will be the continual anthem of heaven.

CHAPTER FIFTEEN

WHERE ARE WE TODAY ON GOD'S PROPHETIC CALENDAR?

We need to grapple with one final question: Where are we today on God's prophetic calendar? Is the end near? Are the lengthening shadows of Armageddon for real? Whether out of deep spiritual concern or mere curiosity, the question intrigues us all. Will the Lord come in our generation, perhaps around the magical year 2000?

INTERPRETING SIGNS

The believer's answer to this question begins by checking for signs the Bible says will portend the end of the age. We note from Bible history that the Lord often designated signs to alert His people to the fulfillment of prophetic events. This He did with Noah and the great flood; with Abraham concerning Israel's entering and leaving Egypt; with Isaiah and the captivity of Jerusalem; with Jeremiah and Israel's return from Babylon; and with Daniel's description of Messiah's coming. Concerning His Second Coming, the Lord Himself enumerated several special events that will signal His return to earth. These various instances remind us that the Lord likes to nudge His people as He prepares to fulfill His promises.

The Place of Signs Today

This being so, we are prone to scan the horizon for signals of the next scheduled event, the coming of Christ for His church. Christian "astrology" has, frankly, blossomed into something of an art form in our time. Catering to this appetite for the sensational, a rash of prophetic seers has surfaced in the past half-century to almost pinpoint the day of the rapture, if not the hour. The question arises as to whether this preoccupation with signs is valid or even wholesome in prophetic studies.

We should be reminded that such extrapolations are really without biblical warrant and fly in the face of many cautions against them. Though Jesus did specify signs to presage His return to the earth, He gave none that would announce His coming to receive the church in the air. That coming is imminent (it can occur at any time) and always has been since Revelation 22:20 ("Behold, I come quickly"). No prophecies or signs need fulfillment before this grand ascent of the church to heaven. In this sense we live in a signless age—a period of prophetic silence. The church today is simply told to "wait for His Son from heaven" (1 Thessalonians 1:10).

This lack of signs to herald the Rapture, however, should not be pressed into wrong service. It should not be used to excuse lethargy or negligence in relating current events to Bible prophecy. Jesus stressed the need for believers to be alert to the prophetic seasons (Mark 13:29). The writer of Hebrews also emphasized this point, saying that an alert church will be able to "see the day drawing near" (Hebrews 10:25). How will that be possible? Not by stargazing for signs, but by studying God's end-time program and being alert to earth's preparation for His coming. As a farmer discerns the approach of summer by the leafing of fig trees, Jesus said, so believers should be alert to the buildup of world events as they swirl into place to fulfill God's program.

With these reminders and cautions, let's look at our world as it relates to conditions of the "last days" both from the view of the seers and that of our society today.

A LOOK AT OUR MORAL WORLD

We are often reminded of how far we have progressed as a liberated and knowledgeable society. Though blotches of corruption may appear here and there, our age exults in its scientific and social advances, unparalleled in history. Even moral deviations are seen as "upward mobility" in achieving a more liberated lifestyle. Traditional values are viewed more and more with scorn by both the media and comedians. They see those principles as outmoded shackles from an unenlightened past. Viewed through these rose-colored glasses, the fast-changing morals and mores of our time are hailed as wholesome, enchanting, and progressive.

The Realistic Picture

Take off those tinted glasses, however, and the chagrin of naked reality appears. The biblical seers looked beneath this enchanting facade and saw the truth. Their frightening disclosure was that "the king has no clothes." And worst of all, he doesn't know it.

As Amos the prophet decreed Israel's fall by holding God's plumb line to their moral house (Amos 7:7–9), so the judgment of our society can be anticipated by its adherence to God's moral standards. Humanistic views to the contrary, our moral world is not destined to evolve into sublimity, but will grossly deteriorate toward the end of the age. Paul declared that "in the last days, perilous times will come." He then gave a most pessimistic view of world conditions just prior to the Lord's return. In it he listed twenty features of personal, social, and religious relapse that will develop (2 Timothy 3:1–13).

His moral pronouncement was that men would become great "lovers"—lovers of self, money, and pleasure. This romance with the ego will bloom into arrogant pride and independence, disrespect for parents and authority, and an addiction to pleasure and immorality. The result will be a bondage to perverseness in sharp contrast to their lack of love for God and His Word.

The Fractured Family

How does our generation fit this dour prophecy? Frankly, you might think Paul tore a page from our daily news. Anarchy and terrorism are on the rise around the globe, often in the name of religion. Family anguish arising from fatherless homes is a desperate plague of our times, spawning endless heartaches and civil disorders. This disjoining of fathers from their children is one of the problems the prophet Elijah was to grapple with in the end times (Malachi 4:6). It's already here—with a vengeance.

Such truncated homes easily domino into further social and moral unrest. Lack of fatherly guidance has bred disrespect for authority, which in turn has spawned gangs and violence. Fast on the heels of these come teenage pregnancies, rampant abortions, homosexual and lesbian lifestyles, and disrespect for life in general. Many of our school grounds today are plagued with violence where guns are smuggled in for protection. Live-in lifestyles are becoming more and more common, while faithfulness to marriage vows is a tired joke of TV sitcoms. A recent term on the grand jury underscored for me again that the root of much crime today stems from the shrapnel of fractured families.

The Sexual Revolution

This deviation from biblical norms is epitomized today in our changing attitudes toward sex. Having legalized free sex, our society now has the temerity to legalize infanticide of the unborn, calling it "abortion" to euphumize its brutality. With the doors of free heterosexual expression open, the gays and lesbians have sued for their "right to choose" their lifestyle. Any who oppose it are charged with discrimination and hate mongering. Increasingly, anti-biblical "lifestyles" are being dignified in the name of an open and pluralistic society.

How do we respond to this modern blitz on morals? The intimidation and challenge it represents require strong assertion of biblical principles. Life is a gift of God that starts at conception (Psalm 139:13–16; Luke 1:41–42). Marriage is a God-given institution in which state alone is allowed the expression of sexual passions (Matthew 19:18).

To those despising God's truth of creation, Paul said, "God gave them over to degrading passions," citing homosexual activities by both women and men (Romans 1:25–27). The result? They received "in their own persons the due penalty for their error."

Moral balance, however, does not call for personal vindictiveness. As Jesus did not come to judge but to show mercy, His people are called to a similar mission. Showing mercy, however, does not mean commending the lifestyle that is contrary to Scripture. It means proper accommodation of victims, but not toleration of its cause. How much we all need the grace and wisdom to discern the difference!

The basic cause of immorality, however, finds its roots in an even deeper source. It is rooted in a twisted attitude of life that worships the lower passions. As Paul prophesied concerning the last days, pleasure today is the essence of life. It has replaced love for God as the center of life. Entertainment, sports, and partying are where the money is—and where the people are. The observance of Sunday or the Sabbath as a day of worship is as archaic as the horse-and-buggy for our "enlightened," entrepreneurial age. That day of divine worship has been rebaptized as a national day of shopping, pleasure, and recreation—and the people love to have it so!

A LOOK AT OUR SCHOLARLY WORLD

As a Jewish scholar, Paul held the plumb line also to our intellectual world. His prophetic scrutiny saw mental disorientation in the "last days." Though he envisioned great advances in learning, he saw the final days as a time of increased blindness to spiritual truth. That blindness will, in fact, eventually harden into fierce opposition (2 Timothy 3:7–8). The apostle saw this rejection of the faith as leading to a state of mental depravity.

We wince at such a forecast and wonder if the apostolic seer misread His vision of our age of "brilliance." The truth is that this paradox has indeed settled into American education, especially in the last fifty years. Though most of our great universities were originally established to train ministers of the gospel, they have now become "command and control centers for the war against Christianity."

This rejection of biblical truth, however, is not a call for believers to wring their hands. Pessimistic timidity is itself an abomination. It is rather a call to a more committed faith in confronting this paradox in education, long ago predicted. It is one of the things the apostle Paul said we should look for in discerning the nearness of the Lord's return. And the latest readings give every evidence that the apostle was again right on target.

A LOOK AT THE RELIGIOUS WORLD

This popularity of secular religion parallels also the Bible's warning of the decline of true faith in the last days. Jesus described His return as a time of scant "faith on the earth" (Luke 18:8). Rather than resorting to prayer, Jesus said, many believers would seek social justice through pressure tactics. The hardships of active faith will be replaced by social schemes that seemingly bring quicker results. This is a reminder that the last days scenario will be one in which many of the saints are so preoccupied with the world that they have little genuine, active faith in God. They will easily give up on prayer.

Paul also described those days as a time "when they will not endure sound doctrine," but "will turn aside to myths" (2 Timothy 4:3–4). Bible doctrine will lose its scintillation for many in favor of myths that entertain rather than convict. In place of biblical truths that grip the heart, many in the church will prefer pleasurable snippets that tickle the ears and soothe the conscience. These entertain the emotions without provoking hard decisions.

The Vulnerable Church

The pity is that much of this superficiality is disgustingly rife today. Though the Bible is still the world's bestseller, for many it is more of a fetish than a vital channel of God's power. Some see it as "good advice" for healthy living, or practical prudence for pious prosperity. Others use it as a pretext to fortify a pet bias on some social or religious issue. In the bargain the Lord's real message in the context is too often missed. As Paul said, it can become merely a facade of godly form without life or power.

We need constant reminders that the Bible is God's richest legacy to man with unlimited potential for spiritual power. So grand is the Lord's regard for it that the psalmist said, "for you have exalted above all things your name and your word" (Psalm 138:2). With this Word alone, Jesus put the devil to flight (Matthew 4:4–10). It is the one thing the Lord promised to bless in ministry, without which there can be no real life or power.

The Religious World

This departure from true doctrine applies even more, of course, to the world at large. Two prominent Bible offshoots illustrate this doctrinal departure, Judaism and Islam. Both grew out of basic truths of God's Word, but both rejected the Christological core of God's redemption in Christ Jesus. Each then developed its own "New Testament" (*Talmud* and *Koran*), giving revisionist interpretations to biblical truths. The crowning error of each is similar; both dethrone the God-Man Jesus, pointing to the coming of another messiah or prophet. Having built a colossus of man-made doctrines, each resorts to human means to implement them—intellectual genius, will power, or military might.

These are classic examples that typify the opposition of false doctrines in the last days. The astounding thing is how they sustain themselves in numbers and commitment. Though both are fractured within, each has a defiant unity that makes it almost impregnable. Islam today is in a period of great numerical growth, unprecedented since the tidal wave of its early centuries. With nearly a billion adherents, they are now the fastest growing religion in the world (having doubled in forty years). Their mosques encircle the globe, seeking to penetrate every race and culture. Though the Bible is the world's bestseller, the *Koran* is the world's most-read book. They claim without apology to have a word from God that supersedes that of the New Testament gospel of Christ.

The Power of the Gospel

These distortions, however, do not mean that true evangelism is dead or even sleeping. The gospel was made for times like these. It has always thrived on opposition, as history abundantly testifies. If the formal shell of Christianity has gone stagnant in many areas, the preaching of the gospel is having a heyday in unbelievable places. The breakup of world communism, for instance, has left millions without moral foundations, creating an ideal vacuum for meeting spiritual needs. Many doors in Eastern Europe have opened to evangelism, allowing unprecedented Bible reading and teaching even in their public schools. The hunger for freedom there has provoked an overwhelming response to the gospel. Morally adrift, many look to the West for both economic and spiritual help in their time of shattered foundations.

Similar breakups of traditional crusts of opposition are evident around the globe. In China a restless population of over a billion is seemingly primed for spiritual liberation. Some fifty million are already said to be underground believers in that vast land.

This priming for evangelism can also be seen in the United States—if we look beyond the media buffoonery. Religious music and expressions have been popularized. "Amazing Grace" and "God Bless America" are becoming national anthems. Congressional and presidential prayer breakfasts continue in high places. Many parachurch organizations are penetrating campuses and work forces. The phenomenon of worldwide crusades is almost legendary, all in the solid stance of the "old time gospel." Much of this aggressive Christianity is, in fact, expressing itself in the face of a rising tide of cynicism.

These many spiritual undercurrents are obviously not all genuine, but they cannot be written off as "religion as usual." They show that God is forcing all strata of society to think seriously about Jesus, even in indifferent America. The name of Jesus has protruded itself into the mind and consciences of the masses in ways only dreamed of twenty-five years ago. Beneath the stagnant crust of religion or irreligion, the Spirit of God is busy completing His work in many individual hearts.

THE POLITICAL WORLD

The struggle of the international world is also of great importance in discerning the end times. As previously noted, its political buildup will involve several coalitions of nations surrounding the Middle East. Four great blocs of power are identified as being involved (Ezekiel 38–39; Daniel 11). The northern bloc of "Gog and Magog" is generally seen to be that of Russia; a southern group of Egypt and her Arab allies appears to fulfill the biblical prophecy of the "south"; and the eastern armies that cross the Euphrates are usually tagged as a coalition of China and Japan. Completing this global polarization is the western alliance of Antichrist from Europe and the West. This last group will constitute a ten-nation federation, which is often seen as developing even now in the European common market. Thus the makings of the four political groups seem to be present and ready for what prophecy calls the end times.

With modern Israel also in place in the midst of this international intrigue, we almost wonder what the Lord is waiting for. Why doesn't He blow the trumpet? Or is all this buildup a mirage?

In evaluating this, it is important to remember that prophecy is not determined by current events, but by Scripture. The prophecy of the end-time assault by Gog and Magog from the far north has not changed. That great battle, however, is one that occurs at the midpoint of the tribulation period. Russia's development as a vicious power in the end times will take place after the church's rapture. It will evolve as Antichrist arises in Europe to challenge the northern bloc of Gog and Magog.

The same should be recognized concerning Antichrist's coming empire. The European common market in development today is certainly interesting, but it has no real relation to the ten-nation coalition of Antichrist in the end times. That organization is also a post-Rapture phenomenon, which will develop during the first three and a half years of Antichrist's rule. Its primary significance today is that it suggests an orbit of related interests.

These considerations indicate that though the international scene today is not precisely that of the end times, it is ideally prepared to slip into that mode as soon as the church is raptured. That rapture will inevitably bring radical changes in world politics. Its sudden occurrence could very well be the spark to alter many international alliances.

THE ECONOMIC WORLD

Though Paul had little to say of economics, he did describe the perils of the "last days" as partially due to the love of money (2 Timothy 3:1–2). Devotion to money inevitably replaces love for God. In an accelerated way greed will doubtless be a divisive factor as the end draws near.

Our world today is governed by economics perhaps more than anything. The stock market reigns over a fragile kingdom whose lifeline is the flow of currency and commodities. That flow, however, is dependent on its monetary reserves, as well as public confidence that tends to fluctuate with the latest rumors. When its reserves dwindle, its guarantees shrink and public confidence gets nervous, fearing a downturn, depression, or even collapse. Investors and buyers who gamble over consumer supply and demand delicately balance all of this. It can be a gambler's Mecca, but it can also domino into financial catastrophe. The ghosts of 1929 keep haunting the market with visions of economic collapse and devastating unemployment.

When applied to government, however, those stakes are much higher, for the whole structure stands or falls on the stability of the national treasury. That dependence was greatly increased during the Great Depression when the Federal Reserve Board began controlling banking, commerce, and much of the economy. As Larry Burkett describes, the Feds then fought the investors' blunders that spawned the Great Depression by assuming the role of "great provider" (*The Coming Economic Earthquake*, 28).

That government rescue was hailed everywhere as it reestablished public confidence and allowed banks to operate without fear of bankruptcy. It resolved the immediate problem of bread lines and restored a measure of dignity to the down-and-out. Strong measures were taken to regulate commerce, business, and trade. To finance this and stimulate industry, a credit system known as "fractional banking" was instituted, allowing businesses to loan on a fraction of deposits. This stimulated industry, but also began a paper mint of financial reserves. It financed itself by resorting to credit, thus inducing inflation. In practical terms, it operated on borrowed money, leaving the "mortgage" for the children to pay. It gave birth to our current plague of rampant deficit spending.

THE RETURN OF ISRAEL

Though the international scene is important, the inauguration of the state of Israel in 1948 is by far the most significant prophetic event of modern times. It is the one phenomenon of our time that makes our age prophetically unique. Though the shadows of four international alliances are important to end-time geopolitics, they are almost meaningless without the political resurgence of Israel. Her regathering to the land is the eleventh-hour mark on the clock of Bible prophecy.

This return of Israel, however, is not to be confused with her final regathering as prophesied. That end-time return, following another great holocaust in the land, will be of a much different character. It will be divinely orchestrated in response to her penitence and reception of Jesus as Messiah-Savior (Zechariah 12:10). That change of heart shows no signs of occurring in Israel today. Though many individual Jews are indeed responding to the gospel, the nation itself is as adamant as ever in its rejection of Jesus as Messiah.

What then is so prophetic about the modern return of Jews to Israel? How is this an eleventh-hour chime of the prophetic time clock?

Its real significance is that it puts Israel in position to fulfill her end-time role. She is now in the land as a recognized nation. But she is also in need of strong support from foreign powers to survive against a massive foe sworn to destroy her. Any shakeup of world powers after the Rapture would make it essential for her to quickly realign with a powerful ally. Though we thrill at her determined action to return to claim her ancient covenant land, we know this is not the return promised by the Lord. That promise had specific conditions that she has not met (Deuteronomy 30:1–3). Her defiant will to survive, however, will find its final expression in that end-time covenant she makes with Antichrist. In her present configuration she could easily move into that end-time role.

SUMMARY

Though the church is not promised prophetic signs prior to Christ's return, it is challenged to be alert to the character of the "last days." Those final days of the church age will be unique in several ways. The most obvious will be their moral degeneracy, spiritual lethargy, scholarly elitism, and religious intolerance of biblical truths. On the political front, a vast realignment of the Middle East is described, especially with respect to the nation of Israel. Our review of these features reveals some astounding developments. Most of these characteristics of the "last days" appear to be present today, some almost marking time. Our accelerated pace of life seems to have quickly ripened conditions for the fulfillment of God's program. Though this ripening process could well be extended, the essential setting appears prepared for that return of the Lord in the air.

The Name of the Game

In observing this accelerated buildup of world events, however, we should not miss the real point of the story. The stage props of modern culture, science, politics, and social turmoil are just the tools of God's workshop. In it He is calling out a people and fashioning them into the image of His Son. Therefore, the dramatic progression of current events does have importance as God arranges His workshop; but it should not be confused with His foremost project. That primary endeavor is the shaping of people for eternity, implanting in them His divine nature for eternal fellowship.

Recognizing this divine purpose serves to bring the buildup of world events into proper perspective. As the world gears up for its inevitable climax, God offers to individuals of every class and clime the "unspeakable gift" of His Son. Receiving Jesus Christ into our lives brings adoption into God's family and deliverance from the kingdom of darkness. It is our heart response to God's saving activity on our behalf. And it brings about this eternal fellowship between the believer and his God, a relationship designed to bring "fullness of joy" and "pleasures forevermore" (Psalm 16:11).

How about you? Have you started this life with God? Have you had a personal meeting with Him in whom you have confessed your need and received this life eternal which He offers in His Son? This prize is really the "holy grail" of everyone's search, but it cannot be bought or earned. It is received by a simple act of faith—and then the divine miracle takes place. That is the Bible's story and God's golden offer to everyone who will receive it.

APPENDIX:

THE MUCH DEBATED TIME OF THE RAPTURE

Concerning the fact of the Rapture there is quite general agreement among those who take the Bible seriously. Biblical statements generously affirm this expectation. A classic point of disagreement, however, is the time of that Rapture as related to other events in the end-time period. Will the church be caught away before the tribulation described by Daniel and Christ? Or will it go through that blitzkrieg to be taken up when Christ comes to set up His everlasting kingdom? How will the church relate to that period known as the "Day of the Lord" in the Old Testament or "the tribulation" in the New?

Various views are taken on these questions, each pleading biblical support. These are the "partial," "pre-tribulational," "mid-tribulational," "pre-wrath," and "post-tribulational" Rapture views. Since the partial Rapture theory (that only the mature will be raptured) divides the body of Christ into the deserving and undeserving, its emphasis on personal merit makes it hardly tenable. It borders on the notion of a "purgatory," and would not only rapture the church, but rupture it, as well. Our study then will focus on the other four prominent views, considering them in reverse order.

THE POST-TRIBULATIONAL VIEW OF THE RAPTURE

The post-tribulation position is perhaps the most popular, maintaining that the Rapture will take place as Christ returns to the earth after the tribulation period. It holds that the church will go through the tribulation, thus denying the imminence of the Lord's return. Many recent refinements of the position admit to a brief hiatus between the Rapture and His return to earth of various short durations. Since the end-time period of world tribulation precedes His return, all alert believers will be able to calculate the approximate time of the Rapture. They can start the countdown when Israel makes a seven-year pact with a great European leader and can check that countdown when this pact is broken three and a half years later and the heightened terror begins. This view sees the rise of Antichrist on the world scene, punctuated by his pact with Israel, as the next prophetic event to look for.

There is no denying that this view has convincing supports with many logical and theological arguments in its favor. Let's review the most prominent of them.

The Traditional View of the Church

This view is frankly held by many, if not most Christians and biblical scholars today. A long list of respected interpreters from the past and present are also associated with this position. The idea of the Rapture taking place before the end-time tribulation was, in fact, rarely considered before the nineteenth century. Tradition appears to overwhelmingly favor this view.

We should recall, however, that the traditions of the elders are not necessarily infallible. Although theological opinions should be thoroughly considered, doctrine must always be validated by recourse to the original sources of Scripture. To use the argument of theological preponderance would also undercut Luther's doctrine of justification by faith alone, for his adversaries could point to an overwhelming church tradition confirming the efficacy of works. It would also favor the Pharisees of Jesus' time on the question of whether Jesus was the Messiah. Human opinions are only valid if they accord with Scripture.

Scriptural Proof Texts

A more convincing argument that the Rapture will be post-tribulational is that the Scriptures themselves often speak of the resurrection and Christ's return in the same passage (Isaiah 26:19–21; Matthew 24:30–31; 1 Corinthians 15:23; Philippians 3:21; 2 Thessalonians 1:7–10; 2:1). It is further claimed that no "proof texts" can be found to distinguish the time of the Rapture from the time of Christ's return to the earth. The argument seems to win by default.

It should be noted, however, that Scripture often mentions several events together that do not necessarily occur together. The Old Testament prophets, for instance, spoke of Christ's first and second comings as seemingly one event (Isaiah 9:6–7; 61:1–2; Zechariah 9:9–10; cf. Luke 1:31–33). Yet they are later seen to be nearly two millennia apart. In the New Testament Jesus spoke of the resurrection of the just and unjust as taking place in "an hour" (John 5:28f.). These He later revealed as occurring a thousand years apart (Revelation 20:4–5). This telescoping of events does not involve error or contradictions, for they left room for their being distinguished in later revelation. The Lord often reveals first the skeleton and later the details, as He unfolds His program throughout Scripture. Though proof-texting is often useful in confirming doctrine, it can be deceptive if naively applied.

The Church Promised Tribulation

A third reason many believe the church will go through the tribulation is that the church is promised tribulation in the world. Jesus said, for instance, "In the world you shall have tribulation" (John 16:33), and many other Bible writers declared the same (2 Timothy 3:12). The book of Acts, in fact, describes the early church in much tribulation and martyrdom. That has often been true of many believers throughout church history, as well as in our own time. The question then arises as to why the church should be spared the great tribulation just prior to Christ's return.

We should first clarify that the question is not whether the church deserves tribulation, but whether it has been promised the end-time tribulation of the wrath of God. Though believers are to expect wrath and tribulation from the world, they are promised deliverance from God's wrath (1 Thessalonians 5:9; Revelation 3:10). The terror of the great tribulation is specifically called the wrath of God and of the Lamb (Revelation 6:16–17). That believers of the end-time will be preserved "through" that time of wrath cannot be demonstrated in the text, for John declares that many will be martyred during that time (Revelation 6:9; 13:7). This strongly implies that these martyrs are not church saints, but those salvaged after the Rapture who suffer martyrdom during the reign of Antichrist. From that the church is promised deliverance.

Grammatically speaking, the end-time tribulation is called "the tribulation" or "great tribulation," contrasting it with tribulation or affliction in general. With few exceptions the term is preceded by the article or an adjective (except for its first mention or introduction in each book, Matthew 24:9; Mark 13:19; Revelation 7:14). The article indicates a specific or previously mentioned tribulation; the reverse is true for general tribulation. This specificity then marks that period off as the long-prophesied time of trial that will be unique in the whole history of man. From this time of divine wrath the church will be delivered.

Resurrection of the Righteous As a Single Event

Three classic passages are often used to show the resurrection of the righteous as a single event. Daniel 12:2 prophesied the resurrection of two groups, one to "everlasting life" and the other "to disgrace and everlasting contempt." Jesus restated this in John 5:28–29 by saying, "an hour is coming in which all who are in the tombs shall hear His voice, and shall come forth; those who did good to a resurrection of life, those who committed evil to a resurrection of judgment." However, He later showed that these will take place a thousand years apart, calling the resurrection of the righteous the "first resurrection" (Revelation 20:5). Yet these passages appear to imply that all the righteous will be raised as one resurrection event after the tribulation, thus denying a rapture of the church before the tribulation begins.

On the surface, this appears conclusive, until the terms are traced to their sources. The "first resurrection" of Revelation 20 refers to the "first" of two "kinds" of resurrections mentioned by Daniel and Jesus, that of the just and unjust. They affirmed the certainty that all would arise, not necessarily all at once. Paul, in fact, described the resurrection of the righteous to be "each in his order," Christ being the "first fruits" (1 Corinthians 15:22–24). Making the resurrection of the righteous a single, all-inclusive event is not the point of any of the writers, but rather the fact of two kinds of resurrection from the dead.

The church is portrayed in Revelation 20:4 as already raised, seated, and assigned judgment roles before the resurrection of tribulation saints takes place.

Though the post-tribulation position is defended by a variety of other minutiae appeals, these are perhaps their most prominent supports. As noted, they make a strong show of credence on the surface, but fail to stand up under careful scrutiny. Especially fragile are the biblical bases supporting the system.

THE MID-TRIBULATIONAL VIEW OF THE RAPTURE

During the past generation another view has surfaced to resolve the problems some see in the pre-tribulational and post-tribulational positions, called "mid-tribulationalism." This view puts the Rapture of the church at the midpoint of Daniel's seventieth week. For these folks, it occurs just before the great tribulation of three and a half years.

The premise of this position is that the seventh trumpet of Revelation 11 is the same as the "last trumpet" of 1 Corinthians 15:52 and 1 Thessalonians 4:16. Both seem to be "last" trumpets. Since this seventh trumpet directly follows the ascent of the two witnesses into heaven at midpoint, they take this to be the time of the Rapture. This rationale, however, defies the obvious contexts which show no relation between the trumpets of Paul and those of John. One announces the blessing of resurrection for the righteous, the other announces the onset of the third "woe."

In several ways this view is similar to the post-tribulational position. It denies the imminence of the Rapture, maintains the church will go through part of the tribulation, and sees God's program for Israel and the church overlapping in the "seventieth week" of Israel. It does differ with the post-tribulational view, however, in denying that the church will go through the last half period of the wrath of God, thereby fulfilling God's promise of deliverance from divine wrath.

Though these compromises appear to solve some problems, they created others with respect to interpretation and consistency. Identifying the rapture trumpet of Paul with the judgment trumpets of John in Revelation 8, 9, and 11 appears to be grasping at straws to support the system. The view has not gained many adherents.

THE PRE-WRATH VIEW OF THE RAPTURE

Somewhat similar to the mid-tribulation position is another, more recent view, called "pre-wrath rapturism." It places the Rapture after the great tribulation, but before the Day of the Lord (a questionable distinction, to say the least). It also puts the "trumpet" judgments after the great tribulation and extends the final "bowl" judgments beyond the "Day of the Lord." This makes the "seventy weeks" of Israel end before the bowl judgments and confuses the bowl judgments with Israel's time of mourning (completely out of context with the bowls).

The view appears to hitchhike on a similar "pre-final woe" position propounded by J. Sidlow Baxter who sought to avoid the difficulties of the other three tribulation views. In the process, however, it adds further fuel to the fire by introducing more distinctions, most of which involve questionable assumptions. Its distinctions between the great tribulation, the Day of the Lord, and the day of God's wrath are especially strained. It also thoroughly confuses Israel and the church in the various passages dealing with the end-time period. Though intriguing, it also appears to present more problems than solutions.

THE PRE-TRIBULATION VIEW OF THE RAPTURE

As previously stated, the pre-tribulational view maintains that Christ will come to catch away the church just before the seventieth week of Israel begins. That will also begin the Day of the Lord and the tribulation period. The "Day of the Lord" is that future period in which God will deal with the world in judgment, following which His reign of peace on earth will take place (please see chap. 4 on the "Day of the Lord"). Related to Israel, it is primarily that prophesied period of the "seventieth week" which Jesus declared would take place just before His return in glory. How then does this pre-trib position defend its view and answer the many questions of the church's relationship to the seventieth week of Daniel? Those questions were providentially addressed by both Jesus and Paul, from which the main bases of the pre-trib position are established.

The Church Accompanies Christ As He Returns in Glory

We turn first to the setting of Christ's coming to the earth. As He returns following the great tribulation, an army will accompany Him from heaven (Revelation 19:7–8, 14). Their "fine linen" as the wife of the Lamb identifies them. They are associated with Him as He comes to judge, make war, and reign over the earth (1 Corinthians 6:2; 2 Timothy 2:12; Revelation 20:4–6).

Prior to this return, however, two key events will have already taken place in heaven. One is the marriage of Christ and His bride, seen as already past, evidently solemnized at God's throne. The marriage feast that follows is distinguished from the marriage and is described by Jesus in Matthew 25:1–13 as taking place on earth. Thus the bride accompanies Him after that marriage as a part of His glory.

A second event that is already past as Christ returns is the giving of rewards to the church (Revelation 19:8). The bride's wedding garments are called "fine linen," embroidered with her righteous deeds. This symbol is the Lord's way of emphasizing how each believer can contribute to Christ's glory on that grand occasion by their faithful service on earth. It follows the custom of each bride making her own wedding dress, but also suggests an eternal garment, not just a wedding or "going-away" outfit.

The implications are almost incontrovertible that the church will have been with the Lord for some time prior to this return in glory. Though these two events could conceivably take less than seven years, there is no reason such momentous ceremonies and celebrations at the

Father's throne should not involve some quality time. Surely the marriage of all marriages will not be a split-second affair, such as a simultaneous rapture and return to earth would require. At that marriage all the incomprehensible splendors the Father can lavish on His Son will doubtless be showered on this heavenly Groom and His bride. It is logical to expect that this will take some time, and the Bible gives every evidence that it will.

Time Gap to Salvage a Millennial People

Besides the need for an interval in heaven between the Rapture and Christ's return, there is also a similar need on earth. During the millennium or messianic age that directly follows His return, a redeemed remnant in mortal bodies will necessarily be on earth. These will be the nucleus of saints that will begin that grand society and to fulfill the messianic promises (Isaiah 11; 35; 65:19–25). Included will be both the righteous remnant of Israel and many Gentile nations of people (Matthew 25:32ff.). Through this salvaged remnant the Lord will fulfill His covenants and bless the world with unprecedented glory (Romans 11:15ff.).

To make the Rapture take place at Christ's return with the judgment of "sheep and goat" nations immediately following (Matthew 25:32) creates an insoluble problem. The "sheep" would then be raptured and the "goats" would go away to eternal punishment (Matthew 25:34, 46). Where then would that redeemed group in their earthly bodies come from? They would be nonexistent by that view. Without such an earthly people the purposes of the Millennium as prophesied could not be fulfilled.

Recognizing a pre-trib Rapture of the church, however, eliminates that problem. By this view a seven-year period will transpire on earth after the Rapture in which a large group of people from every nation will be saved (Revelation 7:9–14). Many of these will be martyred, but many others will survive those trials to be assigned by Christ a place in His earthly kingdom. The fact that these will have missed the Rapture of the church does not suggest a "second chance" for procrastinators. Paul declared that those who have heard and neglected the gospel prior to the Rapture will only be ensnared in a continued delusion (2 Thessalonians 2:11). Others, however, who have not had that opportunity will respond and be saved during that reign of terror to enter the kingdom of Christ's millennial reign.

Again, it might be asked why this should take seven years. Could not this remnant be saved instantly at the second coming, as seems the case with those Israelites in Zechariah 12:10ff.? These appear to make their first response as they see the nail wounds of Messiah.

With a sovereign God, of course, anything is possible, but the question is not what is possible but what is declared. The contexts of Matthew 25 and Revelation 6–18 show that such an instantaneous mass conversion is hardly the case, even for this Jewish remnant. The "wise virgins" of Matthew 25:10 and the "sheep" of Matthew 25:34 who enter the millennial kingdom are those who have made adequate preparation prior to that time. They are not saved at that time, but acclaimed as genuine believers as the lost are sent away. To assume that many will have rejected the gospel even through the tribulation and then are saved as they see Christ returning, is doubtful indeed. Though many will be saved during that tribulation period who have not had a previous opportunity, it will be through a proper reception of the gospel as demonstrated by their readiness to align with Christ's cause in a world of wickedness.

The need for this time gap then makes it almost inevitable that the Rapture occur some time before Christ's return to earth. That provides a time span in which God will deal with the world in judgment, sifting it and calling out "brands from the burning" before that fiery judgment takes place.

The Absence of the Church in Revelation 4–18

John's message in Revelation was given to instruct the church. It has a dramatic movement, first addressing the needs of the churches in Asia Minor and then portraying God's program of consummation. Though the church is the focus of the Lord's exhortations in chapters 1–3, it is not even mentioned in chapters 4–18 as he describes the tribulation. In other words, the Lord introduced the cataclysmic events of the Day of the Lord by first dealing with areas of failure in the churches. Judgment must begin at the house of God (1 Peter 4:17). He reminded them of seven spiritual characteristics of a growing and effective church that needed nurturing in those early churches and continue to instruct us today.

Following these reminders to the churches, the Lord described the coming events of the Day of the Lord as the "things that shall be after these things" (Revelation 1:19; 4:1). Though He spoke of the churches nineteen times in the first three chapters, He made no mention of them in the tribulation chapters till Christ's return with His Bride in chapter 19.

Besides no mention of the church (*ecclesia*) in these chapters, there is also no mention of many church words or concepts. J. B. Smith, in his *Revelation of Jesus Christ,* has noted fifteen such words that do not occur in this section: Father, Holy Spirit, grace, mercy, truth, faith, hope, love, peace, believe, repent (except in the negative), pray (except to the hills), comfort, and good. Though an argument from silence, these omissions are almost thunderous in making their point.

The New Prominence of Israelis in Revelation 6–18

In contrast to the church's absence, Israel is highlighted in these tribulation chapters. The sealed servants of chapter 7 are 144,000 Israelis, specifically named. The satanic attacks on saints are not against the church, but against Israel and her remnant (Revelation 12:12–17; 13:4; 14:12; 17:6; 18:4). The obvious implication is that the church has departed the earthly scene before this judgment, and God is again at work with Israel, completing the predicted activities of her "seventieth week" as outlined by Daniel.

The Church to Escape God's Wrath in the Day of the Lord

Turning to the apostle Paul, we note that he also discussed the Day of the Lord, comforting the church concerning that coming wrath. He declared that though the world will not escape that day of wrath, the true church will (1 Thessalonians 5:3, 9–10). It is important to notice that the wrath alluded to is not eternal wrath in hell, but the wrath to which the world will be subjected in the Day of the Lord (1 Thessalonians 5:2).

To emphasize that point, he noted that, whether living or dead when that day of wrath arrives, all believers will be "with the Lord" (1 Thessalonians 5:10). His stress on "with" here (three successive words emphasizing "with") is most unique, duplicated only in his Rapture statement of 1 Thessalonians 4:17. Both were given to "comfort and edify" the church. He could hardly have been more emphatic in stressing the church's presence with the Lord and absence from the world during the Day of the Lord.

Key Events Preceding the Day of the Lord

Several months later Paul wrote a second letter to the Thessalonians to further clarify that coming day of wrath. Many had recently suffered great persecution, provoking a rumor that that day had already come (2 Thessalonians 1:4). Had he previously taught them that the church will go through the tribulation, they might have rejoiced at the Lord's soon coming rather than being shaken up. As new believers, they needed further instruction about persecution. In answer, the apostle first consoled them that their afflicters would be duly punished in God's time (1 Thessalonians 1:5–9). He then assured them that the Day of the Lord had not come because three key events had not yet taken place.

The Apostasy

In Paul's mind there was one particular event that had to precede the coming Day of the Lord. The *apostasia* (*see* Note) must come first. What, then, is this decisive event that will give incontrovertible evidence that the Day of the Lord is present? The Greek word *apostasia* is generally interpreted as a great latter-day defection from the faith. Preceded by the definite article, the term here speaks of something quite specific of which he had previously spoken. Most interpreters associate Paul's use of it here with various other passages on defection, notably 1 Timothy 4:1; 2 Timothy 3:1ff and 1 John 2:18ff. From these, the doctrine of a spectacular, latter-day retraction from the faith has been constructed, and the word *apostasy* has been defined in dictionaries and lexicons as rebellion or desertion of one's faith.

The problem with making that relationship is that none of these passages speak of a specific end-time rebellion that will precede the Day of the Lord. They all speak of general apostasies of various kinds, many already in progress as they wrote. Though such defections will certainly increase toward the end of the age (Luke 18:8), they are portrayed as developing gradually over a period of time, rather than sudden and climactic as a prophetic sign. This suggests that the notion of a final, climactic desertion of the faith just before the Rapture and end time, is without genuine scriptural support—unless it can be found in this passage (2 Thessalonians 2:3).

At the risk of being out of step with the mainstream, let me suggest the greater likelihood of an alternate view that has gained prominence in recent years. This view interprets the apostasy as the departure of the church in Rapture. Though regarded as novel and far-fetched by most interpreters today, it was at least reflected four centuries ago in the first English translations (rendering *apostasia* in 2 Thessalonians 2:3 as simply departure; e.g., Tyndale, Coverdale, Geneva, etc.). During the past half century, an increasing number of conservative scholars have revived this view (e.g., E. Schuyler English, Kenneth Wuest, Gordon Lewis, John Lineberry, Allen McRae, Earl Radmacher, Duane Dunham, James Montgomery Boise, Leon Wood, and Paul Lee Tan, to name a few). What prompted these researchers to buck tradition and revert to the purely lexical meaning of departure?

The Meaning of Apostasy

The translation of *apostasia* as rebellion has a long history reaching back to the early church fathers (Justin Martyr, A.D. 165). In the process of time the church developed a doctrine of apostasy, calling Emperor Julian "the Apostate," following his renunciation of Christianity in 361. This doctrine is reflected in the writings of the fathers and was further enunciated by later writers as the church confronted many retractions from the faith. With the opening up of further studies in the Greek Old Testament (LXX) and Apocryphal books in modern times, the concept of apostasy has been shown to be strongly rooted in Jewish history. Especially is that seen in the history of the Jewish renegades of intertestamental times.

This theme of an end-time apostasy or declension of faith is certainly a well-supported doctrine of the New Testament. But because of this emphasis in other passages, many assume that the term itself has strong pejorative overtones. They see it as always portraying evil. Since that affects our understanding of 2 Thessalonians 2:3, it is important to check that assumption. Does the term apostasy always mean rebellion? An adequate check should begin with the lexicons, but also include a review of its use in the ancient sources as well, especially the LXX and the Apocrypha.

Ancient Use of the Term Apostasy

From a lexical standpoint, the term is a compound of two root words, *apo* (preposition meaning from) and *histymi* (verb meaning to stand or make stand). It therefore means to stand off or withdraw as a verb, and departure or withdrawal as a noun. Most lexicons assign rebellion as its foremost meaning, based on selected samplings from the ancient writings (Arndt & Gingrich Lexicon; Liddell & Scott; Thayer's; Abbot-Smith; Kittel's Theological Dictionary; Moulton & Milligan; G. W. H. Lampe, etc.).

A check of its verbal use in the LXX and the Apocrypha reveals a wide variety of usages. Hatch and Redpath (*Concordance of the Septuagint and Apocrypha*) list 220 instances of its use, translating forty-one different Hebrew words. Of these, 195 translate the aorist forms *apesty* and *aposty* with their various endings. As a noun it occurs six times in the Old Testament (Joshua 22:22; 2 Chronicles 28:19; 29:19; 33:19; Jeremiah 2:19; Isaiah 30:1), and three times in the Apocrypha (1 Esdras 2:27; 1 Maccabees 2:15; 2 Maccabees 5:8). In the New Testament its verbal forms occur fifteen times, only in the writings of Luke, Paul, and the Hebrew writer (Luke 2:37; 4:13; 8:13; 13:27; Acts 5:37–38; 12:10; 15:38; 19:9; 22:29; 2 Corinthians 12:8; 1 Timothy 4:1; 6:5; 2 Timothy 2:19; and Hebrews 3:12). As a noun it was used twice in the feminine form (Acts 21:21; 2 Thessalonians 2:3), and three times in the masculine speaking of the separation of divorce (Matthew 5:31; 19:7; Mark 10:4). The details of these usages have been included in a footnote.

Significance of the Ancient Texts

An analysis of how these words were used in those texts is rather revealing. Its most prominent use as a verb describes physical or spatial departures (66 of the 220). The next most prominent is that of religious departures (from the Lord, from the Law, from the covenant, etc.; fifty-three times). Interestingly, the much-trumped sense of military revolt is found only eight times. On the other hand, the term also describes the Lord departing from individuals (thirteen times), the opposite of men departing from the Lord. Likewise, it is used of individuals departing or exhorted to depart from evil (twenty-six times), the opposite of departing from God or good.

Besides these more prevalent usages, the term is employed some thirty times, describing an assortment of other departures or separations. A sampling of these expressions can be seen throughout the Bible. In Genesis 12:8, Abram departed (apesty) from Shechem to Bethel; in Numbers 8:25, the Lord commanded the Levites to "retire" (apostysetai) from service at age 50; in Daniel 8:18, the sleep of King Darius fled (apesty) from him as he worried about Daniel in the lion's den. In the New Testament, Paul prayed that his thorn in the flesh "might depart [aposty] from me" (2 Corinthians 12:8), and later quoted the Lord in commanding believers to depart (apostytw) from iniquity (2 Timothy 2:19).

These varied references indicate that the term had a wide range of usages portraying both religious and physical departures. In view of this nearly exhaustive list of those references, it is strange to read Robert Gundry, a leading exponent of the post-trib view, saying that "apostasia and its cognate and earlier forms appear over forty times in the LXX...every time with the meaning of religious or political defection" (*The Church and the Tribulation,* 115). He evidently skipped a few pages in those sources or made his selections by generalizations from lexicons. The truth is that though the term does speak of such defections quite often, it also describes many other kinds of departures.

Interpretive Principles Suggested

This study of the term in the ancient texts suggests several principles essential for a proper understanding of 2 Thessalonians 2:3. The first concerns the inherent nature of the term *apostasia*. In its verb form it speaks of a wide variety of departures from things both good and bad. As a noun its predominant use in the Old Testament (six times) was that of rebellion or defection from the faith. Half of these concern the wicked reigns of Ahaz and Manasseh (though not used of other wicked kings such as Ahab). The term had no inherent bias. Its New Testament use as a noun includes the separation of divorce (masculine) and forsaking the teaching of Moses (feminine). In the later writings of Plutarch and Josephus, the noun describes military rebellions against Nero and the Romans as well as religious defections.

Our first observation then is that the term itself is quite neutral, always dependent on its context to give it meaning. Like the words *apocalypse* and *parousia* (which describe the revelations and comings of both Christ and of Antichrist), the word *apostasia* is a neutral word that depends on its context to give it specific meaning. The vast majority of its uses are followed by the preposition *apo* (from) and are framed in a context that makes the meaning quite obvious.

A second observation concerns its most prevalent usage. Though it describes religious apostasy from the Lord (forty-two times), withdrawal from individuals by the Lord (twenty-two), and military rebellions (eight), it speaks of other kinds of departures even more often. Physical and related kinds of departures are alluded to ninety-three times and departures from evil twenty-five times. As a vehicle of thought, the term is quite unprejudiced toward either good or evil. It describes withdrawals and turnarounds of many kinds. Though it often portrays Israel's degeneracy and military rebellions, it also describes such departures as Anna leaving the temple (Luke 2:37) and the angel departing from Peter (Acts 12:10). The term itself was neutral, always subservient to its context.

A third observation relates to its use as a noun preceded by the article ("the" apostasia). This occurs twice in the Old Testament, once in the Apocrypha, and once in the New Testament (2 Chronicles 29:19; Jeremiah 2:19; 1 Maccabees 2:15; 2 Thessalonians 2:3). The definite article makes it specific in all four cases, and the following pronoun adds to that specificity in the first two. In 1 Maccabees 2:15, however, the term is not followed by such a qualifier. This rare use of the term by itself has been called the "absolute" sense, and since it refers to "religious defection," that is assumed to be its basic meaning.

Because of that unique passage, the term is often seen as a technical term for religious apostasy (e.g., E. J. Bicknell, 74; Robert Gundry, 115; G. B. Stanton, 392; Marvin Rosenthal, 201, etc.). That, of course, would affect its interpretation in 2 Thessalonians 2:3. And since it obviously means "religious rebellion" in 1 Maccabees 2:15, that appears to prove the case for religious apostasy in 2 Thessalonians.

A little reflection, however, may demonstrate the exact opposite. Recall that the first two chapters of 1 Maccabees describe the Greek takeover of Palestine by Alexander to the time of Antiochus Epiphanes. The major part of that introduction deals with the infamous invasion and desecration of the temple by Antiochus in which many Jewish renegades joined him. In recording the courageous exploits of Mattathias and his sons (the Maccabees), the writer describes the whole movement of those Jewish turncoats as the apostasy (1 Maccabees 2:15). They had forsaken the God and covenant of their fathers. In the previous forty-six verses he had thoroughly described that departure as "from God," "from the Lord," "from the covenant," "from the Law," and in many other ways. So bristling and obvious was the nature of this departure, it needed no qualification. Its standing alone without qualifiers only stressed its singular nature. The loaded context made its meaning unmistakable.

Paul's Application

That contextual principle is also used by Paul in 2 Thessalonians 2:3. After thoroughly discussing the Rapture in his previous book, he could speak of it here as "the departure." Each chapter had climaxed with a reference to the Rapture, and chapter 4 gave it its classic expression. Its meaning was unmistakable in its context, for no other departure was even mentioned. As in the paradigm of 1 Maccabees 2:15 where the context clearly defined its meaning, Paul let the context in this passage strongly express its meaning with obvious ellipsis. The subject of the Rapture was his dominant thought as he urged them to holy living.

The Broader Context of the New Testament

To further confirm its meaning, a check should also be made of its broader context in the New Testament. Having recognized the neutrality of the term, we have noted that it could mean either rebellion or simple departure. In checking other New Testament passages, we find it used one other time as a noun in Acts 21:21, and once as a participle in 1 Timothy 4:1. Each of these lacks the definite article, but each has a qualifying phrase identifying its meaning. That meaning in both cases is quite obviously religious apostasy.

As such, those references constitute the main New Testament supports for the view that 2 Thessalonians 2:3 speaks of religious apostasy. Though many passages speak of end-time defections from the faith, only these two use the term apostasy. They were used, however, some five to ten years after 2 Thessalonians was written and were quite unrelated (A.D. 53; 58; 63). Do they then answer the question as to what Paul meant by the apostasy as used in this eschatological passage of 2 Thessalonians?

Further reflection shows the impossibility of such a relationship. Notice the incongruity of each. Relating it to Acts 21:21 would make that coming apostasy another great revolt "from the teaching of Moses." Specifically, that teaching was to abandon the rite of circumcision and the sacrificial offerings as part of the gospel (Acts 21:21–24). That was indeed a part of Paul's gospel, but had no relation to a future religious apostasy in the last days.

A similar futility is evident in relating it to 1 Timothy 4:1. There Paul's concern was the opposite of that in Acts 21. Certain seductive leaders were promoting a return to religious legalism. This Paul called apostatizing from the faith or going back to the strictures of religious celibacy and dietary scruples. That was a fallacy already prevalent in the churches (Colossians 2:16), but certainly not a great sign of the end.

On the other hand, when the apostle did speak of the perilous times of the last days, he carefully described them without ever using the word *apostasy* (2 Timothy 3:1–13). Nor did Peter, John, or Jude as they also warned of the last days (2 Peter 3:3; 1 John 2:18; Jude 1:18). It was evidently not a technical term in their lexicons to designate religious rebellion. Though we use it today as a theological term, it was not so used by the apostles.

The real meaning of religious apostasy in the last days is still a most nebulous idea for those that buy that view. Though many treatises have expounded on it, no one has nailed down precisely what it is. The view of Robert Gundry that it is the rebellion of Antichrist is an ancient one to be sure (Justin Martyr, Dialogue 110.2), but is not generally accepted for several reasons (Gundry, 117–118). First, it would hardly be a comfort or correction to those in Thessalonica who were already afraid that was about to happen. Second, it confuses the two events Paul put in sequence as precursors to the Day of the Lord. He specifically said the departure would occur first, using the superlative adverb *prwtos* (1 Thessalonians 2:3). This is strongly argued by Duane Dunham in his excellent work on the Thessalonian epistles, as it is by Edmond Hiebert, James Moffit, and many others. The two events are shown to follow each other by two verbal clauses that distinguish them.

A third argument against equating the apostasy with the rebellion of Antichrist is its relation to 1 Maccabees (which is part of the ground for that notion). That historic rebellion under Antiochus was not a religious reversal by the pagan ruler, but the spineless surrender of a group of Jewish renegades. Antiochus himself was certainly not a pretender of Judaism who later defected, but an inveterate foe of the Jews and their worship of Jehovah. Likewise, Antichrist's ploys and antics with Israel will be strictly political, certainly not as a converted Jew who later apostatizes.

Another recent attempt to relate this apostasy to Maccabean history is that of Marvin Rosenthal who identifies it, not as the rebellion of Antichrist, but as the apostasy of the Jews who make a covenant with Antichrist. This he calls their "total abandonment of the God of Israel" (*The Pre-wrath Rapture of the Church,* 201). For him the apostasy is strictly Jewish, unrelated to the church. This view he defends by nine analogies between the ancient apostasy of the Jews under Antiochus Epiphanes and the future covenant with Antichrist. Though strained, it is an improvement over the previous in that it separates the two events by three and a half years.

This view, though provocative, is fatally flawed in several ways. 1) It builds mainly on assumptions and extrapolations from texts out of context. To extrapolate apostasy as always meaning total abandonment (from one extra-biblical reference in 1 Maccabees 1:15, while ignoring numerous other usages as simple departure) is hardly unbiased exegesis. 2) It assumes that Paul taught the Gentile church of Thessalonica the intricacies of Jewish Maccabean history during his brief stay there. Though He taught from the book of Daniel (perhaps including references to Antiochus in Daniel 11:21–35), it is doubtful he also expounded on the apocryphal books (2 Thessalonians 2:5). Had he done so, the early church might have canonized 1 Maccabees. Furthermore, his stay there was little more than three weeks, during which time he also had to earn his own living (Acts 17:2; 2 Thessalonians 3:8).

3) It is important to note also that the so-called "covenant" of 1 Maccabees 1:11 (made with Antiochus) is in no way parallel to the future covenant with Antichrist as predicted in Daniel 9:27. While that ancient covenant called for a halt to the holy covenant and its temple sacrifices, the future pact with Antichrist will do the very opposite—call for resumption of temple sacrifices and evidently rebuilding the temple. Any vague analogies are really illusory.

4) A fourth problem with relating the apostasy to the so-called covenant of the Jews with Antiochus is that Paul's Jewish opponents would have seen this as a self-fulfilling prophecy by Paul. They were only too anxious to charge him with doing just that—abandoning circumcision and the Jewish customs which that ancient covenant advocated (Acts 21:21). It is highly doubtful Paul's use of the term had that connotation.

Besides these two futile attempts to pinpoint that coming religious apostasy, no one knows what it is. It is basically generalized as something vile and revolting in morals and religion. If no one knows what it is, it could hardly qualify as the specific prophetic sign Paul intended it to be. The net effect of that view is basically negative, nullifying the specific emphasis Paul made in his previous book that the whole church, both living and dead, will be with the Lord when that coming day of Antichrist arrives (1 Thessalonians 5:1–9).

Summary

The historic sources of the Old Testament (LXX), Apocrypha, and New Testament strongly indicate that the term apostasy is a quite neutral term. It served in many ways to express both spiritual and physical departures. That meaning, however, was invariably dictated by its context, either by a qualifying phrase following or by the definite article pointing back. On two rare occasions the term was used without a qualifying phrase, but with the definite article (1 Maccabees 2:15 and 2 Thessalonians 2:3).

Paul's use of it this way in 2 Thessalonians spoke of a departure of which he had previously given them instruction. His express purpose was to calm them with assurance that the Day of the Lord had not come. The question we then need to ask is: "Would he use this term to remind them of the ancient rebellion of 1 Maccabees 2:15, of which the Thessalonians had practically no knowledge? Or would he use it to remind them of his own recent instruction concerning the coming rapture of the church? Which best fits the context? You be the judge.

The evidence of both the grammar and context of 2 Thessalonians 2:3 appears to overwhelmingly favor the view that the apostasia refers to the departure of the church in rapture. A candid evaluation of the ancient literature, as well as the context of this passage, strongly emphasizes this. As such, this view also answers several other problems in the context. 1) It specifically answers the question of how "our gathering together" relates to the coming Day of the Lord and His parousia (2:1–2). That question needed a clear answer, for it greatly disturbed the church and was one of the reasons Paul wrote the letter. His answer that the church would first depart in rapture was both clear and forthright. 2) This also confirms Paul's declaration in 1 Thessalonians 5:2 that the day of the Lord will come without warning and that the whole church will be "with-with-with" the Lord on that day (1 Thessalonians 4:17; 5:10). It must precede all other fulfillments of prophecies. 3) This view also resolves the question of why Paul failed to include the Rapture as a precursor to the Day of the Lord, if indeed he believed it would be. The answer is that he did so most emphatically—declaring the Rapture to be the first and most celebrated event to precede that day. He saw it as the prime event to begin that end-time calendar, voicing special concern that there be no confusion on the issue (2 Thessalonians 2:3).

The Restrainer Withdraws Himself (2 Thessalonians 2:6–7)

A second event that must precede the day of the Lord is the withdrawal of the "restrainer." The identity of this one has long been pondered, but the fact that He restrains the work of Satan points to the bridling work of the Holy Spirit. Who but God could restrain Satan? (2:9). In doing so, He is not "removed," as if by a higher power, but "removes Himself" (middle voice, aor. subj.). He is not "taken out" of the way.

The evident purpose of His withdrawal at this time is to allow sin to expend itself in an accelerated way. This will force a quick separation of the chaff and wheat in the crucible of tribulation under Antichrist. That He withdraws in association with the raptured church is certainly implied, but the church is not that restraining force. To make it so is to suggest that there was no such restraint before Pentecost. Paul's emphasis here is simply the sudden withdrawal of restraint by the Holy Spirit to allow the quick ascent of the "man of lawlessness."

This withdrawal of the Holy Spirit should be further clarified. He withdraws only as a restrainer of wickedness, certainly not as the sovereign convector and regenerator of sinners. His omnipresence is not in question. He will continue and even accelerate that saving work throughout the tribulation period, for no one could ever be saved apart from His salvaging operation. His withdrawal as the restrainer, however, will open the way for the rule of Antichrist to bring wickedness to a head for divine judgment.

The "Man of Lawlessness" Revealed (2 Thessalonians 2:3, 8)

The third prominent event preceding the Day of the Lord will be the manifestation of the "man of lawlessness." This individual is better known as the Antichrist. His long-prophesied rise on the world scene will inaugurate the events of the end-time period. The time of his manifestation could be either when he first enacts his seven-year treaty with Israel or when he breaks it at the midpoint. The fact that he enacts this infamous peace treaty with Israel and quickly rises to power (as noted in Revelation 6) suggests that Paul is referring to the beginning of that seven-year reign of terror. The implications of that treaty will be worldwide.

SUMMARY AND CONCLUSION

These various considerations from both Scripture and logic strongly favor the view that the Rapture will precede the tribulation. They indicate that the next event on God's prophetic calendar is the coming of Christ to receive His church in the air. Our command is to "wait for His Son from heaven," not for the coming of Antichrist to sign a pact with Israel. Though other views are earnestly defended, we believe this view best harmonizes all the relevant passages.

As previously noted, the pre-trib view does not deny that the church will experience great persecution from the world as the age draws to a close. Such will undoubtedly increase in the progress of time, and the church is told to expect it. What it does deny is that the church will experience that time of unparalleled tribulation that is uniquely described as the "wrath of God." From this fury it will be delivered by the miracle of the Rapture.

This indicates that there will be no "countdown before liftoff." No alerting signs will herald its coming. As far as prophetic fulfillments are concerned, "all systems are go"—He could be raising His trumpet now.

This event of the Rapture then will bring the church age to an end. In one majestic sweep, Christ will retrieve the entire church body and immortalize it by translation. With the church caught away, God will then commence His unfinished business with Israel and the nations in His program of grooming His people for majesty.

NOTE

Rather than listing all the uses of "apostasy" and its cognates in the original sources (which would take several pages), the following examples will demonstrate their varied uses in those passages.

VERB FORMS OF APOSTASIA IN LXX & APOCRYPHA:
Forms: *Aphistymi* (pres. ind.); *apesty* or *aposty* (aor. ind. & subj.)

Departing from the Lord, the Law, the covenant, etc.—42 references
 Joshua 22:18—we have revolted [*apestyte*] from the Lord
Departing from evil—25
 Exodus 23:7—abstain [*apostysy*] from every unjust thing
Departing of people or things—57
 Genesis 12:8—he (Abr) departed [*apesty*] unto...Bethel
Departing of the Lord from individuals—13
 1 Samuel 16:14—Spirit of the Lord departed [*apesty*] from Saul
Loss of hope, peace, mercy, etc.—9
 1 Chronicles 17:13—My mercy I will not withdraw [*apostysw*]
Military revolt—7
 2 Chronicles 21:8—Edom revolted [*apesty*] from Judah

Departing from unclean things commanded—6
 Isaiah 52:11—Depart [*apostyte*]. Touch not the unclean
Departing of sleep from one's eyes—6
 Genesis 31:40—my sleep fled [*aphistato*] from my eyes
Departing of the Word from one's mouth or heart—5
 Joshua 1:8—book...shall not depart [*apostysetai*] from mouth
Removal of someone by the Lord—4
 2 Kings 23:27—I will remove [*apostysw*] Judah from My sight
Departing of one's strength—3
 Judges 16:17—(Samson's) strength left [*apesty*] him
Deserting of evil lovers from one another—2
 Ezekiel 23:22—lovers from whom you were alienated [*apesty*]
Other single usages in verb form—12

Retiring of Levites from service	(Numbers 8:25)
Turning back of good by sin	(Jeremiah 5:25)
Depriving truth from someone	(Sirach 19:2)
Loss of safety on the highways	(Tobit 1:15)
Departing of praise from one's heart	(Judith 13:19)
Leading astray of intelligent men	(Sirach 19:12)
Departing of the whip from one's house	(Sirach 23:11)
Departing of evil conduct as one becomes godly	(Sirach 23:12)
Departing of grief	(Sirach 38:20)
Departing of a memory	(Sirach 38:9)
Departing from one religion to another	(1 Maccabees 2:19)
Leaving an animal	(1 Maccabees 6:36)

Total—192

VERB FORMS IN THE NEW TESTAMENT:
Forms: *Aphistymi* (pres. ind.); *apesty*, *aposty* (aor. ind. & subj.)

Departing from the faith	(Luke 8:13)	—4
Departing spatially or physically	(Acts 12:10)	—9
Departing of the devil from Jesus	(Matthew 4:11)	—1
Departing from evil	(2 Timothy 2:19)	—1

NOUN FORMS OF APOSTASIA IN LXX, APOCRYPHA & NEW TESTAMENT:
Forms: *Apostasia* (fem.); *apostasei*, *apostasion* (masc.)

Joshua 22:22—If in ap. (dep) we transgressed before the Lord
apostasia
2 Chronicles 28:19—he (Ahaz) departed in apostasy (ap.) from the Lord
apostasei
29:19—Ahaz polluted in his reign in his unfaithfulness (ap.)
y apostasia
33:19—God hearkened to all his sins and his unfaithfulness (ap.)
apostaseis
Isaiah 30:1—Woe to the children of rebellion (ap.)
apostatai
Jeremiah 2:19—Your (Israel) idolatries (ap.) shall correct you
y apostasia
1 Esdras 2:27—the people were given over to rebellion (ap.)
apostaseis
1 Maccabees 2:15—who were enforcing the ap. (Jews aligning with Antioch)
tyn apostasia
2 Maccabees 5:8—as to the law rebels (ap.), being hated
apostatys
Matthew 5:32—whoever divorces his wife, let him give her (ap.)
apostasion
19:7—Moses commanded to give certificate of (ap.) and divorce
apostasion
Acts 21:21—that you teach departure (ap.) from Moses
apostasian
2 Thessalonians 2:3—will not come except the departure (ap.) comes first
y apostasia
Plutarch. Galb. 1, 9Z—the departure (ap.) from Nero
apostasian
Josephus, Ant. 13, 219—their departure (ap.) from Rome
apostasian
Justin Dialogue, 110, 2—man of sin called man of apostasy (ap.)
apostasias

VERB FORMS OF APOSTASY IN THE NEW TESTAMENT:
Forms: *Aphistymi* (pres. ind.); *apesty* (aor. ind.); *aposty* (aor. subj. & imp.)

Luke 2:37—she (Anna) never left (aph.) the temple
Aphistato
4:13—the devil departed (ap.) from Him
apesty
8:13—in times of testing fall away (aph.)
aphistantai
13:27—depart (ap.) from Me, all you who do evil
apostyte
Acts 5:37—Judas of Galilee drew away (ap.) much people
apestysen
38—I say to you, stay away (ap.) from these men
apostyte
12:10—immediately the angel departed (ap.) from him (Peter)
apesty
15:38—who (Mark) had departed (ap.) from them in Pamphylia
apostanta
19:9—he (Paul) withdrew (ap.) from them (unbelievers)
apostas
22:29—they (Romans) immediately departed (ap.) from (Paul)
apestysan
2 Corinthians 12:8—that it (thorn) might depart (ap.) from me
aposty
1 Timothy 4:1—some will depart (ap.) from the faith
apostysontai
6:5—if any man departs (aph.) from the truth
aphistaso
(variant text in footnote)
2 Timothy 2:19—let everyone…abstain (ap.) from evil
apostytw
Hebrews 3:12—unbelieving heart in the falling away (ap.) from God
tw apostynai